# Ability Testing of Handicapped People: Dilemma for Government, Science, and the Public

Susan W. Sherman and Nancy M. Robinson, Editors

Panel on Testing of Handicapped People
Committee on Ability Testing
Assembly of Behavioral and Social Sciences
National Research Council

NATIONAL ACADEMY PRESS
Washington, D.C. 1982

NOTICE: The project that is the subject of this report was approved by the Governing Board of the National Research Council, whose members are drawn from the councils of the National Academy of Sciences, the National Academy of Engineering, and the Institute of Medicine. The members of the committee responsible for the report were chosen for their special competences and with regard for appropriate balance.

This report has been reviewed by a group other than the authors according to procedures approved by a Report Review Committee consisting of members of the National Academy of Sciences, the National Academy of Engineering, and the Institute of Medicine.

The National Research Council was established by the National Academy of Sciences in 1916 to associate the broad community of science and technology with the Academy's purposes of furthering knowledge and of advising the federal government. The Council operates in accordance with general policies determined by the Academy under the authority of its congressional charter of 1863, which establishes the Academy as a private, nonprofit, self-governing membership corporation. The Council has become the principal operating agency of both the National Academy of Sciences and the National Academy of Engineering in the conduct of their services to the government, the public, and the scientific and engineering communities. It is administered jointly by both Academies and the Institute of Medicine. The National Academy of Engineering and the Institute of Medicine were established in 1964 and 1970, respectively, under the charter of the National Academy of Sciences.

This report was prepared under Contract 300-80-0616. Its conclusions and recommendations do not necessarily reflect the views or policies of the Office for Civil Rights, the U.S. Department of Education, or any other agency of the federal government.

Library of Congress Cataloging in Publication data

National Research Council (U.S.). Panel on Testing of Handicapped People.
Ability testing of handicapped people.

Includes bibliographical references.
1. Handicapped—United States. 2. Ability—Testing. I. Sherman, Susan W. II. Robinson, Nancy M. III. Title.
HV1553.N43 1982 362.4'042 82-3612
ISBN 0-309-03240-7 AACR2

*Available from:*

NATIONAL ACADEMY PRESS
2101 Constitution Ave., N.W.
Washington, D.C. 20418

Printed in the United States of America

## PANEL ON TESTING OF HANDICAPPED PEOPLE

NANCY M. ROBINSON (*Chair*), Child Development and Mental Retardation Center, University of Washington (clinical psychology)
MARGARET E. BACKMAN, private consultant, New York, New York (psychometrics, rehabilitation psychology)
EMERSON FOULKE, Perceptual Alternatives Laboratory, University of Louisville (psychology)
JOSEPH HIMES, Department of Sociology, University of North Carolina, Greensboro
IRA J. HIRSH, Research Department, Central Institute for the Deaf (experimental psychology)
WILLIAM G. JOHNSON, Maxwell School, Syracuse University (economics)
NADINE M. LAMBERT, School of Education, University of California, Berkeley (school psychology)
JACK C. MERWIN, College of Education, University of Minnesota (educational psychology)
STEPHEN J. POLLAK, Shea and Gardner, Washington, D.C. (law)
NORMAN S. ROSENBERG, Mental Health Law Project, Washington, D.C. (law)
I. RICHARD SAVAGE, Department of Statistics, Yale University
WILLIAM A. SPENCER, Texas Institute for Rehabilitation and Research, Houston (medicine)
HERBERT H. ZARETSKY, Department of Rehabilitation Medicine, New York University Medical Center (rehabilitation psychology)

SUSAN W. SHERMAN, *Study Director*
ALEXANDRA K. WIGDOR, *Senior Research Associate*
NANCY E. ADELMAN, *Research Associate*
RITA L. ATKINSON, *Research Associate*
GLADYS R. BOSTICK, *Administrative Secretary*

**COMMITTEE ON ABILITY TESTING**

# Contents

# Preface

The Panel on Testing of Handicapped People was established, like many committees, because of a dilemma. Conflicting, apparently reasonable codes, which were created with the best of intentions, had brought to a standstill the implementation of federal regulations regarding the testing of handicapped applicants to schools and for employment. On the one hand, such applicants deserved to be protected from being labeled, that is, from having to reveal possibly prejudicial information about the existence of a handicap; on the other hand, the integrity of standardized testing procedures was also in need of protection so that scores obtained under nonstandard conditions could be "flagged" because of their uncertain validity. Yet flagged scores, when reported to admissions officers and potential employers, suggested the existence of a handicap and thereby labeled the applicant.

Recognizing this dilemma, the Office for Civil Rights (OCR) in 1979 sought the help of the National Research Council's Committee on Ability Testing. That committee established the panel to study the psychometric, social, legal, economic, and ethical issues surrounding the use of standardized tests in making decisions about handicapped people, with special reference to postsecondary education admissions. The panel's explicit mandate was to reconcile the testing requirements of the federal regulations implementing Section 504 of the Rehabilitation Act of 1973 with available testing technology and practice. Our report addresses that task.

The report appears, ironically, at a time of cuts in many research budgets, of a decrease in emphasis on the enforcement of federal regulations, and indeed of deregulation of many practices formerly thought to require such regulation. The fate of the Department of Education is uncertain. Yet the report calls for making the regulations under Section 504 workable by strengthening them and for a continuing research endeavor to make more useful and meaningful the results of tests given to handicapped people.

Although the recommendations request a new dedication of resources to a relatively small population of examinees, the extent of the population who might potentially profit from the modification of testing procedures is largely unknown. Just as the elimination of architectural barriers has given access to large numbers of handicapped people previously excluded from the mainstream, access to procedural modifications may encourage others with "hidden" handicaps to request assistance and more of those with obvious handicaps to venture forth.

The panel, appointed by the National Academy of Sciences, consisted of 13 members with expertise in areas bearing on the questions at hand. (Biographical sketches of members and staff appear in Appendix C.) Ten were university faculty members; two were practicing attorneys; and one had worked in test development and research for handicapped people for nonprofit organizations. The disciplines represented include several areas of psychology, law, sociology, economics, statistics, and medicine. Three members were themselves handicapped. No member had a vested interest in the issues to be resolved nor was any of us, in his or her daily work, engaged in the kinds of activities affected by the regulations implementing Section 504.

Between July 1979 and April 1981, the panel met on five occasions. In March 1980 the panel held an open meeting with invited delegates from numerous organizations representing groups of handicapped individuals, colleges, large employers, testing companies, and large professional organizations (see Appendix B). The open meeting and its associated written documents and oral testimony provided a valuable perspective on the complex issues involved and the diversity of positions held. Through the open meeting we also intitiated continuing contacts with a number of particularly helpful people in such organizations as the Office of Personnel Mangement, the Educational Testing Service, and the American College Testing Program.

From the beginning, the responsible staff officers at OCR were exceedingly generous with information and support. James Bennett, Peter McCabe, and John Wodatch provided background information and technical review of an early draft of the report. Despite OCR's shift of locale in 1980 from the Department of Health, Education, and Welfare to the Department of Education, its strong commitment to the project did not falter. The major effect of the shift was some increase in emphasis on postsecondary admissions testing and some decrease in emphasis on employment. At no time, however, was the panel asked to limit its field of inquiry; indeed, the broadest possible support was given for consideration of the spectrum of issues involved.

Position papers were written for the panel by Samuel Guskin of the University of Indiana (a portion of his papers appears as Appendix A) and by Robert Linn of the University of Illinois, whose help we sought in evaluating the practicality of our major policy recommendations.

Ours was a hard-working and unfailingly cooperative panel. Almost every member was involved in drafting and editing sections of the report. Although diverse, even incompatible views were frequently and spiritedly expressed during our deliberations, the discussions were task-oriented, civil, and productive. Particular thanks are due to Ira Hirsh, who headed the panel during several of its final and critical months when I was unable to do so.

We were indeed fortunate to have the assistance of a talented and effective staff. Susan Sherman, the study director, was with us from initial proposal to final report. She was assisted at first by Rita Atkinson, research associate, later by Nancy Adelman, research associate, and by Alexandra Wigdor, study director of the parent Committee on Ability Testing. Each of them contributed significantly to the substance of the panel's deliberations as well as to the report itself. Through all versions of the report, Gladys Bostick, our administrative secretary, was a full partner in the enterprise. We are grateful to the staff of the executive office of the Assembly of Behavioral and Social Sciences: the editorial skills of Eugenia Grohman, associate director for reports, lent style and directness, helping us to say what we intended to say. Heidi Hartmann, associate executive director, provided valuable substantive advice. David Goslin, executive director, provided a steady hand throughout the project.

Finally, I wish to express my personal appreciation to panel members, National Research Council staff, our OCR sponsors, and the many people who educated us as well as to the testing companies, admissions officers, and handicapped applicants who, we hope, will benefit from our work.

NANCY ROBINSON, *Chair*
Panel on Testing of
Handicapped People

# Executive Summary

The Panel on Testing of Handicapped People studied the psychometric, social, legal, economic, and ethical issues surrounding the use of standardized tests in making decisions about the education and employment of people with handicapped conditions. The report examines current testing and selection practices in schools and the workplace in order to describe the experiences of handicapped people and to determine, insofar as possible, the extent to which testing is a barrier to the full participation of handicapped people in American society. The report deals in depth with the legal and psychometric issues relating to the testing of people with handicapping conditions and to the testing requirements of the regulations implementing Section 504 of the Rehabilitation Act of 1973.

The report concludes that current psychometric theory and practice do not allow full compliance with the regulations as currently drafted. The testing requirements of the regulations are based on the assumption that people with handicapping conditions can be tested in a way that will not reflect the effects of these conditions and that the resulting test scores will be comparable to those of nonhandicapped people. Nevertheless, the report concludes that the technical problems of developing and validating tests that accommodate specific handicaps, while very difficult, are not insurmountable.

The report recommends that the Office for Civil Rights require that postsecondary educational institutions subject to Section 504, in their role as members of the corporations that sponsor the large testing programs, instruct the testing companies to develop modified tests to meet the needs of people with sensory and motor handicaps and to perform predictive validation studies on these tests. The validity studies should be completed and reported within four years of the implementation of the panel's recommendations by the Office for Civil Rights. After the four-year research period no test user covered by the regulations may use a modified form of a test whose validity with respect to relevant performance is unknown or for which the necessary refinements in the modified forms have not been made. At the close of the four-year period a working group should be assembled to examine the validity evidence submitted by the testing companies and other investigators to determine the usefulness of modifications for various handicapped groups and to recommend further action in those cases in which the predictive validities are not found to lie within acceptable limits for a modified form for a particular handicapped group.

The report recommends that, in the period before the validation studies have been completed, the locus of control over the flagging of scores to be used for educational admissions should be shifted from the test developer to the handicapped person. When the modified tests have been brought to a condition of equivalent predictive power with the test for the general population, the scores can be translated to a common scale before reporting. At this point, all reasons for flagging will have been eliminated.

In addition to these major policy recommendations, the report recommends other actions to improve the administration and use of tests for people with handicapping conditions, such as modification of tests, dissemination of information regarding the availability of modified forms of tests, and finding solutions to known problems with specific tests or types of tests.

In the long run, much more information is required to ensure adequate measurement of the abilities of people with handicapping conditions. The report describes in some detail the necessary research and places a research effort at the heart of the major policy recommendations. Of utmost importance are studies of test validity and validation procedures (especially for small samples of handicapped examinees), studies of the types of test modifications most appropriate for people with various handicapping conditions, the development and validation of procedures that can supplement or substitute for standardized paper-and-pencil tests, and investigation into the role of test scores in decision making.

# 1
# Ability Testing and Handicapped People

Many of the most important decisions made about an individual in our society—placement in advanced, remedial, or special education programs; admission to college and professional schools; selection for apprenticeship, employment, and military assignment—are made partly on the basis of test results. Some people find the negative effects of test use and test abuse reason for complaint, reform, and even the banning of tests; other people staunchly defend the right of all individuals, without regard to their native language, past experience, or physical or mental disabilities, to take standardized tests and to be considered on the basis of their merits along with all others who take tests. In short, denying a person the opportunity to take a test as part of applying for a position in a school or the work force may be seen as an infringement on his or her civil rights.

For years the testing of handicapped people has left much to be desired. Sensible modifications of tests and test administration procedures have not been widely available until rather recently. Even now, when tests are administered in other than the standard manner to people with handicapping conditions, the meaning of the scores is uncertain. Yet to assert that the test scores resulting from a modified administration of a test cannot be compared directly with others is to further frustrate handicapped people who are trying to demonstrate their abilities and to participate fully in American society.

Full participation in American society has become a major goal of many people with handicapping conditions. It is a theme that runs through federal legislation, such as the Education for All Handicapped Children Act (P.L. 94-142), which talks of placing handicapped children in the least restrictive educational environment possible. This concept has become known as "mainstreaming" or placing children with special educational needs in regular classes as often as possible. The theme reappears in the regulations implementing Section 504 of the Rehabilitation Act of 1973. As stated in the supplementary information accompanying the regulations (Federal Register, May 4, 1977:22676), "[Section 504] establishes a mandate to end discrimination and to bring handicapped persons into the mainstream of American life."

Explicit recognition of the rights of handicapped people was codified in the Rehabilitation Act of 1973 (P.L. 93-112). Regulations implementing Section 504 of that act, promulgated by the U.S. Department of Health, Education, and Welfare in 1977, discussed testing as it is used in admissions to postsecondary educational institutions, in job selection, and in placement in elementary and secondary education programs. The requirements regarding test use are based on the assumptions that handicapped people can be tested in a way that will not reflect the effects of their handicap and that the resulting test scores will be comparable to those of nonhandicapped people. Fully developed test modifications suitable for all handicapped individuals do not currently exist, however, and there is no information about the comparability of available tests for handicapped and nonhandicapped groups. Hence there has been uncertainty as to how to fully comply with the Section 504 regulations.

This report focuses on the testing requirements of the regulations implementing Section 504. In order to place those requirements in proper perspective, the report surveys current testing practices in educational and employment settings (Chapters 2 and 3). Chapter 4 describes the legal context of the regulations, discussing actions toward establishing the civil rights of handicapped people as well as other relevant legislation and case law. Chapter 5 discusses in detail the psychometric requirements of the regulations, describing what steps have been taken to improve tests for handicapped people and what is necessary to ensure valid testing of people with handicapping conditions. Chapter 6 presents the panel's conclusions and recommendations for changes in policies and procedures. Chapter 7 details the panel's recommended research.

The remainder of this first chapter discusses the functions and characteristics of tests, the types of disabilities of major concern to the panel, the social and economic status of handicapped people, the effects of stereotypes and labels on decisions regarding people with handicapping conditions, and the social and individual costs of biased selection procedures.

## THE FUNCTIONS OF TESTS

A "test" is a sample of performance; more specifically, a test is a systematic observation of a person's performance on a specially designed task or set of tasks. The same task is ordinarily used with many people under the same or similar conditions so that comparisons among people can be made.

Tests serve several different functions; two important ones are selection and diagnosis. The selective function of tests, their use in determining who should be allowed (or denied) certain educational and occupational opportunities, is the main focus of this report; the diagnostic function of tests, though important for many handicapped individuals, is considered only briefly. To the extent that diagnostic evaluation shapes a person's educational experiences and vocational goals, it affects such opportunities—but less directly. The more direct effect occurs when tests act as barriers to college, to professional or technical educations, or to jobs, in short, to participation in the mainstream of American society. This report, therefore, is concerned primarily with tests of ability—chiefly cognitive abilities and special skills—since these kinds of tests are generally used for selection purposes.

Many colleges, and most professional and technical schools, require tests as part of their admissions procedure. Some 2 million college-bound high school students take one of two widely used college admissions tests each year. Scores on these tests are weighed, along with high school grades and other criteria, in deciding who will be admitted. Law schools and medical schools require their own special admission tests as do many graduate school departments. Programs that train for most professions—dentistry, nursing, pharmacology, accounting, business administration, to name but a few—require specific tests for admission. If a test score reflects a person's disability, it does not provide an unbiased estimate of a person's potential. To the extent that a test score is not an accurate measure of the abilities that will be required in the program, it fails to measure a person's potential for successfully completing the program.

A similar situation may exist when tests are used to select for jobs, to decide on placement or promotion, to permit entrance into trade unions, or to obtain a license or credential. If a test reflects a person's disability rather than the skills actually needed on the job, it does not accurately reflect the person's potential on the job. In some instances, of course, a test may accurately reflect how well a person would perform on the job: the disability that produces a low test score would also interfere with successful job performance. In still other instances, the abilities tested may have little relation to the necessary job skills, and the person who did poorly on the test might still be able to do the job well. In such cases the tests serve as a barrier; they do not predict successful job performance.

While tests may sometimes be barriers, their use in selection may offer some advantages for handicapped people. Tests provide objective information that may help overcome negative biases against disabled people; they can show a person's strengths as well as weaknesses. And they allow the handicapped person to compete with others for jobs and educational opportunities. Indeed, ability tests were developed originally in order to provide a more objective and relevant basis for selection than social class or physical appearance. A good objective measure of merit may be especially important for handicapped people, who may have had fewer opportunities than nonhandicapped people to demonstrate their abilities.

## THE MEANING OF TESTS

The psychometric concept of validity, which provides an estimate of how well a test measures what it purports to measure, is important in considering the appropriateness of any use of a test and is central to the Section 504 regulations and to the panel's work. There are several different ways to measure the validity of a test, but only one, calibration against the performance to be predicted, is of direct relevance to this report. This type of validity is called predictive or criterion-related validity and is typically expressed as a correlation coefficient, with values ranging from 0 to 1.0. The predictive validity of a college admissions test is typically indicated by the strength of the relationship between scores on the test and first-year college grades, but a criterion other than first-year grades may be used. The predictive validity of an employment test relates scores on the test to performance on the job.

A second characteristic of tests, their reliability, is generally important in interpreting test scores but is far less critical than validity in the current study. Reliability is an index of the stability or consistency of test scores, that is, of the similarity of scores obtained by the same people when tested more than once with the identical test or with equivalent forms of the same test.

## TYPES OF DISABILITIES AND THE DISABLED POPULATION

Various distinctions are often made among the terms "impairment," "disability," and "handicap." One of the most common distinctions is between disability and handicap: a disability is a physical, sensory, mental, or emotional impairment that interferes with the major tasks of daily living; a handicap is the result of an interaction between a disability and an environment that creates obstacles or barriers for disabled people. According to this distinction, a person in a wheelchair is handicapped if narrow aisles in a store prevent entry. If the aisles are widened to permit wheelchair access, the person is still disabled but no longer handicapped.

A second convention distinguishes the terms impairment, limitation of function or handicap, and disability, as follows (Nagi 1979:6-7):

> [Impairment is] a physiological, anatomical or mental loss or abnormality or both. Examples of such impairments are abnormalities and residual losses remaining after the active stage of pathology has been arrested or eliminated, nonpathological congenital deformities and conditions resulting from the disuse of muscles for extended periods.
>
> . . . the most direct way impairments contribute to disability is through the limitations in function or capacity they effect. Limitations in function at higher levels of activity—such as walking, climbing, lifting, bending, reaching, reasoning, seeing or hearing—correspond to what is generally referred to as handicap.
>
> [Disability is] a form of inability or limitation in performing roles and tasks expected of an individual within a social environment. Although short-term sickness may be disabling for a brief period, the term disability is usually applied to inabilities of long or continued duration.

The legislation with which this report is concerned is written in terms of the "handicapped person," and we use the terms disabled and handicapped interchangeably.

Disabilities are so varied in both type and severity that it is often misleading to talk about "handicapped people" as if they were a homogeneous group. The panel's focus on testing, however, does narrow somewhat the population with which this report is concerned:

we consider those disabilities that directly affect test performance. After much debate, the panel decided to focus on the following broad categories: visual impairments; hearing impairments; motor impairments, including speech; learning disabilities; and mild mental retardation. Expressive speech disorders (e.g., stuttering or articulation defects) are included under motor impairments; although such disorders probably would not affect performance on a written test, they would interfere with performance on an oral test. Adults with receptive communication problems, such as difficulty in understanding spoken language, if not diagnosed as aphasic, would usually be diagnosed as either learning disabled or hearing impaired.

Several types of disabilities covered by the legislation receive little attention in this report. One of these is the category of mental illness or psychological disorders. During the acute stages, schizophrenia or severe depression undoubtedly would affect a person's performance on a test. Chronic mental illness, however, would affect job or school performance as well as test scores, and it also presents a situation of enormous individual variability. We also do not focus on health-related impairments, such as heart disease and diabetes. These conditions are likely to affect testing far less than they will affect other situations, primarily employment. Alcoholism and drug addiction were also not considered separately in our work. The interaction of such conditions with test performance is assumed to be minimal except when the person is under the influence of drugs or alcohol or when long-term consumption has produced brain damage. Finally, test anxiety is not included as a separate category because most people experience some anxiety when confronted by a test or examination, and it would be difficult to specify the point at which test anxiety becomes a handicap as defined by the Section 504 regulations.

This report focuses on tests—the ways in which they are modified and validated and their effects on people's lives—and not on specific disabilities. We use examples from specific disabilities and cite data where they are available, and, although we do not discuss all disabilities, we believe the report has relevance for many disabilities. Our focus on test modifications results from our task: it is the test modifications—not the handicapping conditions—that are flagged by testers and that are problematic with respect to both psychometric convention and the federal regulations. Some handicapped people are able to take tests in their standard form, and for them testing is no more (or different) a problem than it is for nonhandicapped people.

## People with Visual Impairments

Most people legally classed as "blind" are not totally without sight. In order to be considered legally blind in the United States, a person must have "central visual acuity of 20/200 or less in the better eye with correcting glasses, or central visual acuity of more than 20/200 if there is a field defect in which the peripheral visual field has contracted to such an extent that the widest diameter of the visual field subtends an angular distance no greater than 20 degrees" (Lowenfeld 1973:29-30). Only about 10 percent of all legally blind individuals are totally blind. Approximately 11 percent have light perception only, and 7 percent have a restricted visual field. Thus, about 75 to 80 percent of the legally blind population have some useful vision (Hatfield 1975). The term "low vision" is often used to describe the condition that lies between blindness and normal vision (Colenbrander 1977).

The National Center for Health Statistics uses a functional definition of blindness in its annual Health Interview Survey. To be "severely visually impaired" a person must be unable to read ordinary newspaper print, even with the aid of corrective lenses; or, if under 6 years of age, be blind in both eyes or have no useful vision in either eye. According to this definition, in household interviews for the year 1977, 1,396,000 people were classified as severely visually impaired. Of these, 990,000 (approximately 70 percent) were 65 years old or older and hence unlikely to be candidates for education or employment (see Kirchner and Peterson 1979a).

Between 30,000 and 40,000 children in the primary and secondary grades are severely visually impaired.[1] About 70 percent of these students attend neighborhood schools; the remaining 30 percent are in residential schools (Koestler 1976). The past 15 years have seen a marked trend toward educating blind children in nonresidential schools: between 1963 and 1978 the figure rose from 55 to 76 percent. This shift to nonresidential schools began even before enactment of the Education for All Handicapped Children Act of 1975, which encourages mainstreaming.

[1]Estimates for school-age blind children vary: the American Printing House for the Blind (APH) reported 29,400 blind students for 1978; the Bureau of Education for the Handicapped reported 32,455 visually impaired students for the 1978-79 school year, plus 2,390 deaf-blind students; the 1977 Health Interview Survey reported 36,800.

Of the school children registered with the American Printing House for the Blind in 1978, 6,221 could read braille; 13,158 could read large type; 1,289 could read both; and 11,797 could read neither. The percentage of blind people who can read braille is reported to be decreasing.[2]

Blind people and people with low vision are employed at every occupational level. The Survey of Income and Education (SIE), which was conducted by the Bureau of the Census, revealed that a little over 80 percent of the blind people in the labor force were employed in 1976. (To be considered as being in the labor force, a person must be either employed or actively seeking employment.) But less than one-third of all blind people were in the labor force at that time compared with three-fourths of the general population. Thus, it appears that blind people experience a serious employment problem (see Kirchner and Peterson 1979b).

## People with Hearing Impairments

Hearing impairment, ranging from mild to profound, is quantified as loss of sensitivity relative to a normal absolute threshold for pure tones at different frequencies whose loudness is measured in decibels (dB). The differences between a person's threshold and a normal threshold is referred to as hearing-threshold level or hearing level in decibels. The audiogram describes hearing level as a function of frequency (pitch), but hearing loss is often characterized by a single number that is the average hearing level at the frequencies of 500, 1,000, and 2,000 Hz (cycles per second). Roughly speaking, the "hard of hearing," who can understand speech with a hearing aid, have hearing levels between 26 and 70 dB. When people speak of the "deaf," they usually refer to two different categories of hearing loss: severe hearing impairment, which is hearing levels ranging from 70 to 90 dB, and profound hearing impairment (sometimes called "totally deaf"), which is hearing levels about 90 dB. Table 1-1 indicates how the ability to understand speech is related to different degrees of hearing loss.

It is estimated that about 14 million Americans have some hearing impairment. Of these, about 7.5 million have significant hearing loss in both ears, and about 1.8 million are deaf (i.e., have profound or severe hearing impairments). Approximately 600,000 people become

[2]Personal communication, Susan Spungen, American Foundation for the Blind.

TABLE 1-1 Hearing Loss and the Ability to Understand Speech

| Average Hearing-Threshold Level for 500, 1000, and 2000 Hz in the Better Ear | | Ability to Understand Speech through Hearing |
|---|---|---|
| Slight handicap | 25–40 dB | Difficulty only with faint speech |
| Moderate | 40–55 dB | Frequent difficulty with normal speech |
| | 55–70 dB | Frequent difficulty with loud speech |
| Severe | 70–90 dB | Can understand some speech or appreciate some speech cues when speech is shouted or amplified |
| Profound deafness | 90 dB | Usually cannot understand even amplified speech |

SOURCE: Adapted from Davis and Silverman (1978).

impaired before the age of 19 years, and 250,000 become deaf prior to the development of speech, usually before age 3 (Davis and Silverman 1978). Generally, the earlier one's hearing is impaired, the more serious the consequences for speech and language development. Individuals who become deaf after learning to talk usually retain the ability to speak; prelingually deaf children have great difficulty learning to talk and learning many things linked to language.

The Annual Survey of Hearing Impaired Children and Youth conducted by Gallaudet College reports that there were about 54,000 deaf children in school for the year 1977-78.[3] About half of these were in special residential or day schools for the deaf; the other half attended neighborhood schools, either in special classes (10,017) or in integrated programs that combined special and regular classes (12,386). As would be expected, profoundly deaf children are more likely to attend residential or day schools; only about 18 percent of those in integrated programs have profound hearing losses (Karchmer and Trybus 1977). Those children who are in integrated (mainstream) programs also are more likely to have learned to speak before becoming deaf.

Several surveys give some indication of the number of hearing-impaired people who participate in higher education. A 1972 study by the Bureau of the Census indicated that 2.7 percent of deaf people aged 25 to 64 had completed 4 years of college. Although a direct comparison with the general population is not possible, an indication of the disparity is given by comparison with the figure of 16.4 percent

[3]Figures from the Bureau of Education for the Handicapped show 41,603 hard-of-hearing and 44,439 deaf children aged 3 to 21 for the 1978-79 school year.

of the population aged 25 to 29 with 4 or more years of college in 1970 (U.S. Department of Health, Education, and Welfare 1975). In fall 1978 there were an estimated 11,256 hearing-impaired students enrolled in colleges and universities, comprising 0.10 percent of the total enrollment at that time (National Center for Education Statistics 1978). According to Bolton (1976b:145):

> . . . more than 3,000 youths aged 16 to 19 leave schools and classes for the deaf annually. Roughly 15 percent enter Gallaudet College, the National Technical Institute for the Deaf, or other college-level programs. Several hundred enroll in technical-vocational schools and community colleges which provide special arrangements for deaf students. An unknown number begin apprenticeships or on-the-job training programs. Many enter the job market at the clerical, semi-skilled, and unskilled levels. Others become unemployed or enter intensive rehabilitation programs.

The principal barriers to educational achievement and optimal vocational placement appear to be related to language development: deficits in direct communication and in linguistic skills. The average deaf 16-year-old has attained a reading skill of an average hearing fourth-grader, and fewer than 10 percent read at or beyond the seventh-grade level (Trybus and Karchmer 1977).

With respect to employment, a 1972 survey by the U.S. Department of Labor found that the unemployment rate for deaf males was close to that for the general population (2.9 compared with 4.9 percent). Unemployment for deaf females, however, was somewhat higher than that of hearing females, 10.2 compared with 6.6 percent (Schein and Delk 1974). Compared with the population as a whole, deaf people are underrepresented in the professions and in technical, managerial, administrative, and service occupations (Schein and Delk 1974). Deficiency in communication skills and the lower education level of the deaf undoubtedly are contributing factors.

Approximately one-third of the deaf students currently in school were born deaf as a result of the rubella epidemic of 1964. Since these students will be of college age in 1983, an increased need for vocational services and programs for the deaf in higher education is likely. Gallaudet College and the National Technical Institute for the Deaf, for example, both expect a temporary 50 percent increase in student enrollment at that time. These students will all be prelingually deaf, and many will have other handicaps, including blindness.

Although maternal vaccination has now largely eliminated rubella as a cause of deafness, this decrease may be offset by the increased number of premature and congenitally deaf infants who survive.

With increased prevention and enhanced treatment of illnesses that produce deafness during youth and young adulthood (e.g., meningitis, measles, other infections), the deaf population of the future may be almost entirely prelingually deaf—except, of course, for the aged. This prediction has significant implications for those concerned with the education and training of deaf people.

## People with Learning Disabilities

"Learning disabilities" is a very heterogeneous and ill-defined category that covers a wide range of difficulties in speaking, understanding speech, reading, and writing. The National Advisory Committee on Handicapped Children developed the following definition, which is used in the Education for All Handicapped Children Act (Wepman et al. 1976:301-302):

> Children with special learning disabilities exhibit a disorder in one or more of the basic psychological processes involved in understanding or using spoken or written languages. These may be manifested in disorders of listening, thinking, talking, reading, writing, spelling, or arithmetic. They include conditions which have been referred to as perceptual handicaps, brain injury, minimal brain dysfunction, dyslexia, developmental aphasia, etc. They do not include learning problems which are due primarily to visual, hearing, or motor handicaps, to mental retardation, emotional disturbance, or to environmental disadvantages.

There seems to be little consensus among physicians or educators about how to identify and classify learning-disabled children. The most commonly accepted indicator is a marked discrepancy between general learning ability, or "intelligence," as measured by standardized tests, and educational achievement, as measured by tests or grades. A typical working definition refers to a child of average intelligence who is about two grade levels behind in achievement. The difficulty, however, lies in determining that the achievement lag is not the result of such factors as poor motivation, emotional disturbance, environmental deficiencies, or simply poor instruction.

In view of the ambiguities and difficulties in defining learning disabilities, it is not surprising that estimates of its prevalence vary widely. The Bureau of Education for the Handicapped estimated that in 1978-79 approximately 2.3 percent of the school-age population between 5 and 17 years of age exhibited a learning disability (a national total of more than 1.1 million children). Other estimates range from 7.5 to 41 percent of various school populations (Minskoff

1973). One study, using multiple criteria and specific decision rules for diagnosis, found that 11 to 20 percent of a control group (aged 7 to 16) were learning disabled (Lambert and Sandoval 1980). The larger estimate covers all underachievers, including students of superior ability but average achievement; the lower figure includes only those who were below grade level in achievement.

To keep "learning disabilities" from becoming a meaningless category that includes all kinds of learning problems, most experts believe that it should be restricted to perceptual or perceptual-motor problems (e.g., see Hobbs 1976). The term "perceptual" here refers to those "mental (neurological) processes through which the child acquires the basic alphabets of sounds and forms" (Wepman et al. 1976:306). The term "perceptual handicap" refers to inadequate ability in such areas as the following (Wepman et al. 1976:306):

> . . . recognizing fine differences between auditory and visual discriminating features underlying the sounds used in speech and the orthographic forms used in reading; retaining and recalling those dicriminated sounds and forms in both short- and long-term memory; ordering the sounds and forms sequentially, both in sensory and motor acts; distinguishing figure-ground relationships; recognizing spatial and temporal orientations; obtaining closure; integrating intersensory information; and relating what is perceived to specific motor functions.

Those who work with college-age, learning-disabled students report that there are a number of otherwise able students whose main difficulty is in the processing of written information. With help in learning how to use alternative methods of processing information (e.g., listening to a recorded text while reading it), many of them can succeed in college.

## Mentally Retarded People

Definitions of mental retardation have changed markedly in the past two decades. The most widely accepted guidelines are those proposed by the American Association on Mental Retardation (AAMD), which also have been incorporated in the *Diagnostic and Statistical Manual* (DSM-III) of the American Psychiatric Association (1980). According to AAMD, "mental retardation refers to significantly subaverage general intellectual functioning existing concurrently with deficits in adaptive behavior, and manifested during the developmental period" (Grossman 1973:11). Significantly subaverage general intellectual functioning is defined as performance that is more than two standard deviations below the mean on a major standardized test, such as one of the Wechsler Intelligence Scales or the Stanford-Binet intelligence test. Approximately 3 percent of the population attain scores at this level or below and formerly were considered retarded on this basis alone.

Lately, however, much more weight has been given to coping ability and its relation to intellectual ability. Under newer conventions, if a person can cope with the demands of everyday life (demands at an ordinary level for a person of his or her age), that person is not considered mentally retarded, regardless of an intelligence test score. During the school years, low intelligence almost always causes academic failure in regular (mainstream) classes. After school years, however, many people of low intelligence do succeed in the everyday world by blending into the marginal community of people of borderline capability or low status and therefore are not considered mentally retarded. Only when they fail (for example, commit a crime) are they properly diagnosed as handicapped. Accordingly, current estimates of the prevalence of mental retardation, particularly at adult ages, run as low as 1 or 2 percent of the population.

To the extent that tests exclude mentally retarded individuals from vocational training or from jobs in which they could succeed if given a chance, then testing could actually increase the prevalence of mental retardation by causing some individuals to remain unemployed or otherwise dependent, that is, unable to cope with everyday life. The people most likely to be affected in this way are the mildly retarded, roughly 2.5 percent of the population. It is unlikely that those who are moderately, severely, or profoundly retarded, who together constitute about 0.5 percent of the population, would be negatively affected by testing for selection. Mildly retarded people, however, often acquire in regular or special education classes the reading and arithmetic skills needed to cope with on-the-job requirements at the unskilled or semi-skilled level, although they might need help in performing such task as filling out application forms and declaring income tax deductions.

## THE SOCIAL AND ECONOMIC STATUS OF HANDICAPPED PEOPLE

The panel examined the position of the handicapped population in American society in an attempt to determine whether handicapped people as a group tended to have lower status, thus suggesting the possibility of discrimination. Relatively low income, educational

TABLE 1-2 Educational Attainment by Selected Handicaps, 1977 (in thousands)

| Educational Attainment Level (individuals 17 years and over) | Handicap: Blind and Visually Impaired[a] | Deaf and Hearing Impaired[a] | Speech Impaired[a] | Orthopedic and Motor Impairments[a] | All U.S.[b] |
|---|---|---|---|---|---|
| TOTAL | 10,737 | 15,364 | 1,081 | 10,201 | 120,870 |
| <9 years | 3,484 (32%) | 4,877 (32%) | 385 (36%) | 2,585 (25%) | 24,053 (20%) |
| 9–11 years | 1,692 (16%) | 2,628 (17%) | 202 (19%) | 1,830 (18%) | 18,372 (15%) |
| 12 years | 2,885 (27%) | 4,261 (28%) | 265 (25%) | 2,984 (29%) | 43,634 (36%) |
| 13–15 years | 1,305 (12%) | 1,746 (11%) | 99 ( 9%) | 1,408 (14%) | 16,197 (13%) |
| 16+ years | 1,177 (11%) | 1,532 (10%) | 77 ( 7%) | 1,216 (12%) | 18,614 (15%) |
| Unknown | 194 ( 2%)[c] | 320 ( 2%) | 53 ( 5%) | 178 ( 2%) | — |

[a]Figures derived from Table 2 in Rehab Group, Inc. (1979) *Digest of Data on Persons with Disabilities.* Prepared under contract to the Congressional Research Service, Library of Congress. GPO #017-090-0050-0. Washington, D.C.: Government Printing Office.

[b]Figures derived from Table No. 226, "Years of School Completed by Race and Sex: 1960–1977 (persons 25 years old and older)," p. K13 in U.S. Department of Commerce (1978) *Statistical Abstract of the United States, 1978.* Bureau of the Census. Washington, D.C.: Government Printing Office.

[c]Column percentage totals may be greater than 100 due to rounding.

achievement, rate of employment, and occupational levels in relation to the general population would tend to indicate exclusion from the mainstream of society. Before presenting the data, however, we must mention some factors that impair our ability to evaluate the situation.

First, the available data do not distinguish among degrees of impairment nor other factors of functional significance. Among the hearing impaired, for example, are some who are totally unable to hear and others with mild or moderate reduction of hearing acuity; some whose loss originated before they began to acquire language (with severe developmental implications), and others with later loss whose language is relatively unaffected. Second, the available data seldom distinguish between people with one handicapping condition and those with multiple handicaps, which impose additional burdens. Simply counting the number of people with a single one of the enumerated conditions does not reveal the entire portrait of disability. Third, inclusion of mentally retarded people in the handicapped population lowers its overall occupational and educational attainment because those people by definition are unable to succeed in coping independently with the demands of mainstream society (Grossman 1977). Fourth, because children born to parents of lower socioeconomic status suffer a higher incidence of handicaps than those born to parents of higher status (Richardson and Higgins 1965), family background must be taken into account in any analysis of the educational and social status of handicapped individuals.

## Educational Achievement

Data on the educational attainment of handicapped people are presented in Table 1-2. (Note that the handicapped and nonhandicapped samples are not strictly comparable because the sample of handicapped people includes people over 17 years of age and the nonhandicapped sample includes those over 25.) The most striking difference between the handicapped and the nonhandicapped population is in the percentage of people in the lowest educational category (less than 9 years of schooling), but there are marked differences at all levels.

The large difference in educational attainment was one of the major factors prompting federal legislation, namely the Rehabilitation Act of 1973 and the Education for All Handicapped Children Act. Many of the handicapped people who are counted in Table 1-2 attended school when mainstreaming was not emphasized, special needs presumably were not met, and special education classes were dead ends. Many of those people probably encountered attitudinal as well as physical and program barriers. These factors have created substantial disadvantages in both the ability to compete for employment and satisfaction to be gained through personal intellectual growth.

The overall effects of relatively low educational achievement may be particularly severe for handicapped individuals, who might be able to compensate for physical limitations by acquiring new skills. Rehabilitation agencies, for example, often offer education and training as a compensatory device to improve the employability of handicapped people.

### Income

Table 1-3 presents comparative family income figures reported by four categories of handicapped individuals, again compared with all U.S. families. According to the Bureau of the Census, median family income for the United States in 1977 was $16,009, considerably higher than that for any of the seven categories. We cannot determine from these data what proportion of income is derived from wages, disability insurance, or other sources, nor do we have an income breakdown by sex. Nationally, 11.6 percent of the total population were estimated to have incomes below the poverty level (defined for a nonfarm family of four as $6,191 in 1977). Table 1-3 indicates that the proportion of handicapped people with incomes below the poverty level was 2 to 3 times greater than for the population as a whole.

The income of severely disabled people, defined as those who cannot work at all or cannot work regularly, is of course even lower than the income of partially disabled people, who are limited in the kind or amount of work they can do but are able to work competitively to some degree.

### Occupational Status

As shown in Table 1-4, handicapped people work much less often in white-collar jobs than do U.S. workers as a whole, and much more often they are unemployed or not in the labor force. There is little doubt that, whatever the reasons, handicapped people have substantially lower occupational status than other workers.

## Frequency of Employment

Participation in the labor force is closely related to the degree of disability. Severely disabled people, by definition, are largely unable to work except in sheltered employment situations. Partially disabled people may be limited in the kind of work they can do, and possibly in the amount as well, but they are considered potentially capable of competitive employment. Table 1-5 illustrates the degree to which partially disabled people are able to maintain employment of some kind (even though that employment may be of low status). The data distinguish between severe and partial disability and between men and women. Partially disabled and nondisabled men have a relatively similar employment profile, with only minor differences in the ratio of part- to full-time employment. Partially disabled women, however, are much more likely than nonhandicapped women to have part-time rather than full-time employment or to be either unemployed or not in the labor force at all. From the available data, we cannot determine whether the differences derive from different expectations for women, differential educational and employment opportunities, or other factors.

## Conclusions

Clearly, the place of handicapped people in the American social structure is restricted and disadvantaged. Although many people with limited or partial disabilities are able to participate in essential activities and thereby achieve positions that are not strikingly different from the general population, those with more severe handicaps are often largely excluded from the mainstream and are subordinated in the status hierarchy. Women appear to be generally less successful than men with the same degree of impairment, particularly in employment.

The marginal and inferior positions of some handicapped people in the social structure may have adverse implications for their performance on ability tests. Handicapped people may not have acquired adequate background knowledge and formal education for successful performance in test situations. They may come to the place and time of the test with less experience in taking tests and with a feeling of discomfort because their previous experiences have been in segregated facilities. They may face the test experience with frustration, anxiety, and a sense of threat, perhaps in part because

TABLE 1-3 Annual Family Income by Selected Handicaps, 1977 (in thousands)

| | Handicap | | | | |
|---|---|---|---|---|---|
| Annual Income | Blind and Visually Impaired[a] | Deaf and Hearing Impaired[a] | Speech Impaired[a] | Orthopedic and Motor Impairments[a] | All U.S. Families[b] |
| TOTAL | 11,415 | 16,219 | 1,995 | 11,507 | 57,215 |
| < $3,000 | 1,309 (12%) | 1,584 (10%) | 210 (10%) | 1,201 (10%) | 2,054 ( 4%) |
| $ 3,000– 4,999 | 1,671 (15%) | 2,111 (13%) | 259 (13%) | 1,436 (12%) | 3,289 ( 6%) |
| $ 5,000– 6,999 | 1,225 (11%) | 1,738 (11%) | 217 (11%) | 1,138 (10%) | 4,147 ( 7%) |
| $ 7,000– 9,999 | 1,328 (12%) | 1,900 (17%) | 218 (11%) | 1,334 (12%) | 6,237 (11%) |
| $10,000–14,999 | 1,686 (15%) | 2,644 (16%) | 349 (18%) | 1,967 (17%) | 10,552 (18%) |
| $15,000–24,999 | 1,930 (17%) | 2,912 (18%) | 398 (20%) | 2,203 (19%) | 18,128 (31%) |
| $25,000+ | 1,139 (10%) | 1,733 (11%) | 174 ( 9%) | 1,225 (11%) | 12,808 (22%) |
| Unknown | 1,127 (10%)[c] | 1,597 (10%) | 170 ( 9%) | 1,003 ( 9%) | — |

[a]Figures derived from Table 2 in Rehab Group, Inc. (1979) *Digest of Data on Persons with Disabilities*. Prepared under contract to the Congressional Research Service, Library of Congress. GPO #017-090-0050-0. Washington, D.C.: Government Printing Office.

[b]Figures derived from Table A, "Families and Unrelated Individuals by Total Money Income in 1977," p. 2 in U.S. Department of Commerce (1979) *Consumer Income: Money Income in 1977 of Families and Persons in the United States*. Bureau of the Census. Current Population Reports, Series P-60, No. 118, March 1979.

[c]Column percentage totals may be greater than 100 due to rounding.

TABLE 1-4 Type of Occupation by Selected Handicaps, 1977 (persons over 17, in thousands)

| | Handicap | | | | |
|---|---|---|---|---|---|
| Type of Occupation | Blind and Visually Impaired[a] | Deaf and Hearing Impaired[a] | Speech Impaired[a] | Orthopedic and Motor Impairments[a] | Total U.S.[b] |
| TOTAL | 10,425 | 15,328 | 1,043 | 9,750 | 90,546[c] |
| White Collar | 2,009 (19%) | 2,840 (19%) | 122 (12%) | 2,142 (22%) | 45,187 |
| Blue Collar | 1,421 (14%) | 2,472 (16%) | 245 (23%) | 1,590 (16%) | 30,211 |
| Service | 465 ( 4%) | 688 ( 4%) | 79 ( 8%) | 528 ( 5%) | 12,392 |
| Farm | 129 ( 1%) | 276 ( 2%) | 9 ( 1%) | 151 ( 2%) | 2,756 |
| Unknown | 32 (<1%) | 57 (<1%) | 4 (<1%) | 35 (<1%) | — |
| Not in Labor Force (including unemployed) | 6,369 (61%)[c] | 8,995 (59%) | 584 (56%) | 5,304 (54%) | — |

[a]Figures derived from Table 2 in Rehab Group, Inc. (1979) *Digest of Data on Persons with Disabilities*. Prepared under contract to the Congressional Research Service, Library of Congress. GPO #017-090-0050-0. Washington, D.C.: Government Printing Office.
[b]Figures derived from Table 643, "Labor Force and Employment: 1947 to 1978," in U.S. Department of Commerce (1978) *Statistical Abstract of the United States, 1978*, 99th ed. Bureau of the Census. Washington, D.C.: Government Printing Office.
[c]Column percentage totals may not equal 100 due to rounding.

TABLE 1-5 Employment Status of Handicapped and Nonhandicapped People

| | Employment Status | | | |
|---|---|---|---|---|
| | Full Time | Part Time | Unemployed | Not in Labor Force |
| Severely disabled | | | | |
| Men | 8 | 8 | 3 | 81 |
| Women | 4 | 4 | 1 | 91 |
| Partially disabled | | | | |
| Men | 80 | 11 | 4 | 5 |
| Women | 31 | 21 | 6 | 42 |
| Nondisabled | | | | |
| Men | 86 | 6 | 3 | 4 |
| Women | 49 | 15 | 4 | 32 |

SOURCE: Derived from Social Security Administration (1980) *Work Disability in the United States: A Chartbook.*

of past failures. Any or all of these conditions may lessen their chances for optimal performance in the testing situation.

## THE EFFECTS OF STEREOTYPES AND LABELS

Stereotypes and labels affect the lives of handicapped people, particularly in selection processes. "Gatekeepers" in the mainstream of society, such as teachers, school counselors, rehabilitation workers, examiners and test assistants (readers, signers), and admissions and employment officers, are likely (as are other people) to attach labels and to apply stereotypes as they interact with and affect the lives of handicapped people.

When a handicapped applicant and a gatekeeper interact, the latter may assume one of several postures. The gatekeeper may take a realistic (objective) stance, based on an accurate evaluation of the individual applicant; or he or she may employ either a negative or a positive stereotype. A negative stereotype emphasizes the lack of ability of handicapped people, characterizing them as weak, dependent, incompetent, and unsuccessful. Positive stereotypes exaggerate the competencies of handicapped applicants and describe them as normal, independent, superior, successful, and so on. The research literature suggests that the negative stereotype response is the most prevalent pattern, although positive stereotyping also occurs. Unrealistic and biased expectations are of crucial importance when testing information is used.

There are various ways in which handicapped people can deal with negative expectations. They may, for example, accept, internalize, and comply with the beliefs and expectations. Alternatively, they may avoid contacts with particular people or situations in which they are likely to encounter bias (e.g., by residing in segregated communities), stress or claim that the disability is only temporary, direct attention to abilities and assets that offset the stereotype, or oppose the stereotypical constraints and reject the ascribed inferiority and discrimination.

The portion of the regulations implementing Section 504 that prohibits pre-selection inquiry is an effort to enable handicapped people to encounter the gatekeeping situation without the hazards of stereotyped responses. Yet the flagging of test scores as having been administered in nonstandard fashion, as allowed by OCR's interim policy, is de facto labeling of examinees as handicapped. Indeed, since the flagging of scores does not identify the precise modifications of standardized procedure that have occurred, it is labeling at its vaguest and therefore potentially most damaging.

Standardized testing is only one part of an assessment procedure. Other information that sometimes is requested in applying for educational or employment positions includes written questionnaires, essay material, transcripts of educational records, letters of reference, resumes or autobiographies of educational and work experience, and, frequently, face-to-face contacts. (The personal contacts may be interviews, performance tests, or probationary placements.) Many of these sources of information have the potential for revealing the presence of a handicapping condition. This is particularly true for school reports (if the applicant attended a special class or school), reports of extracurricular activities, letters of reference, autobiographies, and face-to-face contacts. Yet this identification need not take place. Indeed, some individuals with health impairments, reading disabilities, or mental disorders may be able to conceal the handicap even during face-to-face interviews.

Handicapped applicants may or may not desire to inform decision makers about their handicap. Some applicants, particularly those with achievements, may want to take advantage of a positive stereotype, capitalizing on the tendency of an evaluator to overestimate an individual's qualifications when he or she is viewed as having overcome an obstacle in attaining a goal. A person who is temporarily rather than permanently handicapped may want to ensure that attention is directed to the handicap in order that its transient nature be known (Levitin 1975). Another person may believe that he or she will be more accurately evaluated with the assistance of a report by a rehabilitation counselor, physician, or therapist. Still another may wish to waive some requirements that pose particular problems.

Other handicapped applicants however, may not wish to disclose the fact that they are impaired. They may fear an uninformed discrimination against handicapped people; they may want to avoid (illegal) rejection because of the cost of accommodating their handicaps (for example, through supplying readers or translators); or they may want the personal satisfaction of succeeding in open competition. The regulations implementing Section 504 preserve the right of the applicant to conceal the existence of a handicapping condition until a selection decision has been made.

Because the research literature regarding the operation of labels in decision making in college admissions, employment, and licensing was of such direct relevance to the provisions of Section 504, the panel reviewed the literature bearing on this issue (see Appendix A).

Briefly summarized, the research literature on the effects on decision making of knowing a person is handicapped shows varied results. Knowing that an individual is handicapped may, in different situations, have negative, positive, or negligible effects. In short, research does not support the common assumption that knowledge of a person's handicapping condition works to that person's disadvantage. Opinions expressed in the panel's open meeting were similarly varied.

## THE SOCIAL AND INDIVIDUAL COSTS OF BIASED SELECTION PROCEDURES

To the extent that selection procedures for admitting or hiring handicapped people are biased, either because of tests that fail to predict future success or more subtle processes of labeling and stereotyping, both society and handicapped individuals suffer. It should be pointed out that either a negative or a positive bias may create serious costs to the individual concerned, as well as to others. A negative bias is likely to exclude a handicapped person from activities and opportunities he or she is competent to handle, with consequences such as unrealized assets, nonproductivity, boredom, truncated educational and career progression, and so on. A positive bias may also have serious costs if the individual is placed in a situation that exceeds his or her capabilities. The inevitable failure may be damaging in both the long and short term and may affect others as well—professors and friends who give extra help to a floundering college student, employers who lose money, the public unprotected from an incompetent professional, and so on. In other words, inaccurate labels, stereotypes, expectations, and actions, whether negative or positive, are expensive to all concerned.

It is difficult to quantify the costs, however. Strictly speaking, the economic cost of biased selection procedures to society stems from the misallocation of resources that could be better used in an alternate fashion. The two most important misallocations are the inefficient use of people in producing commodities and the inefficient use of education and training in preparing future workers. Conversely, the reducton or elimination of bias in selection procedures creates societywide economic benefits since it improves the allocation of resources. Let us look at these two potential benefits of improving tests for handicapped people in greater detail.

The first type of benefit is the more efficient use of workers in the work force. Employment tests provide a proxy for the expected productivity of the workers and, thereby, an indicator of the maximum wage that an employer could pay without reducing profits. A firm, in order to maximize profits, will not knowingly pay a wage that is greater than a worker's contribution to the firm's revenue. A firm will reject, therefore, all applicants whose expected contribution to revenue is less than the wage to be offered, which in this example can be assumed to be the same for all workers. To the extent that the impairments of handicapped applicants reduce their test scores below those of nonhandicapped applicants, the handicapped applicants are disadvantaged in the selection process. If the true productivity of the rejected handicapped applicants is greater than that of those (presumably nonhandicapped) who are hired, the cost to society is the difference between the productivity of the handicapped applicants and the productivity of those who are hired.

The second type of benefits emanates from the elimination of bias in educational tests. Such benefits are more difficult to enumerate than those related to employment, because the benefits of education can be viewed as likely increases in employability and income following school and as nonpecuniary benefits to the individual, such as increased social status, heightened appreciation of the arts, and a personal enjoyment of school life. Although the nonpecuniary benefits may be very important to handicapped people, particularly those who value highly participation in the mainstream, one can argue that the employment benefits of educational attainments are even more important to handicapped people. As was mentioned earlier, acquiring skills is one important way—perhaps the most important way—that handicapped people can compensate for their impaired physical abilities as they compete for places in the labor force.

If, because of impairments, test scores are biased measures of the true probability of success in an educational program for handicapped people, then some handicapped applicants who are more likely to succeed than some nonhandicapped applicants will be rejected. Thus, some less promising applicants will receive the benefits of an education, and the return on the investment in the postschooling years will be less than that that could have been produced by the handicapped applicants. The difference between the returns for the handicapped and the nonhandicapped students is the measure of the social cost of the rejection of the handicapped students. In addition, if one takes the position that education is the difference between employment and unemployment for handicapped people, then the return on the investment in education for handicapped people is marginally much higher than that for nonhandicapped people, and one could even argue that handicapped people who had a lower probability of success should be admitted to school in favor of nonhandicapped people.

The aggregate benefit to society resulting from improved resource allocation due to improved testing of the handicapped might be rather small, on the order of less than 1 percent of the GNP. (For example, the economic costs of racial and ethnic discrimination have been estimated at 2 to 3 percent of the GNP.) Nevertheless, the benefit of improved procedures may loom rather large, making the difference between employment and unemployment or between poverty and moderate income levels. And the nonmonetary benefits, such as the psychological satisfaction that a handicapped person might obtain from working in a job that is considered in the mainstream, may be very great, though essentially nonquantifiable. Moreover, society may place a positive value on the creation of equal opportunity for all and on achieving a greater degree of equity between the handicapped and nonhandicapped, above and beyond the value of the more efficient use of resources or the improved economic status of individual handicapped people.

It is with all of these considerations in mind—the low social and economic status of handicapped people, the barriers that poor tests can place in their way, the opportunities that appropriate tests can create, the benefits to society and to handicapped people of increased education and employment opportunities—that we proceed with our discussion of testing of people with handicapping conditions.

# 2
# Admissions Testing for Postsecondary Education

Although the primary focus of this chapter is on tests that are used to make admissions decisions for postsecondary education, we first describe the exposure of handicapped students in elementary and secondary schools to standardized tests. The reason for beginning with this discussion is that some people have suspected that handicapped students may have very limited or, at least, very different exposure to standardized tests in the elementary and secondary grades and, therefore, may be at a disadvantage relative to their nonhandicapped peers when they encounter college admission tests. Then we move to a discussion of college admission tests. We look at how those admissions tests are modified (described in detail in Chapter 5), the numbers of handicapped people who take the tests, how the scores are reported by the testing companies, and how the scores are used in making admissions decisions. We next discuss tests that are used for admission to graduate and professional schools. Finally, we present what little evidence there is on the validity of all these tests for handicapped applicants and consider that evidence in the context of the validity of tests for nonhandicapped applicants.

## PRIMARY AND SECONDARY SCHOOLS

Testing has long been an integral part of schooling, but the use of standardized tests to measure ability or achievement has been increasing since the early 1900s. Public school children today are given standardized tests for many reasons: to diagnose the strengths and weaknesses of an individual student in order to design an appropriate educational program; to help the teacher decide when a student has learned a particular skill and is ready to progress to other instruction; to place children in the type of program that will best meet their needs; to give guidance and counseling for future education and career plans; to certify minimum competencies; and to evaluate the merits of particular educational programs (such as bilingual or compensatory education programs). The extent to which handicapped children experience this testing is a matter of interest because, if handicapped children are tested less frequently than nonhandicapped children, they are apt to lack test-taking skills and, consequently, to be at a disadvantage when required to take college admission, employment, or certification tests.

Handicapped children who are able to participate in the regular school program for most of the day generally share in the testing experiences of their nonhandicapped classmates. The testing procedures for those children who spend most of their time in special classes vary, according to the school district and the nature of the handicap. In some large, urban schools (e.g., in New York City and Detroit) handicapped children are tested on the same schedule as those who are not handicapped, with modifications made according to each child's individualized education program. In others (e.g., Baltimore) all special education children are excluded from the regular testing program.

## Testing for Placement

For a handicapped child, tests play an important role in determining an appropriate educational program and in deciding whether mainstreaming or a special classroom will be most beneficial.[1] The regulations implementing the Education for All Handicapped Children Act (P.L. 94-142) require that a full and individual evaluation of a child's educational needs be conducted before a handicapped child is assigned to a special education program. Although the procedures vary from school to school, the evaluation of a student usually is

[1]This is one of the issues being investigated by the National Research Council's Panel on Selection and Placement of Students in Programs for the Mentally Retarded (Heller, et al. 1982).

made by a group of people—school psychologist, special education teacher, physician, speech therapist, and other specialists—and includes assessment of the child's health, physical abilities, social and emotional status, general intelligence, and academic performance. A number of tests usually are administered and may include an "intelligence test" as well as tests of basic skills, psychomotor abilities, adaptive behavior, and so on, depending on the nature of the child's handicap. Anywhere from two to fourteen tests may be given, taking from one to ten hours to administer (Anderson 1982).

If, on the basis of this assessment, parents and school personnel agree that the child should receive special education, an "individualized education program" (IEP) is developed—usually by a group consisting of parents, teachers, and other professionals. The IEP is supposed to include a description of the child's current educational performance and adaptive behavior, the type of special services desired, long-range goals and short-term objectives, criteria for evaluating whether the objectives are achieved, and a time schedule for evaluation of progress. In developing the plan, additional tests may be given, and the evaluation of progress (which should be made annually but must take place at least every three years) may also be based partly on test results.

It is clear that handicapped students in special education programs are not inexperienced in test taking. However, many of the tests that are used to make placement decisions are individually administered and differ significantly from the kind of group-administered paper-and-pencil tests that are routinely taken by regular students—the kind that more closely resemble college admission and employment tests.

## Testing for Competency

A relatively new area of testing that is creating problems for handicapped students and raising legal issues in regard to P.L. 94-142 and the Section 504 regulations is minimum competency testing (MCT). Reports of declining test scores and of high school graduates who can barely read and write have generated concern that today's students are not receiving an adequate education. In response to this concern, an increasing number of school districts and states are developing programs to assess a set of basic academic skills that each student is expected to master. Approximately 32 states have mandated some form of minimum competency testing for pupils in the primary and secondary grades.[2] In addition, 156 local school districts have instituted minimum competency testing—some prior to, or as a supplement to, state legislation and some in states that have no mandated state program (Gorth and Perkins 1979).

The purposes of the MCT programs vary. Some states use the test results primarily to determine which pupils need remedial work and to make decisions regarding the school curriculum. Others tie the mastery of competencies to high school graduation or grade-to-grade promotion. Most minimum competency testing programs are directed toward regular education students and have been implemented—sometimes hastily, under pressure from state legislatures or school boards—with little thought given to how the requirements would affect handicapped students (National Association of State Directors of Special Education 1979). Consequently, only a few MCT programs systematically address the needs of handicapped students.

Policies regarding minimum competency testing of handicapped students vary among states and among local school districts. The most common practice is to exempt some or all special education students from the minimum competency tests: for example, Maryland exempts all special education students while North Carolina exempts only the trainable mentally retarded and those students with multiple handicaps. A few states use the student's IEP to determine whether or not the student should take the tests. Minimum competency tests are modified for handicapped students as a state policy in about a third of the states. In New York, for example, special education students are allowed extended time, braille, or use of a calculator or reader, depending on their handicap. Most states, however, leave the responsibility to the local school districts. The state usually prepares a list of accommodations that are appropriate for different handicapping conditions, but it does not indicate criteria for determining the extent of accommodation or the severity of handicap that requires accommodation (Rosewater 1979). Another option, devising tests with different content for handicapped students, has been used only infrequently. Florida has separate tests for hearing- impaired students and for educable mentally retarded students. Several local programs

[2]Some sources (e.g., Pipho 1979) cite 36 MCT programs. However, defining MCT programs as those that set desired performance standards and also specify consequences that affect students as a result of meeting, or not meeting, the standards (e.g., remediation, the receipt of a high school diploma), a study conducted at National Evaluation Systems, Inc., sponsored by the National Institute of Education (Gorth and Perkins 1979), counted 32 such MCT programs.

make provisions for tailoring the tasks required on the test to the needs of individual students (for example, making a business transaction by telephone instead of letter). Several programs make no specific provisions for handicapped students but treat each case on an individual basis. Other procedures include allowing handicapped students to delay testing or letting the student decide whether to take the regular test or be exempted.

Most of the states that link diplomas with MCT scores have not yet specified whether handicapped students are to be included or excluded from their programs. The practices of schools in awarding regular or special diplomas to handicapped students (irrespective of MCT programs) were recently surveyed by the National Association of State Directors of Special Education (1979). Regular diplomas are issued to handicapped students in 31 states, while 17 states allow for local board discretion in awarding diplomas to handicapped students. Special diplomas may be issued to handicapped students in 15 states, depending on local board decisions; 9 states issue special certificates of high school attendance; and 17 states provide for local board discretion to issue such certificates.

Minimum competency testing programs are currently the subject of vigorous controversy (see Haney and Madaus 1978; Madaus and McDonagh 1979; McClung 1977) and litigation (e.g., *Debra P.* v. *Turlington*; *Green* v. *Hunt*). In light of the challenges, a number of states in which competency testing is mandated have not yet implemented their programs (including Utah and South Carolina), and some states (including Florida and North Carolina) have had to change their policies as a result of court decisions.

Three major potential difficulties with minimum competency testing programs come to mind with regard to handicapped students, but all three also affect nonhandicapped students to some extent. First is the definition of the skills that are to be included in the tests, including the decision as to whether those skills are defined to be the same for handicapped and nonhandicapped students. Validity is a concept that has been applied only rather loosely to minimum competency tests, and there are virtually no rigorous, empirical validation studies of the skills to be included. The importance of the inclusion of certain skills and the omission of others, which has received considerable attention for the general population, should receive equal attention for handicapped students. The second potential difficulty is the way in which a cutoff score to distinguish passing from failing scores is determined and, again, whether the cutoff score should be the same for all students, be they able-bodied, handicapped in regular classes, or handicapped in special education classes. The arbitrary nature of the setting of a cutoff score is particularly troublesome. The third difficulty is the policy of using the score of one test as the sole determinant for awarding diplomas, a critical fact in people's lives. The use of one test score without additional information is strongly discouraged by nearly all professionals who work with tests.

It seems clear that careful planning and consideration of all the ways in which MCT programs will affect special education students are essential if discrimination against handicapped people is to be avoided.

## COLLEGE ADMISSIONS

### Policies of Test Makers

In the United States, there are several types of postsecondary schools, each of which has different admissions policies and requirements. Almost all (9 of 10) four-year colleges and universities require either the Scholastic Aptitude Test (SAT) or the American College Testing Program (ACT) assessment as part of their undergraduate admission procedures (Skager 1982). These tests, administered nationwide, are usually taken by high school seniors either at their own school or at testing centers. The results are mailed from the central testing agency to the student and to colleges that he or she specifies.

#### *The Scholastic Aptitude Test*

The Scholastic Aptitude Test (SAT) is composed of a verbal section, which focuses on verbal reasoning, verbal relationships, and reading comprehension, and a mathematical section, which tests for knowledge of algebra and geometry and requires skill in computation, application of principles, and problem solving.

The College Board, which sponsors the SAT (as well as achievement tests in particular subjects, which are also required by many colleges), publishes a special booklet, *Information for Students*, that covers services for handicapped students. The booklet informs the student that a disability should not automatically lead to a request for special testing. Students whose disabilities do not affect reading or writing abilities and who would not require extended time are instructed to follow regular procedures. There is also a separate information sheet for counselors and admissions officers regarding services and procedures to be followed. The information sheet for counselors and admissions officers calls attention to the limited knowledge about the impact of accommodations, that is, changes in standard conditions, on test scores and the resulting uncertainty in interpreting the scores. It also notes that all administrations that involve extended time, special test editions, or the use of a reader, manual translator, or an amanuensis are considered nonstandard and lead to the designation "NON-STD" on the student's score report. The college that receives the score report knows that standard administration procedures were not followed, but it does not know the nature of accommodation made or the type of handicapping condition.

A special "Test Order Form/Test Record" for handicapped examinees calls for information on (1) the nature of the disability; (2) whether the disability is permanent or temporary; (3) the test edition and practice material desired; (4) a sign-off by the student (parent or guardian, if necessary) to indicate both acceptance of conditions outlined in *Information for Students* and understanding that "NON-STD" will appear on score reports to indicate that standard administration procedures were not followed; and (5) a sign-off by a school official that affirms the existence of the handicap and that the testing and reporting procedures have been explained to the student.

The College Board reports that the number of students requesting special administrations of the SAT has nearly doubled over the past five years—from 1,554 people during the 1974-75 testing year to just over 3,000 for 1979-80 (see Table 2-1). Nearly all of this growth can be attributed to large increases in the number of nonstandard administrations using regular editions of the test; regular editions are used primarily by students with learning disabilities who request extended time. Requests for the braille edition of the test have decreased fairly steadily, from 179 administered in 1974-75 to 81 in 1979-80; requests for large-type editions have remained relatively constant, slightly under 600 a year until 1979-80, when they increased to nearly 700. The use of the cassette version of the SAT has increased substantially since it was introduced in 1978, primarily by students with learning disabilities.

### *The American College Testing Program*

The American College Testing Program (ACT) assesses competencies in four subject areas: English, mathematics, social studies, and natural sciences. While the ACT subtests are intended to be tied more closely to academic curricula than are the SAT tests, scores on the ACT and

TABLE 2-1 Special Administrations of Scholastic Aptitude Tests

| | | Test Form | | | |
|---|---|---|---|---|---|
| Year | Total | Braille | Large Type | Regular Type | Audio-Cassette |
| 1974–75 | 1,554 | 179 | 542 | 833 | — |
| 1975–76 | 1,900 | 151 | 602 | 1,147 | — |
| 1976–77 | 2,068 | 166 | 595 | 1,307 | — |
| 1977–78 | 2,220 | 132 | 597 | 1,491 | — |
| 1978–79 | 2,463 | 102 | 584 | 1,710 | 67 |
| 1979–80 | 3,083 | 81 | 699 | 2,051[a] | 252 |
| 1980–81 | 4,500[b] | n.a. | n.a. | n.a. | n.a. |

[a] Of the 2,051 special administrations, 1,493 students reported a perceptual handicap (presumably most were specific learning disabilities), 395 reported a physical handicap, and 163 reported a visual handicap.

[b] The data for 1980–81 are not comparable to those for previous years. The breakdown for this year was done by the characteristic of the test taker, rather than the test. Of the total, 2,702 were "perceptually handicapped," 888 were "visually handicapped," 500 were "physically handicapped," and 410 were "other noncategorized."

NOTE: n.a. = not available.

SAT are highly correlated; applicants who score well on one test will tend to do about as well on the other.[3]

The information booklet for students taking the ACT, entitled "Taking the ACT Assessment," notes that students in certain categories should not complete the regular registration folder. Students are informed that if they are handicapped or confined they may request a special administration by writing to ACT and that all requests are considered individually. ACT reports that almost all requests are accepted. The booklet comments on the availability of braille, large-type, and cassette editions of the ACT assessment for visually handicapped or dyslexic students. It notes that other arrangements may be made for students who are unable to write the test or to complete the test at a regular test center.

A special brochure, "The ACT Assessment Special Testing Guide,"

[3] The sum of the ACT English, natural sciences, and social studies subtests had a correlation of .82 with the SAT verbal test in a sample of about 15,000 applicants who took both tests (Skager 1982).

sets forth conditions and procedures under which special administrations will be conducted. It informs the student that if a special testing that involves extended time is elected, the word "special" will appear on report forms under "Type of Test." On the Special Registration Form for Handicapped Applicants, students are asked to provide a brief description of their handicap or disability and to indicate which edition of ACT assessment is desired. The person who supervises the administration is asked to confirm that the applicant is handicapped. The student is required to select as a supervisor a teacher or a counselor who is able to read and write English.

Practice material is available only in regular form. ACT reports that teachers often read the regular sample questions to visually impaired students and that some schools for the blind have reproduced the sample questions in braille. Since most special administrations are untimed, ACT does not feel that the lack of practice material is a problem. However, in view of the evidence that "coaching" or other forms of practice can significantly improve test scores (Federal Trade Commission 1978, 1979; Messick 1980), this point is debatable.

The American College Testing Program reports that about 1,000 handicapped people each year request and receive special test administrations in order to submit their applications to college. In addition, many students take the ACT for placement purposes after they have been admitted and arrive on campus. About 1 percent of all on-campus test administrations each year are special administrations.

It is important to note that, in contrast to the College Board's policy for marking "NON-STD" on *all* scores reported for special administrations, ACT assessment scores are marked "special" only if the tests are taken under untimed conditions. (About 60 percent of all special administrations are untimed.) The only other information regarding handicaps that might appear with a score report would be an affirmative reply to the statement, "I have a physical handicap or disability that may require special provisions or services from the college I attend," which appears on the student profile section given on a voluntary basis to examinees. However, only about 10 percent of the 3,120 institutions that received score reports in 1978-79 requested that applicants' responses to that item be printed on the 1979-80 score reports (Maxey and Levitz 1980). In addition, some people who are not permanently disabled (e.g., someone in a hospital or someone who temporarily cannot write because of surgery or an accident) are permitted to take the tests with extended time and thus would be included in the "special" category. Beginning in 1980-81, the score report for students who ask for a specially arranged

TABLE 2-2 Special Administrations of the ACT Assessment, 1978–79

| | | Test Form | | | |
|---|---|---|---|---|---|
| Handicap | Total | Braille | Large Type | Regular Type | Audio-Cassette |
| Hearing Impaired | 26 | — | — | 26 | — |
| Dyslexic | 155 | — | — | 77 | 78 |
| Learning Disabled | 325 | — | — | 183 | 142 |
| Visually Disabled | 430 | 83 | 266 | 24 | 57 |
| Physically Disabled | 207 | — | — | 195 | 12 |
| TOTALS | 1,143 | 83 | 266 | 505 | 289 |

NOTE: Numbers include both timed and untimed administrations; ACT reports that about 60 percent of all special administrations are untimed. Special administrations given on campus are included only if they involved modified test forms, i.e., braille, cassette, or large type. ACT is not informed of other special arrangements for on-campus testing, e.g., untimed regular-type tests.

SOURCE: Data provided by Philip Rever of the American College Testing Program.

administration of the ACT assessment under timed conditions will have an indicator that will say "arranged."

The numbers of different special administrations of the ACT, both timed and untimed, for the 1978-79 testing year are shown in Table 2-2.

### *Other Admissions-Related Tests*

Three additional tests sponsored by the College Board have some bearing on college admissions. The Preliminary Scholastic Aptitude Test/National Merit Scholarship Qualifying Test (PSAT/NMQT) is taken by college-bound high school juniors who wish to compete for National Merit Scholarships or to gain familiarity with the SAT. The PSAT/NMQT is available in braille and large type; a reader, manual translator, or amanuensis is permitted. During the 1979-80 testing year, 338 special editions were requested (73 braille and 265 large-type). Requests for these special versions have increased over the past five years, in contrast with the SAT, for which braille requests have decreased and those for large type have remained fairly constant. This may be because the SAT is available on cassettes and the PSAT/NMQT is not.

Advanced Placement Program (APP) examinations may be taken

by high school juniors and seniors who wish to get college credit for college-level work completed in high school. There are no special editions of the 24 APP examinations, but special arrangements may include extra time or the assistance of a reader or amanuensis. In such instances the following statement appears on all copies of the grade report: "Candidate handicapped. Exam administered under special conditions." Each year, approximately 25 handicapped students take the APP.

The College-Level Examination Program (CLEP) enables nontraditional students entering college to get credit for college-level skills and knowledge acquired outside the classroom. Four of the five CLEP general examinations are available in cassette editions with accompanying line figures for test questions that require interpretation of graphs, charts, and tabular material. All other tests, including the 47 subject examinations, are provided only in regular editions, but they may be administered with the assistance of an amanuensis or reader. The CLEP humanities test, which includes a number of pictures in the questions on art history, is being prepared in a special edition for visually impaired test takers; questions that do not require visual stimulus material are substituted for those that do. Up to twice the regular time is permitted for handicapped students. Score reports indicate that the examination was administered under nonstandard conditions. Approximately 20 handicapped and 93,000 nonhandicapped people take one or more CLEP examinations annually.

## Policies of Admissions Officers

While college admission is widely viewed as a highly competitive process, with scores on admissions tests playing a crucial role, several recent surveys suggest this is not the case. In fact, most colleges and universities are not highly selective. A survey based on the responses from about 200,000 freshmen who entered 362 institutions of higher education in the fall of 1979 found that more than 75 percent were accepted by either their first or second choice (Cooperative Institutional Research Program of the University of California, Los Angeles and the American Council on Education 1980).

A national survey of undergraduate admissions policies (sponsored jointly by the American Association of Collegiate Registrars and Admissions Officers (AACRAO) and the College Board [AACRAO-College Board 1980]) found the median percentage of applicants accepted by both private and public four-year institutions for 1978 to be more than 80 percent. For two-year colleges the median acceptance rate was more than 90 percent. Since there is good reason to suspect that the schools that responded to the questionnaire (about 63 percent of the public and 57 percent of the private schools) may constitute a sample biased in the direction of more selective institutions, the 80 percent acceptance rate for the four-year colleges and universities may well be an underestimate.

On the basis of their replies to the survey, each institution was categorized as nonselective (accepts all applicants who meet certain minimal requirements) or selective (accepts only a limited number of applicants). Data for the 255 selective four-year public institutions show that 23 percent accepted more than 90 percent of their applicants for the 1978-79 school year, 24 percent accepted 81 to 90 percent, and 25 percent accepted 71 to 80 percent; only 11 percent accepted fewer than 50 percent (AACRAO-College Board 1980).

These figures give a misleading picture, in one sense, because they do not consider self-selection by applicants. That is, a distinguished institution may accept a large percentage of its applicants because only outstanding students choose to apply. A study by Venti and Wise (1980) supports this interpretation. They conclude that, while SAT scores may greatly affect admissions decisions, particularly in highly selective schools, their effect on the decisions of applicants is much stronger. Nevertheless, the overall impression is one of increasing accessibility. It is estimated that about a third of U.S. institutions of higher education have essentially an "open door" policy (Skager 1982).

The majority of public and private institutions in the AACRAO-College Board study (1980) report that high school grades are considered more important as admissions criteria than test scores, although test scores rank a close second. Other types of credentials commonly required for some or all applicants include personal interviews (required by 42 percent of the public and 54 percent of the private four-year institutions) and letters of recommendation (required by 33 percent of the public and 82 percent of the private four-year institutions). Judgments about such personal qualities as motivation and moral character were considered important, as was evidence of special skills, work experience, community involvement, and leadership qualities. Venti and Wise (1980) also conclude that test scores do not appear to be the major constraint on the college opportunities of high school graduates.

Most schools apparently weigh admission test scores in reaching an overall judgment regarding admissibility but do not set a cutoff score. Fewer than half of the four-year institutions participating in the

AACRAO-College Board study had minimum SAT or ACT scores below which "an applicant is generally not considered for admission": 38 percent of public and 42 percent of private institutions using the SAT; 29 percent and 30 percent, respectively, for those using the ACT. When a cutoff score is used, it is surprisingly low. Average cutoff scores for the total SAT were about 750 (of a possible 1,600) for public and private institutions. For schools using the ACT, the mean minimum composite scores were 16.2 and 16.4 (of a possible 36) for public and private institutions, respectively.

The overall picture for admissions at the undergraduate level is one of considerable flexibility in the use of test scores along with other information (Skager 1982). Most institutions admit the majority of their applicants, and most applicants are admitted to the college or university of their choice. With the anticipated decline in the college-age population and increased concerns for affirmative action, undergraduate admissions seem likely to become even more open and less selective in the future.

## Handicapped Students in College

Compared with their numbers in the college-age population, handicapped people are underrepresented in college. A 1976 survey by the National Center for Education Statistics (U.S. Department of Education 1980:38) found that among the college-age population (18 to 25 years of age) only 29 percent of handicapped people were enrolled in school compared with 36 percent for the college-age population as a whole. In addition, a much higher percentage of handicapped than nonhandicapped students attend two-year (as opposed to four-year) institutions: while 36 percent of all students enrolled in colleges and universities in 1978 attended two-year institutions, 50 percent of the mobility-impaired and almost 57 percent of the acoustically impaired students attended two-year institutions (U.S. Department of Education 1980:38).

To what extent is the underrepresentation of handicapped people in college a result of selective admissions? Unfortunately, there is little information about admissions policies for handicapped students. The only relevant question on the AACRAO-College Board survey had to do with exceptions to the formal admissions requirements made by selective institutions: 39 percent of the public four-year, 30 percent of the private four-year, and 25 percent of the private two-year institutions said that exceptions could be made for "physically handicapped students."

According to James Dunning, director of admissions at the University of California, Irvine, admissions officers in most colleges make every effort *not* to discriminate against handicapped applicants.[4] He believes that scores resulting from a nonstandard administration are treated as if they were regular scores, unless they are to the student's obvious detriment. When those scores are low, applicants' records are reviewed further in an attempt to assess accurately their abilities; if special test administrations are not flagged, Dunning suggested, low-scoring handicapped applicants may be unwittingly denied admission.

## ADMISSION TO PROFESSIONAL AND GRADUATE SCHOOLS

### Policies of Test Makers

#### *The Graduate Record Examination*

The test most frequently required for admission to graduate school programs, the Graduate Record Examination (GRE), is published by the Graduate Record Examinations Board and administered by the Educational Testing Service. It includes an aptitude test composed of three subtests (verbal, quantitative, and analytical reasoning), and advanced tests in 20 fields.

An asterisk next to the test date on a handicapped applicant's score report directs attention to a footnote saying "special testing condition; see enclosed memo." The memorandum describes the special conditions under which the test was taken, urges cautious use of the scores, and recommends that other indicators of achievement be emphasized. The Educational Testing Service notes in its information bulletin for applicants that "our intent is to remind the graduate schools that each handicapped student should be considered individually, in light of the particular disability involved and the student's academic record."

Overall figures for the administration of the GRE aptitude test show a downward trend over the past 5 years, from 300,000 tests in 1975-76 to 275,000 in 1978-79. About 400 handicapped applicants take the GRE aptitude test each year under special conditions; an additional 100 take one of the advanced tests only. Of the 409 special

[4]Dunning spoke at the open meeting of the panel (see Appendix B), representing the American Association of Collegiate Registrars and Admissions Officers.

administrations of the aptitude test in 1978-79, 215 were regular type, 113 large type, 39 braille, and 42 cassette. Of the 215 handicapped applicants who used the regular-type edition, about 55 percent were reported by test supervisors to have "physical disabilities" and 45 percent to have "visual problems." Some applicants included under "visual problems" may have had learning disabilities, but this was not a category used in the supervisor's report form. The most frequent accommodation was extra time; readers and amanuenses were seldom used. People with visual problems often used special aids, such as the Opticon.

### *The Miller Analogies Test*

The Miller Analogies Test (MAT), published by the Psychological Corporation, is also used for graduate admissions on a national scale—sometimes along with the GRE and sometimes in its place. The test consists of a series of problems stated in the form of analogies, mostly verbal. Each analogy has four parts, or terms, three of which are given with the remaining term to be selected from four choices. Many of the terms are quite esoteric, so the test requires an extensive vocabulary.

About 80,000 people take the MAT each year; some 20 to 30 of these use braille editions, while 35 to 45 use large-type editions. Presumably almost all of these special administrations took extra time, but the Psychological Corporation does not record that information. It also does not keep count of the number of handicapped individuals who take the test with a reader or amanuensis or under standard conditions. The Psychological Corporation indicates a nonstandard administration when reporting scores for all accommodations, and they enclose a cautionary statement concerning interpretation.

### *The Medical College Admission Test*

Applicants to all but two of the 126 U.S. medical schools are required to take the Medical College Admission Test (MCAT), which is developed by the American Institute for Research under the sponsorship of the Association of American Medical Colleges and is administered by the American College Testing Program. The test, which replaced an older version in 1977, assesses (a) science knowledge in biology, chemistry, and physics; (b) the ability to solve problems in these three science fields; (c) reading skills; and (d) quantitative skills.

Handicapped applicants are informed, in the *MCAT Announcement*, that they must submit a letter from a physician documenting their handicapping condition and the need for special arrangements. There are no modified editions of the MCAT, but the assistance of a reader or an amanuensis is allowed, as is extended time if requested—up to two days compared with the regular one day (6½ hours actual test time). If any of these arrangements is used, the test report is marked by an asterisk. The asterisk could signify temporary disability, such as a broken arm, but since applicants are almost always interviewed before being accepted, whether or not score reports reveal one's handicap is usually irrelevant.

Approximately 54,000 administrations of the MCAT are given yearly; about a third of them are repeat testings. The average applicant takes the test twice, and many take it three to five times. Of the 26,000 applicants who took the MCAT in the fall of 1979, only about 10 requested special accommodations. According to ACT, which administers the MCAT, about half of those requesting special accommodations are dyslexic individuals who ask for extended time. The rest typically have low vision or a temporary disability.[5]

*The Law School Admission Test*

All of the 168 law schools approved by the American Bar Association require the Law School Admission Test (LSAT), which is developed, administered, and scored by the Educational Testing Service under the authority of the Law School Admission Council. The test yields a single score reflecting the ability to understand and draw inferences from reading and to reason logically about both verbal and quantitative problems. There is also a separate section, with a separate score, on writing ability.

During the 1978-79 testing year, 115,284 applicants took the LSAT; about one-third of them were repeat testings. Most law schools require that applications be submitted through the Law School Data Assembly Service, which provides each school with a summary of the applicant's academic work, copies of college transcripts, LSAT scores, and a numerical index—based on undergraduate grade-point average and the LSAT score—that predicts first-year law grades for each applicant.

The only modification in test format is a large-type edition with

[5]This information comes from Ken McCaffrey, Director of the MCAT program at ACT, in a personal communication with the panel.

large-type answer sheets. A handicapped person may take the regular edition of the LSAT with the assistance of an amanuensis or in a separate testing room. Neither readers nor extra test time is permitted, although additional rest time between sections is allowed. Braille and cassette versions, which had fewer questions than the regular LSAT and were untimed, were discontinued in 1976. The decision to drop them was made by the Law School Admission Council, which believed that the modified tests could not be validated and were not in compliance with the Section 504 regulations. At the same time, a large-type edition of the regular LSAT to be administered with standard time limits was made available.

The *Law School Admission Bulletin* points out that the options available for testing handicapped people are limited and suggests that applicants whose handicap makes it impossible to take the test with the options offered should so notify the law schools to which they are applying. Schools may want applicants to take the large-type version or they may waive the test. Even if a school waives the test, it may want applicants to submit data through the Law School Data Assembly Service. The Law School Admission Council recommends that law schools consider handicapped students individually in deciding whether to require them to take the LSAT and in making admissions decisions.

For applicants who take the large-type LSAT each year—there have been 20 or fewer in recent years—the scores reported to the law schools are accompanied by a note stating that "This candidate took the Large Print edition of the Law School Admission Test under conditions for the visually handicapped." A letter given to the applicant to forward to the school describes the conditions of testing, notes that the score earned should be viewed as representing the "lower limits" of ability as measured by the LSAT, and suggests that the student's school record and personal recommendations be given greater weight. Scores from applicants who require an amanuensis or separate testing room are not flagged in any way.

### *The Graduate Management Admission Test*

The Graduate Management Admission Test (GMAT) is developed and administered by the Educational Testing Service according to policies set by the Graduate Admissions Council, an organization composed of 55 graduate schools of management, all of which require the GMAT. The test is also required by some 500 schools or departments in the fields of business administration, accounting, public administration, and public health. Approximately 190,000 tests were administered in 1978-79 (about 207,000 is the estimate for 1979-80). Use of the GMAT has increased steadily in the past 5 years as applicants who might earlier have selected other types of graduate or professional training have shifted to business and management fields.

Editions of the GMAT in braille, large type, and on cassette first became available in 1979-80. The assistance of an amanuensis or a reader is permitted, as is up to six hours of extra time. The score results for handicapped examinees include a memorandum describing the nature of the test conditions and the fact that norms are not available for interpreting the scores.

During the 1979-80 testing year, 74 special administrations of the GMAT were given: 33 were large-type, 7 were cassette, and 3 were braille versions; 26 applicants took the regular test with extra time, and 5 took the regular test within the standard time limits but required a separate room or special seating.

## Policies of Admissions Officers

It is difficult to determine the proportion of graduate school applicants who are required to take the GRE, because requirements for graduate admission often vary from department to department, even within the same university. A large graduate institution might incorporate 30 different schools and departments, each with its own admissions requirements. However, among the largest and most prestigious graduate institutions (members of the Association of Graduate Schools), the GRE is likely to be required for some or all applicants for a majority of programs (Skager 1982).

Decisions about acceptance to graduate school usually are made by a faculty committee of the department or program involved. Consequently, it is difficult to obtain a definitive picture of how important test scores are in the process. The only national study of the use of the GRE in graduate admissions (Burns 1970) indicates that scores are weighed along with other data, and that cutoff scores—below which applicants are automatically rejected—are seldom used.

Admission to medical school is extremely competitive. For example, most of the 48 private medical schools in this country admitted less than 10 percent of their applicants in 1977-78 (Gordon 1979). And medical school applicants are a highly self-selected group: for example, the mean undergraduate grade-point average of those applying to medical school in 1978-79 was 3.3 (Thomae-Forgues and Erdmann 1980).

Almost all U.S. medical schools interview prospective students, so admission is essentially a two-stage process. Undergraduate grades, MCAT scores, letters of recommendation, background information, and state residency (in the case of many public institutions) are considered in determining who will be interviewed. (Medical schools typically interview about 2.5 times the number of applicants who will eventually receive offers of admission.) Final decisions regarding admission presumably are based on impressions gained during the interview of the applicant's personal qualities as well as on further exploration of academic background and relevant experience.

The Special Advisory Panel on Technical Standards for Medical School Admission appointed by the Association of American Medical Colleges prepared a set of guidelines for medical colleges specifying the technical (nonacademic) standards for applicants seeking the Doctor of Medicine (M.D.) degree (Cooper 1979). These standards, which physicians should meet to ensure good patient care, include adequate somatic sensation, vision, hearing, speech, equilibrium, exteroceptive sense (touch, pain, temperature), proprioceptive sense (position, pressure, movement), and motor function. The advisory panel stressed that the M.D. degree is a broad, undifferentiated degree, and that medical students should be potentially capable of performing any of the tasks required of a physician. Thus, they argued, it is not acceptable to admit a blind student, for example, on the grounds that he or she plans to become a psychiatrist and therefore will not be required to perform many of the physician's tasks that depend primarily on vision.

The guidelines are only recommendations, and they are probably more conservative than the policies of some medical schools. In view of the fact that there are so many more qualified applicants than available places in medical schools, however, it seems unlikely that any but the most exceptional handicapped student would be admitted to medical school. The Association of American Medical Colleges has no data on the number of handicapped applicants admitted to medical school; the only available information relates to a few handicapped individuals who have graduated from medical school.

With guidelines as explicit as those from the special advisory panel and with the demand for admission to medical schools far exceeding the number places available, it is reasonable to conclude that while the MCAT is undoubtedly an obstacle for some handicapped people, it probably does not constitute the major barrier to medical school admission.

While law school admissions generally are not as competitive as medical school admissions, there are still many more academically qualified law school applicants than can be admitted. Compared to graduate and medical schools, law schools have a more mechanical admission process. Few law schools interview applicants, and the quantitative index provided by the Law School Data Assembly Service (based on undergraduate grade-point average and LSAT score) is used as a screening device. There is some indication that test scores are weighted more heavily than grade-point average in determining the index (Schrader 1976).

The Law School Admission Council recommends that law schools waive the LSAT for certain handicapped applicants, but there are no data showing how many do so. Because LSAT scores are not flagged, those handicapped applicants who receive low scores could be rejected automatically unless the law school's attention is drawn to the other evidence of ability.

## PREDICTIVE VALIDITY OF POSTSECONDARY ADMISSIONS TESTS

The primary purpose of college admissions tests is to identify applicants who will succeed academically. It is presumed that applicants with high test scores will earn higher grades and be more likely to graduate than those with low test scores. In this section we describe the available evidence on this issue, the validity of admission tests for the general population and for handicapped applicants.

### College Admissions Tests

In a sample of 310 validity studies of the SAT, the median correlation between scores on the verbal section of the test and freshman grades was about .38 and that for the mathematical section was about .34 (analysis by Linn 1982 based on data from Schrader 1971). The ACT composite scores have a correlation of about .38 with freshman grades; multiple correlations of the four ACT subtest scores with freshman grade-point averages are about .50 (American College Testing Program 1973).

Correlations in this range allow for considerable error in prediction. For example, with a correlation of .50, under ideal circumstances only 44 percent of those in the top fifth of the distribution of test scores will be expected to be in the top fifth in terms of grade-point average (Linn 1982). Thus, people with the same scores on college admissions tests are likely to have wide variability in their grade-point averages. These correlations, however, to some extent underestimate the degree of relationship between test scores and college grades because the group in college is fairly homogeneous. College students generally are more able than the population at large. If the entire college-age population were tested and admitted to college, the correlations between test scores and freshman grades would be higher. In addition, as Venti and Wise (1980) note, test scores affect an individual's decision of whether to apply to college as well as the choice of college. This further attenuates the correlation between test scores and college grades.

While ACT and SAT scores do provide some basis for predicting freshman grades, neither of these tests has been found to be a better, or even as good, a predictor of freshman grade-point averages as high school grades or high school rank in class (Schrader 1971; American College Testing Program 1973). Nevertheless, a combination of test scores and high school grade-point average does predict college grades better than either of those two variables alone. For both the ACT and the SAT, the multiple correlation for high school grades plus test scores is about .59, compared with .50 for high school grades alone. Furthermore, it can be argued that the scores provide an adjustment for the variability in the quality of education and in the meaning of grades from different high schools.

Although the available data are quite meager, they do give some indication of how well grades and test scores predict the college achievement of handicapped students. The available data come from a study of handicapped and nonhandicapped students who have taken the ACT assessment (Maxey and Levitz 1980). (The handicapped applicants are those who took the regular ACT assessment on a national test date, not those who took modified editions or untimed tests.) It should be noted, first, that data collected by ACT show that handicapped students, on the average, have earned lower high school grades and earn lower college grades than nonhandicapped students (Maxey and Levitz 1980); see also Table 2-3. (Students are asked to report their high school grades when they register to take the ACT assessment.) The high school grades for these handicapped students were, on average, 0.21 grade points lower than the national norm. In their first year of college, the grades of these handicapped students were, on average, 0.17 grade points lower than for nonhandicapped students (Maxey and Levitz 1980).

For handicapped students in this sample the correlation between high school grades and freshman grade-point average is .43; the correlation between ACT composite scores and freshman grades is

TABLE 2-3 Mean Self-Reported High School Grades for Students Taking the Regular Edition of the ACT, 1976–80

| Year | Mean Grades: Handicapped Students | Mean Grades: Nonhandicapped Students | Number: Handicapped Students | Number: Nonhandicapped Students |
|---|---|---|---|---|
| 1975–76 | 2.68 | 2.94 | 9,112 | 62,113[a] |
| 1976–77 | 2.80 | 2.96 | 337[a] | 66,562[a] |
| 1978–79 | 2.74 | 2.95 | 555[a] | 73,376[a] |
| 1979–80 | 2.75 | 2.95 | 717[a] | 80,145[a] |

[a]Number is a 10 percent sample of the identified populations.

SOURCE: Maxey and Levitz (1980) and personal communication, Maxey (1981).

.46. Thus, for this sample of handicapped students, test scores are a slightly better predictor of college performance than are high school grades. For nonhandicapped students in this study, the reverse is true: the correlation for high school grades with freshman grades is slightly higher (.46) than the correlation of the ACT composite score with freshman grades (.44). For both groups, a combination of the ACT composite scores and high school grade-point average predicts college grades equally well (.59) (Maxey and Levitz 1980).

While the above data suggest that ACT scores are a valid predictor of college performance for this sample of handicapped students, they do not provide any information about the validity of the tests for students with different disabilities, or for those with more severe disabilities. (The reader should remember that the study included only those handicapped students who took the regular ACT assessment.) In one study conducted in the late 1960s, 41 deaf students at the National Technical Institute for the Deaf (NTID, part of the Rochester Technical Institute) were compared with 103 hearing students who enrolled in the program. The mean score on the verbal part of the SAT for the deaf students was 291, with a range of 200 to 416. This contrasted with a mean verbal score among their hearing peers of 485, with a range of 301 to 727. Thus, the lowest score of the hearing students was close to the mean of the scores of the deaf students. On the quantitative section of the SAT, the mean score was 392 for the deaf students and 564 for the hearing students, with ranges of 253 to 577 and 343 to 752, respectively. While the mathematics scores of the deaf students were substantially higher than their verbal scores, they were also low relative to the mathematics scores of their hearing peers. The top quantitative score among the deaf students was not much higher than the mean for the hearing students. The proportion of deaf students who would have been admitted to Rochester Technical Institute on the basis of their SAT scores would undoubtedly have been quite low; however, SAT scores were not considered in the admission of NTID students. At the end of the third term the deaf students trailed the hearing students by an average of less than 0.5 grade point, and the attrition rate of these "high-risk" students was less than that of the hearing students (Walter 1970).

The support received by the deaf students at NTID (tutoring, interpreting, etc.), which presumably raised what their college grades would otherwise have been, may have greatly reduced the predictive power of the SAT. Nevertheless, these findings indicate that the SAT was not an effective predictor for the deaf students in this program. The Educational Testing Service is nearing completion of a study of the validity of the SAT for deaf and hearing students at California State University at Northridge. Early analyses of the data indicate that the SAT is as good a predictor of college grades for the hearing-impaired as for the nonhandicapped students (Jones and Ragosta 1981). Gallaudet College, a college for deaf students, has developed its own admissions test battery; it has been found to be a much better predictor of grade-point average over four years of college than the SAT (Greenberg and Greenberg 1971).

### Graduate Admissions Tests

The correlations between admissions test scores and academic performance in graduate, medical, or law schools are generally lower than those for undergraduate schools because the severely limited variability in test scores and grades attenuates the correlation coefficients. In general, predictions based on academic performance in college (undergraduate grade-point average) are about as good as predictions based on test scores, but the combination of test scores and undergraduate grades is a better predictor than either alone (Willingham 1974).

## CONCLUSIONS

What can we conclude about the nature of the admissions process for handicapped people? For the general population there emerges a picture of a few highly selective colleges and universities but with a majority of colleges and universities accepting a relatively large proportion of their applicants. Most college applicants are admitted by the school of their first or second choice (although perhaps in part because students tend to apply to schools where they are likely to be admitted). High school grades have been shown to be the single best predictor of freshman college grades, with test scores improving the prediction rather little. Based on these findings some may conclude that postsecondary admissions tests are of no consequence for most college applicants, including those with handicapping conditions. Nevertheless, the panel believes it is unsafe to conclude that tests are unimportant for handicapped college applicants for the following reasons:

- Test scores *are* used in admissions decisions by many schools.
- Tests may offer an opportunity for handicapped applicants to demonstrate their abilities.
- Tests may, in some situations, work to the detriment of some handicapped applicants.
- The right to take appropriate tests has been accorded handicapped people by federal regulations.

# 3
# Testing for Job Selection

There are several points at which testing could serve as a barrier to the participation of the handicapped in the world of work. For an increasing number of occupations, licensing or certification procedures are required, and written tests have become a common vehicle for measuring competence. Federal, state, and local civil service systems rely heavily on screening through testing. Unions and management alike use tests to screen candidates for entry-level jobs or occupations. Frequently, handicapped people also encounter tests in rehabilitation agencies when they prepare for jobs. In these situations, the use of tests may hinder handicapped people from joining the work force in a capacity for which their education and training have otherwise been adequate and appropriate, or it may facilitate their moving into productive roles in American society.

Primarily because tests have tended to screen out blacks, Hispanics, and members of other minority groups, employment testing has been under close scrutiny since the mid-1960s. One focus of the concern has been the job-relatedness or validity of the tests. (See Chapter 4 for a discussion of the relevant legal issues and Chapter 5 for a discussion of psychometric considerations in validation studies.) One significant consequence of the closer scrutiny of employment testing has been a tendency to overestimate the historical importance of tests in the total hiring process. A second consequence has been the unprecedented volume of social resources that have recently been invested in employment testing—from test development to litigation.

A third consequence has been a decline in test use, particularly among small employers, in the wake of confusion about the precise interpretation of federal guidelines on employee selection procedures.

The panel has obtained information from public and private sector employers, rehabilitation agencies, and licensing and certification officials regarding the degree to which handicapped individuals encounter tests in employment settings. We have learned that there is sparse information about employment testing in the private sector, even for the general population. This lack of information is of concern because the private sector is a much larger, more amorphous part of the world of work than the public sector. In this chapter we present a synthesis of the information we obtained, but we caution against overgeneralization based on these data, particularly those regarding the private sector, in which the enormous number and diversity of employment settings limit inference from one case to another. Whenever possible we compare employment testing procedures for handicapped people with those for the general population. Following the descriptions of testing in the various employment settings, we discuss issues that are common to those settings relating to hiring or promotion practices that may tend to limit the occupational opportunities of handicapped people. Finally, we give a brief sketch of the practices and policies of a few other nations trying to improve the status of people with handicapping conditions.

## THE PUBLIC SECTOR

### Employment Testing at the Federal Level

The public sector, which includes federal (including the military), state, and local government agencies, is the locus of the most comprehensive and systematic testing programs for selection and placement in employment. At the federal level, the Office of Personnel Management (OPM, formerly the Civil Service Commission) has in recent years administered hundreds of thousands of examinations yearly for clerical and entry-level professional positions in the federal government. Most of the exams are intended to predict how a candidate without much experience will perform in a job that requires no special training. Although OPM's Professional and Administrative Career Examination (PACE) has been supported by ongoing test development and validation, including considerable work on modifications for handicapped examinees, it is being phased out in favor of tests or other selection devices developed for each of the 118 jobs formerly covered by the PACE.[1]

The Rehabilitation Act of 1973 and the Vietnam Era Veterans' Readjustment Assistance Act of 1974 require every federal agency to facilitate hiring, placement, and advancement of handicapped people. However, interest in the special problems associated with the testing of handicapped candidates for civil service positions dates back to the 1950s. Some of the most constructive steps toward solving the psychometric problems associated with the testing of handicapped people have been undertaken by research divisions of OPM and its predecessor.

Recently the emphasis in the federal government has been on alternate routes (i.e., not tests) to careers with the federal government. Many mid-level and senior positions are open to all applicants through what is termed the "excepted service." No civil service rating is required for these openings; candidates are evaluated on the basis of education, training, and experience. OPM's Office of Selective Placement Programs also administers two entry-level programs that are particularly relevant to handicapped job seekers. Through the Schedule A appointments program, applicants may arrange for special procedures or accommodations in hiring requirements, including exemption from tests. Schedule B appointments provide similar arrangements specifically for the "mentally restored," people who have received psychiatric treatment.

In addition to the variations on the traditional competitive testing method of entry into the civil service, the federal government has also instituted temporary or trial work periods. Upon successful completion of 700 hours on a full- or part-time job, the candidate becomes a regular government employee. Another entry route to the federal civil service, instituted in 1971, is the counselor certification technique. Under this arrangement, a report from a rehabilitation counselor who has inspected the worksite, job requirements, and client's qualifications can be substituted for passing an examination (Schein et al. 1980).

In 1977, 6.85 percent of the federal work force reported having a handicapping condition; the figure for 1978 was 6.74 percent (U.S. Office of Personnel Management 1980). The percentage of handi-

[1]This change is the result of a consent decree between OPM and a number of plaintiffs who claimed the test was discriminatory because of its adverse impact on blacks and Hispanics.

TABLE 3-1 Programs for Employing the Handicapped in State Government, 1971

| Program | Number of States |
|---|---|
| Civil Service or Merit System | 48 |
| Temporary Appointments for the Handicapped | 18 |
| Special Appointments in Lieu of Testing | 24 |
| Appointments Reserved for Specific Disabilities | 11 |
| Training Program for Supervisors Handling the Handicapped | 13 |
| Special Testing Arrangements for the Handicapped | 44 |

SOURCE: President's Committee on Employment of the Handicapped (1971).

capped employees who said they were severely disabled rose by about 5 percent between December 1977 and December 1978. The OPM report also notes marked change in the distribution of handicapped employees across the government salary levels. Based on these figures, OPM's report concludes that attitudinal and procedural barriers to employment and advancement of the handicapped in federal government are diminishing. Unfortunately, it is not possible to determine from this report the means by which disabled individuals entered federal service and whether tests were used in the selection process.

## Employment Testing at the State Level

State governments also rely heavily on tests to maintain their legislatively mandated merit systems of hiring. A survey conducted jointly by the Office of Personnel Management and the Council of State Governments (1979) indicated that more than three-fourths of the states used written tests as part of the selection process for clerical, professional, and technical jobs, while more than one-half tested applicants for blue-collar and management/administrative positions. State and local governments differ from the federal government, however, in that they typically do not maintain research departments for test development and validation but rather rely on research done by others, usually in industrial or academic settings (see below).

A 1971 survey of hiring practices for handicapped job applicants in all 50 states showed great variety (see Table 3-1). A total of 44 states provided special testing arrangements for handicapped candidates. Temporary and special appointment categories parallel

Schedule A and B appointments and the 700-hour trial work period instituted by the federal government.

State employment services have turned to the United States Employment Service (USES) of the U.S. Department of Labor for help in developing and validating tests used in vocational counseling and in the selection of applicants for specific jobs. For example, USES research has demonstrated that by using the six subtests of the General Aptitude Test Battery (GATB) plus an as yet unvalidated test called the Nonreading Measure of General Ability, counselors and personnel staff are provided with an adequate assessment of a deaf person's aptitudes. However, users of this combination of tests are cautioned that scores thus obtained cannot be compared with the norms established on nonhandicapped takers of the GATB. For another example, USES research into the applicability of the GATB for mentally retarded people indicates that the battery is appropriate for those individuals termed "slow learners" or borderline mentally retarded but not for blind people.

The rest of this section is devoted to more detailed information on programs for assessing handicapped employees in several states. We do not claim that these examples constitute a representative sample of state practice, but we do feel that they indicate the variety of responses to federal legislation concerning handicapped people.

New York State has long had a civil service law that prohibits discrimination against the disabled in any part of the civil service testing or employment process.[2] This law specifically refers to the right of a handicapped person to extra time and the services of an amanuensis in taking tests, and additional accommodations are offered to handicapped examinees. Until 1977, the section of the law that tried to protect the disabled was interpreted to mean that a handicapped person could not be certified by an officer with hiring authority until the Commission for the Blind and Visually Handicapped or the Office of Vocational Rehabilitation had confirmed that the job in question was an appropriate setting for that person. This procedure was viewed as a protection for the handicapped person against appointment to a "no-win" situation. In practice, however, it was frequently so time-consuming that job openings were filled before the certification process could be completed. Now, job candidates

[2]Information about New York State is based on a personal communication from Donald Hoyt, coordinator of oral testing, New York State Department of Civil Service.

who identify themselves as handicapped are notified of the availability of rehabilitation services at the time they receive their test results and are certified for employment in the same manner as all other candidates. If a personnel officer believes a handicapped applicant can perform a given job, he or she refers the person to a health services physician, who investigates the situation and either supports the agency's assertion or recommends accommodations in the job. In most cases, the agency first attempts to make the needed modifications, viewing the referral as a last resort.

The state of Michigan has instituted a six-month trial appointment program for handicapped people who would be at a competitive disadvantage in the regular civil service examination process. This trial period takes the place of the regular examination for a position and serves as the probationary period required of all employees. In order for applicants to qualify for this program, they must be certified as meeting guidelines of the Michigan Bureau of Rehabilitation, the state Commission for the Blind, or the Veterans Administration. Following certification, the applicant's name, with a "handicapped" designation, is placed at the top of the employment list that is circulated to state agencies. This process, however, by no means guarantees a disabled person a six-month trial appointment, nor does it mean that no testing is involved. The rehabilitation services counselor must determine that the candidate is able to perform a job adequately (often through testing) and must keep apprised of current state job openings that are appropriate or could be reasonably restructured to accommodate a particular handicap. The brochure publicizing the program notes that a handicapped person may also enter the civil service through the regular examination process with assistance provided at exam centers.

In California, handicapped people who wish to take the examination for civil service job openings are given the options for testing accommodations that have become available in most large testing programs. Civil service classifications have been developed for the readers and interpreters who provide necessary support services to visually, hearing-, and speech-impaired applicants and employees.

## EMPLOYMENT TESTING IN THE PRIVATE SECTOR

According to a joint 1975 survey by Prentice-Hall, Inc., and the American Society for Personnel Administration (the P-H survey, Prentice-Hall, Inc. 1975), the single most important variable governing the use of tests for employee selection or promotion in the private sector is the size of the business establishment. Firms with more than 1,000 employees tend to rely on testing programs to a greater extent than smaller firms. The size of a business also affects the source of the tests it uses. Small firms, particularly those with fewer than 500 employees, tend not to use tests, and when they do, they either develop their own tests according to commonsense rules or buy tests from commercial publishers. Almost half of medium and large businesses rely exclusively on tests purchased from outside publishers. The most popular approach in the largest companies (those with more than 25,000 employees) is a testing program that combines in-house and published tests.

The size of a firm affects the prevalence of validation studies. In the P-H survey, only 17 percent of businesses with fewer than 100 employees had validated the tests they used. The proportion increased to 40 percent for companies with 5,000 to 9,999 employees and to 67 percent for firms with more than 25,000 employees. Most firms had spent less than $5,000 on validation studies, although a few cited expenditures of more than $20,000.

The P-H survey data indicate that tests are more widely used in nonmanufacturing businesses, such as public utilities, banks, insurance companies, retail sales, and communications, than by manufacturers. A survey of testing practices, which was conducted by the Bureau of National Affairs in 1976, revealed that, of the companies that use tests, more than 80 percent use them for office positions, while only 20 percent use them for production jobs, and 10 percent for sales and service jobs (Miner 1976).

Conducting an adequate survey of private sector employment practices with regard to handicapped people would be an enormous undertaking, one far beyond the scope of the panel's mandate. In order to form some impression of how the business community selects handicapped employees, the panel contacted several large companies who reportedly hire substantial numbers of handicapped people. In general, as noted above, the amount of paper-and-pencil testing for all job candidates, handicapped and nonhandicapped, varies greatly from one company or corporation to another and from one type of occupation to another. It appears, however, that tests are frequently waived for handicapped applicants.

The major barrier to comparable employment testing of handicapped people cited by several large corporations is the fact that most of the tests they use are speeded. If extra time is allowed, the meaning of results obtained under nonstandard conditions is unknown. One large corporation makes accommodations, such as an amanuensis, braille versions of tests, and extra time, but informs candidates that scores obtained *within* the time limits will be considered as well as the total achieved in the extended time. Another large company waives tests if a standard administration is not possible.

Differential validation research on testing of handicapped people is virtually nonexistent in the private sector and is considered unfeasible because of the small numbers of handicapped employees in similar jobs. Such studies would require that a number of people with a similar handicapping condition take the same form of an employment test and be placed in highly similar jobs at approximately the same time. Consequently, rigorous predictive validation studies seem rarely if ever possible for only one employer; alternatives might include multijurisdictional validation studies and a longitudinal case-study approach. In either case, better records on the employment of handicapped people would be needed.

## TEST USE IN REHABILITATION AGENCIES

Both state and private vocational rehabilitation agencies frequently play major roles in helping handicapped people receive training and get jobs. Such agencies act as intermediaries between disabled applicants and potential employers, whether in the public or private sector. As we have seen, the federal and some state civil service systems have established programs whereby certification by a rehabilitation counselor may be substituted for civil service examinations. Some private sector employers have similar arrangements with vocational rehabilitation services. In a questionnaire distributed to recipients of the Employer of the Year Award, which is presented by the President's Committee on Employment of the Handicapped, respondents indicated that their most common sources for recruitment of handicapped people were vocational rehabilitation agencies and state employment offices (President's Committee on Employment of the Handicapped, no date).

Although the rehabilitation system often spares a client the experience of competitive test taking for jobs that is required of nonhandicapped applicants, tests of various kinds frequently play a large role in the assessment procedures used by these agencies to certify a disabled person. Some rehabilitation professionals point to a difference between their use of tests and that of an employer; they view tests in the rehabilitation setting as concentrating on "abilities, assets, potentials and strengths, what the person can, rather than can't do" (Barron 1980). Rehabilitation testing also focuses on discovering areas of weakness and on providing the necessary training to strengthen a person's general employment potential.

Norms are available on only some of the tests used by rehabilitation agencies. The tests are used to inform counselors as well as placement officers, but rarely is there an interest in comparing test scores for handicapped and nonhandicapped people, as there is in college admissions.

Rehabilitation agencies have conducted much research and development on assessment procedures. Rehabilitation services have long been developing and using the "work sample," a performance test in which a person performs tasks similar to those required on a job. People who experience difficulty with written tests often possess the aptitude and ability to perform actual tasks with great skill. Two such systems are TOWER (Testing, Orientation, and Work Evaluation in Rehabilitation) and Micro-TOWER, both of which are used by rehabilitation agencies throughout the country to screen clients for training and placement in clerical, factory, food service, paraprofessional health service, and similar positions. The TOWER system, developed in the 1930s by the International Center for the Disabled (ICD), is an individualized test consisting of 94 work samples that takes 4 to 5 weeks to complete (Rosenberg 1977). More recently, ICD developed Micro-TOWER, a shorter group-administered version of TOWER. This aptitude battery includes work samples in five areas—verbal, numerical, motor, spatial, and clerical perception—and can be completed in less than a week. The Micro-TOWER test has been normed for physically disabled, psychiatrically disturbed, brain-damaged, and educable mentally retarded populations; however, predictive validity studies have not been conducted. The developers of the test allude to several considerations that have hampered validation efforts: (1) uncertainty as to whether or not the level of Micro-TOWER samples is high enough to allow for prediction of successful employment; (2) problems with obtaining sufficient samples for specific jobs; and (3) difficulties in securing the cooperation of unions and employers (Backman 1977).

Vocational rehabilitation agencies also use a number of other tests to measure aptitudes. For example, a private rehabilitation agency in New York uses the following set of tests in its prevocational evaluation of clients:

*Interest*
Geist Picture Interest Inventory
Strong-Campbell Vocational Interest Blank

*Achievement*
Wide Range Achievement Test
Differential Aptitude Test
Nelson Reading Test
Gates-MacGinitie Reading Test
Form E (Grades 7-9)
Form F (Grades 10-12)

*Aptitude*
Minnesota Clerical Test
General Clerical Test
Bennet Mechanical Comprehension Test
Revised Minnesota Paper Form Board

*Dexterity*
Bennett Hand Tool Dexterity Test
Crawford Small Parts Test
Stromberg-Carlson Dexterity Test

The Wide Range Achievement Test is a reading achievement test that is easy to administer and is reported to have high reliability and validity with undifferentiated populations (Lloyd 1979). The Differential Aptitude Test, which is published by the Psychological Corporation, measures verbal reasoning, numerical reasoning, space relations, mechanical reasoning, clerical speed and accuracy, and language usage. It was normed on 50,000 students in Grades 8 to 12 in 43 states and has extensive validity information in its manual, but no research regarding its use with handicapped populations has been undertaken (Miller 1979). Other more specialized tests are also used, for example, to determine eligibility for computer programming courses and jobs.

## LICENSING AND CERTIFICATION

Licensing and certification requirements were designed to regulate the competence of individuals allowed to practice a particular profession. The two terms are often used interchangeably, but they technically refer to two distinct processes: licenses are issued by government agencies to individuals who are thereby granted permission to engage in a given occupation; certification is granted by nongovernmental agencies (e.g., professional associations) to individuals who have fulfilled requirements established by the profession to regulate itself. Today more than 2,000 occupations have licensing or certification requirements (Pottinger et al. 1980). Types of professions that are typically regulated by state government agencies and that have tests as part of the licensing requirements include architecture, barbers and beauticians, certified public accountants, dentistry, electrical contractors, engineers, marriage counselors, plumbers, medical examiners, nursing, optometry, pharmacology, city planning, psychology, and veterinary medicine.

A survey by Hiscox and Nafziger (reported in Pottinger et al. 1980) determined that relatively few of the occupations that require licensing or certification include testing as a component of the process for the general population. Rather, there is usually an educational requirement in combination with on-the-job experience or an internship or practicum. Experience can sometimes be substituted for other requirements.

According to the Hiscox and Nafziger survey, the validity or reliability of the tests that are used is of very little concern to the licensing or certifying bodies. Frequently, test administration procedures are not even standardized. A limited survey conducted by the National Center for the Study of Professions found that the only claim to validity that could be made for most licensing and certification tests was a kind of content validity based on the fact that experts in a given field had agreed on what are appropriate items (reported in Pottinger et al. 1980).

The panel attempted to estimate the demand for modified certification and licensing examinations by contacting several involved states, professional organizations, and testing companies. In general, the number of handicapped applicants who seek licensing or certification in any one profession appears to be quite small, although there is some variability. For example, in one large industrial state, 11 of 330 candidates taking a recent licensing test for psychologists identified themselves as handicapped. "Handicapped" in this context was broadly defined and may have included individuals with heart conditions, cancer, and so forth. Another state estimates 250 requests for test accommodations in a year; another reports only 10 accommodations of an estimated 80,000 examinations administered. Panel correspondence with licensing and certification bodies that use tests prepared by the Psychological Corporation indicates that very few handicapped individuals have applied to take modified examinations in such fields as electroencephalographic technology, personnel administration, occupational therapy, and cosmetology.

Requests for special consideration are handled on an individual basis. The types of accommodations most frequently offered include readers, interpreters, extra time, and separate testing rooms. Braille tests are generally not available.

In cases in which licensing or certification tests are produced, normed, distributed, and scored by testing companies, the usual procedure is for the accrediting board or association to pass on any requests for special testing arrangements to the testing company, which then arranges for the appropriate modifications to be available at the designated time and place. Types of modifications appear to be more limited than in college admissions testing, with a reader or amanuensis and extended time the most common accommodations. Extra costs are absorbed by the professional association or board rather than by the candidate.

Some licensing and certification agencies model their tests after the Multi-State Bar Examination, a two-part test for the licensing of lawyers. For this examination, the Educational Testing Service (ETS) produces and scores a multiple choice section that is used in 42 states; each state determines the cutoff score for the multiple choice section and writes, administers, and scores its own essay section of the test. ETS reports that visually impaired applicants can be accommodated with a reader, but in general, determinations about accommodations would be at the discretion of the individual state bar associations. California, for example, has printed a braille version of its examination.

In recent years there has been a growing concern about the lack of knowledge about the predictive validity of tests used in licensing and certification. The major difficulties cited as stumbling blocks to converting tests to performance-based measures are the familiar ones of exorbitant costs and problems in defining performance criteria. Federal and state governments have become increasingly involved in regulation of the licensing process and in a few limited cases have funded development of performance-based measures of occupational competency (Pottinger et al. 1980).

Concern about the validity of tests for licensing and certification is intensified when tests are modified to accommodate handicapped people. When licensing boards use nationally normed and standardized tests, they are often reluctant to alter the guidelines for test administration procedures provided in the test manual. One agency, however, which uses its own psychometricians and has many years of experience in evaluating the outcomes of special test administrations, has concluded that the time allowed for all candidates exceeds what is necessary and, therefore, any extra time has little effect on the overall validity of scores. We did not find any actual research efforts designed to establish the validity of any type of special test administration.

In general, the procedures used by licensing and certification bodies are extremely diverse. Few handicapped applicants have requested testing modifications, but the reasons for the small number of requests are unknown. Licensing boards regulated by state agencies have been most active in providing testing accommodations, but they too have received a limited number of inquiries. The panel's concern about licensing and certification is not abated by the small numbers of handicapped people requesting modifications of licensing or certification examinations, both because the reasons for the limited number of requests are unknown and because as more handicapped people complete educational programs and apply for employment, it is likely that the number of requests will increase.

## ISSUES IN EMPLOYMENT TESTING

Several issues are common to the testing and employment of handicapped people in the public and private sectors. The first relates to the knowledge and sophistication of handicapped applicants and employees. Because they may need to use options not offered to the general population, handicapped individuals need to be particularly well informed regarding the ramifications of their choices. For example, test waivers and alternate selection processes, while providing some opportunities, may put handicapped employees at a disadvantage in other ways. This would be the case if a person were hired on a six-month trial basis at a lower salary level than if the standard employee selection route, perhaps including testing, had been followed. In addition, employers may not provide full benefit packages to those who are under a probationary contract.

Handicapped people also need to be well informed regarding the legally constituted complaint process under federal or state fair employment regulations. Arnold R. Vasbinder, state coordinator of placement services for the New York State Office of Vocational Rehabilitation, has reported that no complaints about improper testing of handicapped people have been registered with the Office of Federal Contract Compliance.[3] He contends that this is in part because mentally retarded and learning-disabled individuals are not likely to understand the complaint procedures and very probably do not know that the law affords them some protection. If no complaint is filed, businesses are not required to show the job-relatedness of tests or selection procedures or to improve practices that put handicapped people at a disadvantage.

The second issue concerns the practices in employment selection that result in identification of an applicant as handicapped. The panel has observed that most public sector affirmative action programs for handicapped people presuppose self-identification of those with

[3]Testimony at the panel's open meeting (see Appendix B).

handicapping conditions, thereby suggesting that the pre-employment identification of a person as handicapped is not considered significant. Or it may be that the concern about privacy is outweighed by the necessity of achieving compliance with federal or state laws through programs that are designed to employ handicapped people. In any case, it appears that because of other practices, the flagging of scores that identify a job applicant as having a handicapping condition is less an issue in testing for employment than in testing for admission to postsecondary education institutions.

The third issue involves the need for specialized training of psychologists, guidance and employment counselors, and other professionals whose responsibility it is to evaluate and provide realistic advice to handicapped job seekers. In some cases such personnel are school-based, either in secondary or postsecondary institutions. More frequently, however, handicapped people will receive employment information, evaluation, and counseling through rehabilitation services or state employment offices. Yet personnel employed by rehabilitation services are not necessarily specialists in evaluating the abilities of handicapped people. Vasbinder reported to the panel that the current practice in New York is to purchase testing services from private licensed psychologists (see Appendix B). According to Barron, many of these psychologists have neither training nor previous experience in assessing the aptitudes of handicapped people (1980:342):

> There are many examples of clients whose testing experiences or contact with helping professionals has increased rather than diminished their insecurities, has lowered rather than improved the chances that their assets and potentials would be discovered and capitalized on, because the psychologists involved were convinced by limited exposure and experience that handicapped people were incapable of leading any but marginal lives. Or, the psychologists were certain the clients were deeply disturbed because they did not understand the behavior in the context of the disability.

A representative of the Alexander Graham Bell Association for the Deaf cited two surveys that support this view. McCrone and Chambers (1977) found that in 11 states, professionals who were used by state vocational rehabilitation agencies to perform psychological evaluations of clients were not supervised by doctoral-level psychologists as required by the Rehabilitation Act of 1973 and recommended by the American Psychological Association (APA). Spear and Schoepke (1979) surveyed the psychology training programs of all APA-approved schools and found (with an 87 percent response rate) that 26 percent of all program directors had never heard of the Rehabilitation Act of 1973. Another 28 percent had heard of it but were not familiar with its requirements. Only 10.5 percent of all clinical and counseling doctoral candidates reported having taken a course on the psychological aspects of disability.

New York has instituted a program for training psychologists hired by the Office of Vocational Rehabilitation in the testing of specified disability groups. Another approach to the problem now under consideration is the possibility of requiring that the academic programs of doctoral candidates in clinical psychology programs include course work in the psychology and testing of disabled people.

The fourth issue is the concern that is universally referred to as the greatest barrier to the employment of handicapped people: employers' attitudes, that is, their bias against handicapped people. Handicapped individuals, advocacy groups, placement personnel in rehabilitation agencies, the President's Committee on Employment of the Handicapped, and employers who have had successful experiences with handicapped employees all point to the need for continuing efforts to break down stereotypes, preconceptions, and fears concerning employment of handicapped people. Many of the efforts of the president's committee are geared to confront precisely this problem.

Employers' reluctance to consider handicapped applicants for job openings is often expressed in terms of apprehension about work-related issues, such as absenteeism, lower productivity, safety factors, and increased insurance costs. But E. I. DuPont de Nemours and Company, which has many disabled employees (particularly veterans), conducted a major study of the performance of its handicapped employees (Wolfe 1973-74) that showed: (1) no increase in workmen's compensation costs; (2) minimal physical adjustments for some handicapped employees and no adjustments for most; (3) an average or better safety record for 96 percent of the handicapped employees; (4) an enthusiastic reception of disabled employees by other employees; and (5) relatively high ratings on job performance, job stability, and attendance. A significant positive correlation was found between severity of handicap and job performance ratings.

Overcoming employer resistance to hiring handicapped workers is the focus of many programs and organizations. The National Center on Employment of the Deaf (NCED) of the National Technical Institute for the Deaf in Rochester, New York, emphasizes four major areas in its efforts to provide job opportunities for deaf people: (1) academic preparation in technical and professional fields; (2) on-the-job training through cooperative work experiences; (3) job development through personal contacts and seminars; and (4) publicity. A person's academic record and job interview are considered by NCED to be the two most important criteria in a successful job placement. Testing is rarely a barrier to the employment of a deaf person who has completed a course of study at National Technical Institute for the Deaf.[4]

Projects With Industry (PWI), a nationwide program that is partly supported with federal funds, takes an approach similar to NCED's in developing jobs for handicapped people. PWI has more than 50 projects involving more than 2,000 industries; the programs frequently are organized and administered by rehabilitation agencies. PWI seeks to provide consultation to employers regarding employment of handicapped people and offers technical assistance on removal of architectural barriers and the feasibility of job modifications. An advisory council composed of representatives from participating companies addresses major issues, such as change in the job market or projected areas of employment growth. Job-ready handicapped individuals, who are referred to PWI by a state vocational rehabilitation service, receive instruction in effective methods of seeking employment and placement assistance.

## A BRIEF INTERNATIONAL PERSPECTIVE

In considering the problems associated with employment of handicapped people and the role that testing plays in their employment, the panel briefly reviewed the policies and practices of other nations to see if they might suggest alternatives for this country.

Most Western European nations attempt to ensure employment of handicapped people through a system of quotas that obliges employers to hire a percentage of people in various categories, including the physically and mentally handicapped and older workers. In the United Kingdom, the Disabled Persons Employment Act of 1947 requires that, in companies employing more than 20 people, 3 percent of those hired must be disabled. Handicapped job seekers must register with the Department of Employment in order to be considered for positions. Under this plan, the proportion of disabled people in the labor force remained at 3 percent or higher until 1961 but has since been declining, to less than 2 percent in 1979. The number of

[4]Personal communication from Dr. R. S. Menchel, employment opportunities analyst, National Center on Employment of the Deaf.

employers fulfilling their quota obligations has also steadily declined over the past 15 years. Two of the reasons cited for the failure of this system are a very small number of prosecutions for failure to meet the quota and the practice by the Department of Employment of issuing large numbers of exemption permits to employers covering blocks of time of up to six months (Jain 1979). Problems arise because many disabled people do not register with the Department of Employment and because it is difficult for officials to refute an employer's judgment that an applicant is not the right person for the job ("And in Britain. . . ." 1979).

West Germany also relies on a quota system to ensure employment for its handicapped people. Firms that employ more than 16 people must have at least 6 percent handicapped employees on the payroll. Failure to do so carries a monthly financial penalty; the money is used to provide free technical adaptations at work sites employing handicapped people and to support vocational training for disabled people (President's Committee on Employment of the Handicapped 1980). In addition, West Germany's Chambers of Handwork and Industry and Trade (similar to American unions) have set up a program designed to extend apprenticeship training to about 60 percent of the 46,000 young people enrolled in special schools (Organization for Economic Cooperation and Development 1979).

The practices of France, Sweden, and the Netherlands with regard to employment of handicapped people have been studied by G. D. Carnes (1979). The French system is similar in many ways to both the British and West German approaches to finding employment for the disabled population. A law mandates a 3 percent quota for industry (10 percent for veterans), but, as in England, enforcement of the statute is rare except within the civil service system. Employers of more than 5,000 people are also required to guarantee reemployment of any rehabilitated employees following illness or accident.

In the Netherlands, the government is responsible for planning, organizing, and financing rehabilitation programs; private sector voluntary societies provide actual services to clients. A 3 percent quota appears in the country's laws but is reportedly no better enforced than elsewhere. Sheltered workshops, which are criticized for their low turnover rate, provide work for much of the disabled population in the Netherlands.

Sweden does not have a quota system for the employment of its handicapped citizens but has attempted to guarantee work for its handicapped population by instituting a system of reimbursements to employers who hire handicapped individuals. In the case of a young, entry-level physically handicapped worker, an employer receives 90 percent of the employee's wages from the government for the first year and 50 percent in succeeding years. Rehabilitated workers who have difficulty finding work through the open job market also are eligible for this type of work, with employers receiving supporting grants of 75 percent of their salaries for the first year, 50 percent for the second year, and 25 percent in each year thereafter. About 200 state-subsidized sheltered workshops are scattered throughout the country.

The Swedish government maintains a clinic for occupational testing where evaluation of a severely disabled client may take up to six months. Considerable psychological testing of rehabilitation clients also takes place in specialized institutes. Research into testing of the handicapped is conducted at these sites, but an Organization for Economic Cooperation and Development report on the Swedish rehabilitation system notes that the tests and selection procedures are not validated (Jain 1979).

Carnes (1979) reported a significant degree of dissatisfaction with the Swedish system. Work disincentives, which undermine the rehabilitation system, are built into the disability payment structure. Attitudinal barriers also remain a problem. Advocacy groups composed principally of militant disabled individuals are increasingly vocal and influential in pressuring the government to institute changes in the laws and services that protect handicapped people.

The panel's review of the policies of other nations regarding the employment of handicapped people has been neither thorough nor extensive. It leads us to believe, nonetheless, that the policies of the Western European nations that we reviewed do not offer particularly promising solutions to problems in the United States. We believe that the direct application of their policies to the United States is neither desirable nor feasible.

# 4
# The Legal Context of Section 504

With the passage of Section 504 of the Rehabilitation Act of 1973, the federal government took a major step toward extending civil rights protection to people with handicapping conditions. The act marked the first time that federal statutory law formally recognized the principle that people with disabilities are entitled to the same protection against discrimination that other people have. Section 504 thus represented a fundamental shift in federal policy toward handicapped people: from the provision of financial entitlements to the prohibition of discrimination on the basis of handicap in any program or activity receiving federal financial assistance.

This chapter discusses administrative and judicial interpretation of Section 504. Although we focus particularly on testing practices, since that is the nub of the panel's charge, it is useful to place our analysis of Section 504 within the larger context of civil rights law.

## THE HISTORICAL CONTEXT OF CIVIL RIGHTS LAWS

### The Prohibition of Discrimination

Contemporary conceptions of civil rights in the United States have been defined largely with reference to the experience of black Americans. Under slavery, blacks suffered what might be called absolute discrimination: they had no right to hold property, no freedom of contract, no freedom of movement, none of the political rights of citizenship (to vote, to hold office, to serve on juries), no right to sue or to testify in court, no right to marry or establish a family. The Fourteenth Amendment to the Constitution and the Civil Rights Acts of 1866 and 1870 extended to former slaves equal legal standing with other citizens of their gender, as well as remedies at law to protect those rights. But the efficacy of such constitutional and statutory protections was undermined in the following decades by a proliferation of state and local laws and customs that, by the end of the nineteenth century, had produced a segregated society in which blacks occupied a distinctly inferior status—legally, politically, economically, and socially (Woodward 1957).

Beginning with the Supreme Court's 1954 landmark decision in *Brown* v. *Board of Education*, the federal government moved to overturn the legacy of separate treatment by asserting federal rights to equal treatment under the law, to which local laws and customs would have to conform. The statutory centerpiece of this initiative was the omnibus Civil Rights Act of 1964 (P.L. 88-352). In keeping with the task of dismantling discriminatory legal barriers, the thrust of the act was prohibitory in character: it made it illegal to discriminate among people on the basis of "race, color, religion, sex, or national origin" (although not all sections of the act included all categories).

The Civil Rights Act addressed five major areas in which blacks had, by law or by custom, suffered unequal and exclusionary treatment: (1) political participation, including voting rights; (2) access to public accommodations, such as hotels, theaters, and restaurants; (3) access to publicly owned facilities, such as parks, playgrounds, and office buildings; (4) education; and (5) employment. In each area, the act prohibited the use of unlawful considerations, such as race or ethnic origin, on the assumption that equal treatment would substantially ameliorate the disadvantaged condition of blacks and members of other specified groups.[1]

In addition to defining prohibited activities, the Civil Rights act of 1964 included detailed provisions for implementing various sections of the act. Title VII, for example, which enumerated unlawful employment practices, established the Equal Employment Opportunity Commission (EEOC) as one of the means of implementing its provisions. Title VI, which prohibits exclusion on the grounds of race, color, or national origin from any program or activity receiving federal financial assistance (the prototype, along with Title IX of the

[1]For a more detailed analysis, see Wigdor and Garner (1982) and Wigdor (1982).

Education Amendments Act of 1972 which prohibits such exclusion on the basis of sex, for Section 504 of the Rehabilitation Act), directed each agency that disburses federal funds to promulgate implementing regulations and authorized specific compliance activities, including procedures for terminating grants.

## Testing and Civil Rights

Title VII of the Civil Rights Act, which deals with equal employment opportunity, has been the basis of the most important challenges to the use of standardized tests. As a consequence, the administrative requirements and legal precedents established under Title VII that affect the use of standardized tests are important to the developing interpretation of the obligations imposed by Section 504.

Because ability tests are frequently the most visible part of the decision process in hiring, placing, promoting, or dismissing employees, the federal agencies implementing Title VII quickly converged on testing—which is defined broadly enough to cover any selection procedure that involves choice among candidates—as the most important locus of discriminatory activity. Guidelines on employment testing procedures evolved into more and more complicated statements of technical validation methods.[2] In order to present a uniform federal policy on the obligations of the employer, the agencies joined together in 1978 in adopting uniform guidelines.[3]

The EEOC, which came largely to dominate federal policy, interpreted Title VII discrimination to consist not only of employment practices of which the overt intent was to discriminate or to treat

[2]There are seven such guidelines: Equal Employment Opportunity Commission (1966) Guidelines on employment testing procedures, *Fed. Reg.* 31:6414; Office of Federal Contract Compliance, Department of Labor (1968) Validation of employment tests, *Fed. Reg.* 33:14392; Equal Employment Opportunity Commission (August 1, 1970) Guidelines on employee selection procedures, *Fed. Reg.* 35(149):12333-12336 (reissued, *Fed. Reg.* 41:51984, 1976); Office of Federal Contract Compliance, U.S. Department of Labor (1971) Employee testing and other selection procedures, *Fed. Reg.* 36(192):19307-19310; Office of Federal Contract Compliance, U.S. Department of Labor (1974) Guidelines for reporting criterion-related and content validity, *Fed. Reg.* 39(12):2094-2096; U.S. Department of Justice, Department of Labor, Civil Service Commission (1976) Federal Executive Agency guidelines on employee selection procedures, *Fed. Reg.* 41(227):51734-51759; Equal Employment Opportunity Commission, U.S. Civil Service Commission, U.S. Department of Labor, U.S. Department of Justice (1978) Uniform guidelines on employee selection procedures, *Fed. Reg.* 43(166):38290-38315.
[3]*Uniform Guidelines on Employee Selection Procedures* 43 *Fed. Reg.* 38290-38315.

people of protected status differently from others, but of all practices that have an "adverse impact" on members of the protected classes.[4] This policy, announced in the agency's first set of guidelines,[5] has become the basic formula for federal oversight of personnel selection. If an employer, union, or employment agency uses a test or other selection device that results in proportionally lower selection rates for minorities and females than for white males, the procedure will be considered discriminatory and declared unlawful *unless* the employer can "validate" the test in accordance with the requirements set forth in the *Guidelines*. This policy put federal officials and courts in the position of having to decide what constitutes technical adequacy, a position that has brought its share of difficulties. And it placed employment testing at the center of controversy as evidence accumulated in the late 1960s that neither black nor Hispanic applicants performed as well *as a group* on tests of cognitive functioning as did white applicants. In general, group mean scores for black or Hispanic test takers are one standard deviation lower than the mean score of white applicants (Linn 1982).

### The Griggs Decision: Employment Testing

The judicial standards for applying Title VII to employment testing were defined by the U.S. Supreme Court in 1971 in *Griggs* v. *Duke Power Co.* (401 U.S. 424). The Court focused its attention on the consequences of a selection process rather than on intent or motive: if tests are shown to have an exclusionary impact, then the inference follows that discrimination has taken place.

The analytical framework spelled out in *Griggs* has provided the ground rules for Title VII litigation (and has influenced judicial thinking in other spheres of civil rights litigation as well). First, the plaintiff bears the burden of presenting evidence strong enough to support an inference of discrimination by showing the exclusionary effects of a selection process. That evidence is usually statistical, frequently the comparison of pass/fail or hire/reject rates by race or other classification mentioned in the act. Second, proof of disparate impact triggers the employer's burden to rebut the inference of

[4]Peter C. Robertson, "A staff analysis of the history of EEOC guidelines on employee selection procedures." Submitted to General Accounting Office, August 29, 1976. Unpublished document. Available in the files of the Committee on Ability Testing, National Academy of Sciences.

[5]*Guidelines on Employment Testing Procedures*, 35 *LW* 2137(1966).

discrimination by showing that the challenged test is a "reasonable measure of job performance." Showing the test to be a measure of job-related qualifications establishes, unless rebutted, that the basis of the selection decision is a legitimate, nondiscriminatory purpose (such as work force efficiency) and not one of the forbidden considerations. The demonstration of job-relatedness, as it has come to be called, is normally understood to mean establishing the "validity" (in the psychometric sense of the word) of the test for the position in question.

The *Griggs* decision paved the way for federal courts to look to the EEOC *Guidelines on Employee Selection Procedures* as the standard against which a challenged selection procedure should be judged. Since *Griggs*, a significant body of precedent has made it clear that some sort of formal validation study is necessary to justify the use of a test when a system selects disproportionately, with resulting adverse impact on specified groups. This requirement for a demonstration of technical validity has recently been asserted in a number of cases involving educational testing, specifically the use of intelligence tests for the placement of pupils in classes for the educable mentally retarded,[6] and the use of a minimum competency test as a criterion for high school graduation.[7] A basic assumption underlying *Griggs* was that, in an entirely neutral marketplace, people will be selected for employment in roughly the same proportion as they are represented in the population. In *Teamsters* v. *United States* in 1977, the Supreme Court stated it explicitly: ". . . absent explanation, it is ordinarily to be expected that nondiscriminatory hiring practices will in time result in a work force more or less representative of the racial and ethnic composition of the population in the community from which employees are hired."[8]

The problem with that assumption is that it does not face squarely the present reality of disadvantage. Even the most conscientious employer is caught between the possible illegality of preferential treatment (a legally acceptable affirmative action policy is just beginning to emerge) and the very great difficulty of finding an objective selection procedure that will be free of disparate impact. Given the rigor of the validation requirements of the *Guidelines* and the willing-

[6]*Larry P.* v. *Riles* 343 F. Supp. 1036(1972), 502 F.2d 963 (1974), 495 F. Supp. 926 (1979); *Parents in Action on Special Education* v. *Hannon* Civil Number 74 C 3586 (1980).
[7]*Debra P.* v. *Turlington* 474 F. Supp. 244 (1979), 644 F.2d 397 (1981).
[8]431 U.S. 324, 339.

ness of the courts to accord them a great deal of deference in judging the sufficiency of challenged tests, most tests are not surviving legal challenge.

These ambiguities in the *Griggs* opinion reflect an ambivalence that runs through American society about the meaning of equality. In the name of equal rights, society rejects the idea of preferential treatment or quotas; in the name of social justice, it insists on equal outcomes. By writing into law the EEOC policy of defining discrimination in terms of disparate impact, the *Griggs* opinion tipped the balance in the direction of the latter yet confounded that result by maintaining the rhetoric of equal opportunity. A similar ambivalence has characterized administrative and judicial interpretation of the Rehabilitation Act of 1973, to which we now turn.

## THE REHABILITATION ACT OF 1973

Until the last decade, federal legislation affecting people with handicaps was oriented toward rehabilitation and social welfare services. Concern about the rehabilitation and employment of disabled veterans following World War I led to a modest piece of legislation that was expanded in 1920 to include physically handicapped people, whether or not they were veterans.[9] This legislation was incorporated essentially unchanged into the Social Security Act of 1935.[10] The first significant alteration of the 1920 congressional mandate was the Vocational Rehabilitation Amendment of 1943, which broadened the definition of eligibility to include the mentally ill and the mentally retarded and expanded the scope of rehabilitation services.[11] Further extensions to the concept of rehabilitation and the inclusiveness of the legislation were enacted through amendments in 1954, 1965, and 1968.[12]

The Rehabilitation Act of 1973,[13] of which Section 504 is a part, is

[9]P.L. 66-236, 41 Stat. 735 (1920) [repealed 1973].

[10]P.L. 74-271, Sec. 10001, 49 Stat. 620, (1935) [Current version 42 USC Sec. 1381-1382, 1970, and Supp. V 1975].

[11]Vocational Rehabilitation Amendment of 1943, P.L. 79-113, 57 Stat. 374 Sec. 10 [repealed 1973].

[12]Vocational Rehabilitation Amendments of 1954, Secs. 2-5, P.L. 83-565, 68 Stat. 652 [repealed 1973]; Vocational Rehabilitation Amendments of 1965, Sec. 2-13, P.L. 89-333, 79 Stat. 1282 [repealed 1973]; Vocational Rehabilitation Amendments of 1968, P.L. 90-391, 82 Stat. 297 [repealed 1973].

[13]P.L. 93-112, 29 USC 701 *et seq.* Descriptive portions of the discussion of legislative and regulatory history of Section 504 of the Rehabilitation Act of 1973 rely heavily on the 1981 draft revisions of the Handbook for the Implementation of Section 504 of the Rehabilitation Act of 1973 (CRC Education and Human Development, Inc. 1981; hereafter referred to as *Handbook*).

a direct descendant of the previous rehabilitation legislation. Titles I, II, and III of the act provide the statutory basis for the Rehabilitation Services Administration (RSA), now housed in the Department of Education; authorize the rehabilitation programs that the federal government will support; and delineate the relationship between federal, state, and local agencies in providing rehabilitation services to handicapped individuals. Title IV outlines the responsibilities of the secretary for administering Titles I, II, and III, for evaluating programs and projects authorized by the act, for implementing specific studies, for dissemination, and for reporting to Congress.

Title V, which bears the unassuming name of "Miscellaneous," has a very different provenance from the other four titles. The principles and programs outlined there are drawn from the federal civil rights initiatives of the 1960s. Indeed, the central provisions—affirmative action in the hiring of handicapped people in executive agencies of the federal government (Sec. 501); elimination of architectural and transportation barriers (Sec. 502); affirmative action hiring programs by federal contractors (Sec. 503); and nondiscrimination under federal grants (Sec. 504)—were originally offered in the House and the Senate as amendments to the Civil Rights Act of 1964.[14]

Section 504 of the Rehabilitation Act of 1973 provides in its entirety that:

> No otherwise qualified handicapped individual in the United States, as defined in section 7(6), shall solely by reason of his handicap be excluded from the participation in, be denied the benefits of, or be subjected to discrimination under any program or activity receiving Federal financial assistance.

The language of Section 504 parallels both Title VI of the Civil

[14]117 Cong. Rec. 45974 (December 9, 1971); 118 Cong. Rec. 525, 526 (January 20, 1972). The substance of the House and Senate bills was subsequently incorporated into the Rehabilitation Act of 1972, which was passed by Congress but vetoed by President Nixon on grounds unrelated to the civil rights aspect of the legislation (118 Cong. Rec. 32317 (October 27, 1972)). The protective clauses reappeared once again in a Senate bill (119 Cong. Rec. 9597-9598 (1973)), also vetoed by President Nixon (119 Cong. Rec. 16676, 18127 (1973)), before final inclusion in the Rehabilitation Act of 1973.

Congress has continued to decline to afford the broader coverage of Title VII of the Civil Rights Act of 1964 to the handicapped: H.R. 13199, 93d Cong., 2d Sess., 120 Cong. Rec. H1393 (daily ed. Mar. 4, 1974); H.R. 12654, 93d Cong., 2d Sess., 120 Cong. Rec. H6717 (daily ed. Feb. 6, 1974); H.R. 461 and H.R. 1107, 95th Cong., 1st Sess., 123 Cong. Rec. H193, H209 (daily ed. Jan. 6, 1977).

Rights Act of 1964,[15] which mandates nondiscrimination under federal grants on the basis of race, color, or national origin, and Title IX of the Education Amendments of 1972,[16] which prohibits discrimination under federal grants on the basis of sex. But as a number of commentators have pointed out (Engebretson 1979, Ray 1979-80), Title VI and Title IX were accompanied by detailed instructions designating the implementing authorities, instructing them to issue regulations, outlining the compliance procedures they were authorized to use, and clarifying Congress' position on a number of substantive issues that were bound to arise in the regulatory process. Section 504 was enacted without specific guidance as to how the law was to be implemented and without articulation of the remedies available to handicapped people who believe they are the subjects of discrimination. Moreover, the legislative history of Section 504 was very brief, establishing simply that Section 504 is a civil rights statute, the primary purpose of which is to eliminate discrimination against qualified handicapped people and to increase their opportunities to participate in and benefit from federally funded programs. Thus, the ban on discrimination against handicapped people became law without any extensive elaboration of congressional purpose and intent.

The law's sponsors attempted to remedy this situation during the passage of the Rehabilitation Act Amendments of 1974 (P.L. 93-516) by the means of writing a *post hoc* legislative history. A report of the Senate Labor and Public Welfare Committee declared that Section 504 was not just hortatory but was mandatory in form and that Congress intended that implementing regulations and enforcement procedures be put in place.[17] The report also indicated that because the U.S. Department of Health, Education, and Welfare (HEW) had experience in dealing with handicapped people as well as enforcement experience under Title VI and Title IX, the secretary of HEW should assume responsibility for coordinating the enforcement efforts of

[15]42 USC s. 2000d (1976). The clause reads: "No person in the United States shall, on the ground of race, color, or national origin, be excluded from participation in, be denied the benefits of, or be subjected to discrimination under any program or activity receiving Federal financial assistance."

[16]20 USC s. 1681 (1976). The clause reads: "No person in the United States shall, on the basis of sex, be excluded from participation in, be denied the benefits of, or be subjected to discrimination under any program or activity receiving Federal financial assistance. . . ."

[17]S. Rep. No. 93-1297, 93d Cong., 2d Sess. (1974), reprinted in [1974] U.S. Code Cong. and Ad. News 6373, 6391.

departments and agencies affected by Section 504. The administrative responsibility for enforcement of the act was not formally assigned to HEW, however, until 1976, when President Ford issued Executive Order 11914.[18] By this time the agency was also under court order to issue regulations within a specified period of time.[19] The provision of an explicit remedial section in the statute was not enacted until the 1978 Amendments to the Act; Section 505 made the "remedies, procedures, and rights set forth in Title VI of the Civil Rights Act of 1964" available to any person aggrieved under Section 504 of the Rehabilitation Act.[20] At this same time, an attorney's fees provision, Section 505(b), and a provision establishing an Interagency Coordinating Council to promote implementation and enforcement of Section 504 and regulations thereunder, Section 507, were added to the act.

## ADMINISTRATIVE INTERPRETATION OF SECTION 504

The HEW secretary, Caspar Weinberger, assigned responsibility for implementing Section 504 to the Office for Civil Rights (OCR), probably because of that office's existing network of field offices and compliance resolution procedures for implementing the related nondiscrimination provisions of Title VI of the Civil Rights Act of 1964 and Title IX of the Education Amendments of 1972.[21] The final regulations promulgated guidelines for ending discrimination on the basis of handicap in five areas: (1) employment practices; (2) accessibility to physical facilities; (3) preschool, elementary, and secondary education; (4) postsecondary education; and (5) health, welfare, and social services. The specific rules for compliance in each area were influenced by a number of basic policy decisions about the coverage and meaning of the statute.

First, OCR's enforcement authority is limited to recipients of federal financial assistance; these recipients typically include public schools, public and private universities, and state agencies. (The 1978 amend-

[18]41 *Fed. Reg.* 17871.

[19]*Cherry* v. *Mathews*, 419 F. Supp. 922 (D.D.C. 1976). In *Cherry*, HEW maintained that it had authority to issue regulations, and the only dispute was how soon the agency would issue the final regulations.

[20]P.L. 95-602, s. 120(a), 92 Stat. 2982 (1978).

[21]According to Engebretson (1979:67), based on an interview (Feb. 15, 1978) with John Wodatch, acting branch chief, Handicapped Discrimination Branch, Office for Civil Rights, Department of Health, Education, and Welfare.

ments to the act extended the nondiscrimination provisions of Section 504 to the federal government and the United States Postal Service.) Section 504 is not, like Title VII, a general antidiscrimination law: it does not reach the private sector except as private institutions receive or benefit from federal financial assistance.

Within that limitation, however, the agency considers the mandate of the Rehabilitation Act to be a civil rights mandate, and not program specific (CRC Education and Human Development, Inc. 1981:20). Thus, the agency feels that if a state education agency accepts any federal funds—not just those earmarked to assist handicapped people—it must comply with Section 504 (CRC Education and Human Development, Inc. 1981:291). On the basis of its interpretation of Section 504 as a civil rights mandate, OCR decided to include specific rules prohibiting employment discrimination by recipients of federal financial assistance. It was encouraged in this interpretation by the conference report accompanying the 1974 Amendments.[22] The correctness of this reading of the statute undoubtedly will have to be determined by the U.S. Supreme Court, however, as a number of recent decisions in the Second, Fourth, and Eighth Circuits, most notably *Trageser* v. *Libbie Rehabilitation Center, Inc.*,[23] have held that Section 504 does not generally cover employment discrimination against handicapped individuals. The courts have ruled that Section 504 protects the handicapped against employment discrimination only when the principal purpose of the federal funds received by the employer is to provide employment. Despite these decisions, OCR has decided to enforce its interpretation (except in states in the Second, Fourth, and Eighth Circuits) until there is more definitive judicial ruling on the matter (CRC Education and Human Development, Inc. 1981:113-116).

Second, the protections offered by Section 504 are limited to "qualified handicapped persons." Unlike Title VI, which protects all people from discrimination on the basis of race, color, and national origin, Section 504 protects only qualified handicapped individuals from discrimination on the basis of handicap. This limitation points up an important dissimilarity between Section 504 and other civil rights legislation. The premise of the 1964 Civil Rights Act was that equal treatment would end racial discrimination, that distinctions

[22]H.R. Conf. Rep. No. 93-1457, 93d Cong., 2nd Sess., p. 25 (Oct. 9, 1974).

[23]590 F.2d. 87 (4th Cir., 1978); but see, *Hart* v. *County of Alameda Probation Department*, 485 F. Supp. 66 (N.D. Ca., 1979).

based on race are arbitrary and not correlated with essential differences. The language of Section 504, on the contrary, implies, and the regulations assert, that only those handicapped individuals who are capable of learning or performing the essential functions of a job with reasonable accommodation to the handicap are covered by the provision.

Third, the decision was made that nondiscrimination means equal treatment. This issue was one of the most difficult faced by the drafters of the regulations.[24] Early civil rights legislation was based on the assumption that discrimination meant unequal treatment and, conversely, that equal treatment would end racial discrimination (although administrative and judicial interpretation has tended to modify the equal treatment doctrine in the direction of equal outcome, as we noted above). The equal treatment standard seemed even less appropriate to the special circumstances of people with handicaps than to disadvantaged minorities. Yet Congress provided no guidance for a standard of differing treatment to achieve the goal of equality.

The first draft of the regulations took the position that, because of the real differences in the situation of handicapped and nonhandicapped people, equal treatment would not result in equal opportunity for the handicapped. The preamble made a clear distinction between Section 504 and other civil rights statutes:[25]

> Section 504, however, differs conceptually from both Titles VI and IX. The premise of both Title VI and Title IX is that there are no inherent differences or inequalities between the general public and the persons protected by those statutes, and, therefore, there should be no different treatment in the administration of federal programs. The concept of section 504, on the other hand, is far more complex. Handicapped persons may require different treatment in order to be afforded equal access to federally assisted programs and activities, and identical treatment may, in fact, constitute discrimination. . . .

During the period of comment on the draft regulations, however, there was a great deal of opposition expressed to the turning away from the fundamental policy of nondiscrimination that had informed the whole civil rights movement. Many representatives of handicapped people feared that a policy of differential treatment would in practice become arbitrary treatment. Convinced by these arguments, OCR

[24]The discussion of the emergence of OCR's policy on equal treatment is drawn from Engebretson (1979:70-77).

[25]41 *Fed. Reg.* 20296 (1976).

adopted the traditional civil rights policy of equal treatment as the centerpiece of the final regulations.

The regulations differ from other civil rights guidelines in recognizing that special treatment may in exceptional circumstances be necessary in order to provide services that are as effective as those provided for others, but differential treatment is allowable only when equal treatment has been shown to be inappropriate. Thus, for example, the basic policy regarding public education is for mainstreaming of handicapped pupils. Yet the regulations recognize that in some cases a handicap can be a legitimate grounds for exclusion from the regular education program. By providing due process procedures and requiring an individualized education program for such a pupil, the grounds of decision will be the characteristics and educational needs of the particular handicapped child and not general and arbitrary assumptions about "the blind" or "the deaf."

### Employment Testing

Section 84.13(a) of the regulations prohibits employers from using tests or other selection criteria that screen out, or tend to screen out, handicapped people, unless two conditions are met: (1) the employer can show that the tests or criteria are job-related and (2) the director of the Office for Civil Rights is unable to identify alternative tests or criteria that do not have a tendency to screen out handicapped applicants. Section 84.13(b) further refines the prohibition by requiring an employer to consider whether a given test is actually measuring a handicapped individual's impediment rather than the person's aptitude or ability to perform a job. Appendix A of the regulations cites the example of a job applicant with a speech impediment who is given an oral test. Unless the job in question specifically required oral communication skills, an employer could not justify the use of an oral examination for such a handicapped person. The purpose of the provisions encompassed by Section 84.13 of the regulations is to prevent employers from excluding handicapped people from their work force by using tests and other selection criteria that, while appearing to be neutral screening devices, in fact have the effect of disqualifying a disproportionate number of handicapped people when there is no reasonable business justification for using the particular test or criterion.[26]

[26]Unless otherwise noted, attributions of agency intent in the following discussion of the testing subsections of the regulations are based on the exposition in the OCR *Handbook.*

Because OCR was concerned that the small numbers of handicapped people would make it very difficult to establish differential or disproportionate impact statistically, the agency adopted a more subjective standard for triggering Section 84.13(a) enforcement. The standard is keyed to a showing that a test or other criterion tends to screen out handicapped people. The standard is applied as follows: if a handicapped person files a complaint against an employer based on alleged discriminatory testing procedures and if there is evidence that the test "substantially limits the employment opportunities of handicapped people," then the burden of proof in compliance proceedings shifts to the employer (the recipient of federal funds) to show that the test is job-related.[27] While the Section 504 regulations do not set forth standards for determining job-relatedness, the section-by-section analysis makes it clear that some formal validation study is contemplated (although it does not express a preference for the form of the study). Although judicial interpretation of validation requirements under Title VII has not provided a great deal of guidance about what constitutes a sufficient validation study, the emerging standard is that a test or other selection device must measure the critical areas of knowledge or skill and that there must be a significant relationship between performance on the test and performance on the job.

If an employer does make a successful showing of job-relatedness of a test or other procedure that has an exclusionary effect on handicapped applicants, then the regulations place an obligation on the director of the Office for Civil Rights to identify an alternate, less discriminatory instrument that the employer could use.[28]

## Testing at Preschool, Elementary, Secondary, and Adult Education Levels

In accordance with judicial precedents established early in the 1970s[29] and with the Education for All Handicapped Children Act, Subpart

[27]Section-by-section analysis, 42 *Fed. Reg.* 22689 (May 4, 1977). The agency's section-by-section analysis, appended to the final regulations, states that Section 84.13 (a) is an application of the principle established under Title VII of the Civil Rights Act of 1964 in *Griggs* (42 *Fed. Reg.* 22688).1

[28]This is a deviation from the Equal Employment Opportunity Commissions *Guidelines on Employee Selection Procedures* and earlier versions of the Section 504 regulations, which place this obligation on the employer.

[29]*Mills* v. *Board of Education of the District of Columbia*, 348 F. Supp. 866 (D.D.C. 1972), *Pennsylvania Association for Retarded Children* v. *Commonwealth of Pennsylvania*, 343 F. Supp. 279 (E.D. Pa. 1972), *Lebanks* v. *Spears* 60 F.R.D. 135 (E.D. La. 1973).

D of the regulations for Section 504 requires the provision of a free appropriate public education for all qualified handicapped people. It requires further that handicapped students be educated with nonhandicapped students to the maximum extent possible consistent with their needs (the so-called least restrictive environment principle) and that education agencies seek out previously unserved handicapped children. For the purposes of Subpart D, the term "qualified" is defined in terms of age and disability, as follows:[30]

> With respect to public preschool, elementary, secondary, or adult educational services, a handicapped person (i) of an age during which nonhandicapped persons are provided such services, (ii) or any age during which it is mandatory under state law to provide such services to handicapped persons, or (iii) to whom a state is required to provide a free appropriate public education under Section 612 of [the Education for All Handicapped Children Act].

The definition does not connote the concept of competitive selection in the sense that "qualified" is applied under the employment and postsecondary education subparts of the regulation. An "appropriate" education, however, carries the implication of evaluation and placement—processes in which testing has traditionally played a major role. Section 84.35 of Subpart D establishes placement procedures described in the section-by-section analysis as "designed to ensure that children are not misclassified, unnecessarily labeled as being handicapped, or incorrectly placed because of inappropriate selection, administration, or interpretation of evaluation materials."[31] By requiring public and private schools that receive federal funds to follow rules that require consideration of information drawn from a variety of sources in making pupil placement decisions, HEW sought to eliminate undue reliance on standardized scholastic aptitude tests that, the agency believed, had led to disproportionate assignment of racial and linguistic minorities to special education classes.[32] Other sources of information that might inform the placement decision are enumerated in Section 84.35(c) and include achievement tests, teacher recommendations, reports of physical condition, and investigations of social and cultural background and adaptive behavior.

Section 84.35(b) of the regulations provides general rules for the use of tests and other evaluation materials that are used to assess a

[30] 42 *Fed. Reg.* 22678 (May 4, 1977).

[31] 42 *Fed. Reg.* 22691 (May 4, 1977).

[32] The section-by-section analysis cites "Issues in the Classification of Children," a report by the Project on Classification of Exceptional Children in which HEW participated.

student's need for special education or related services. A recipient institution must ensure that

- tests and other evaluation materials have been validated for the specific purpose for which they are used and are administered by trained personnel in conformance with the instructions provided by their producer;
- tests and other evaluation materials include those tailored to assess specific areas of educational need and not merely those that are designed to provide a single general intelligence quotient; and
- tests are selected and administered so as best to ensure that, when a test is administered to a student with impaired sensory, manual, or speaking skills, the test results accurately reflect the student's aptitude or achievement level or whatever other factor the test purports to measure, rather than reflecting the student's impaired sensory, manual, or speaking skills (except when those skills are the factors that the test purports to measure).

The regulation does not further define "validation," although one can assume that a formal, technical validation procedure is intended. Furthermore, the case law has not established clear standards for judging the sufficiency of a validation effort (see "Judicial Interpretation of Section 504," below). Nevertheless, the validation requirement is likely to have an important influence on school testing practices.

To date, few, if any, validation studies have been undertaken by local and state education agencies, and little attention has been paid to assessing the applicability of a test producer's validation to local conditions. Moreover, validation of tests for handicapped populations has been rare (for achievement tests as well as tests that yield an intelligence quotient). Schools that receive federal funds will be open to compliance investigations when pupils of racial or linguistic minority status are placed in special education classes for the educable mentally retarded or the emotionally handicapped in disproportionate numbers and when the parent or guardian of a handicapped pupil protests a placement decision and there is evidence in the school system of a "pattern or practice" of disproportionate placements.[33]

[33]The doctrine is drawn from Title VII of the Civil Rights Act of 1964, which gives the U.S. Department of Justice jurisdiction to bring civil action against employers whose behavior evidences a "pattern or practice of resistance to the full enjoyment of any of the rights secured by this title" (P.L. 88-352, Title VII, Sec. 707(a)).

## Testing for Admission to Postsecondary Education

Section 84.42 of the regulations implementing Section 504 prescribes requirements for the admission and recruitment of handicapped students to institutions of postsecondary learning. Because colleges, universities, graduate schools, and professional schools typically use and sometimes rely heavily on scores from nationally standardized examinations in making admissions decisions, these provisions have particular significance for a study of testing in relation to handicapped populations.

Unlike the provisions concerning employment testing practices, the regulations on admissions testing use the language of disproportionate effects, which indicates OCR's expectatation that statistical demonstrations of disparities in selection rates will be possible in college and graduate admissions. The regulations state that in admitting students, institutions may not make use of any test or criterion for admission that has a "disproportionate, adverse effect" on handicapped persons unless (1) the test or criterion, *as used by the recipient*, has been validated as a predictor of success in the program or activity in question (emphasis added), and (2) alternate tests or criteria that have a less disproportionate, adverse effect are not shown by the OCR director to be available.

The regulations further require, in words nearly identical to provisions in the sections dealing with employment testing and school testing, that the recipient institution shall assure itself that tests are selected and administered so as to ensure that

> ... the test results accurately reflect the applicant's aptitude or achievement level or whatever other factor the test purports to measure, rather than reflecting the applicant's impaired sensory, manual, or speaking skills (except where those skills are the factors that the test purports to measure) . . . (See Chapter 5 for a discussion of the psychometric implications of that requirement.)

The central provision of the regulation is that qualified handicapped applicants may not, solely on the basis of handicap, be denied admission to a postsecondary educational institution or be discriminated against in recruitment practices. Recipient institutions may not lawfully limit the number or proportion of qualified handicapped students admitted nor make preadmission inquiry as to any handicapping condition.[34] The apparent objective of the preadmission

[34]Exceptions are allowed when an institution that has been found to be out of compliance with Section 504 is attempting to correct the effects of past discrimination

inquiry prohibition was to place all applicants on an equal footing during the admissions process; to date, OCR has not enforced the ban on preadmission inquiry against such designations. It is the policy of the testing companies that produce the major postsecondary admissions tests to make note of nonstandard testing conditions when reporting scores (see Chapter 2). This designation of a nonstandard administration has the effect of informing the admissions officials that the applicant is probably handicapped.

Because of the testing companies' strong disinclination to alter their policies for apparently good technical reasons, OCR adopted an interim policy, which has three parts (see Chapter 5).[35]

First, pending a resolution of the issues (noted above), the Office for Civil Rights will not find an institution out of compliance if that institution requires the submission of test scores by applicants, even though there is a strong possibility that these tests do not reflect a handicapped applicant's ability. In order to ensure that it is in compliance, however, the institution must guarantee that admissions decisions take into account other factors, such as high school grades, recommendations, and so forth. (Such consideration of other factors is, in fact, recommended by the major testing services.)

Second, until such time as a more viable policy can be worked out, the testing services will be allowed to continue to notify users that tests were taken under nonstandard conditions, but it is stressed that this is an interim policy only. OCR recognizes that this procedure may violate the prohibition of preadmission inquiry; it will be allowed only until the interim policy can be modified, and OCR suggests that recipients be prepared to modify their admissions requirements in the future. OCR has initiated discussions with the major testing services in order to resolve the apparent problems with the testing of certain handicapped people.

Third, whenever information is given regarding tests required for admission, an institution must include a statement that special testing arrangements can be made for handicapped applicants and that there are alternate admissions criteria for handicapped applicants who are

---

or when an institution is voluntarily seeking to increase the participation of handicapped students in its programs.

[35]*Recruitment, Admissions and Handicapped Students: A Guide for Compliance with Section 504 of the Rehabilitation Act of 1973*. Published by the American Association of Collegiate Registrars and Admissions Officers and The American Council on Education under contract with the Office for Civil Rights, Department of Health, Education, and Welfare. Washington, D.C., April 1978.

unable to take the required tests. Both the Educational Testing Service and the American College Testing Program have brochures describing special testing arrangements. Admissions personnel are supposed to review and evaluate the suggestions made in these brochures, in preparation for developing other testing arrangements in the future.

Since the first articulation of the interim policy, which has been confirmed in successive editions of the *Handbook for the Implementation of Section 504 of the Rehabilitation Act of 1973*,[36] the U.S. Supreme Court's decision in *Southeastern Community College* v. *Davis* (442 U.S. 397 (1979)) has recognized that there may be physical qualifications that are necessary for participation in a particular academic program. Moreover, in the *Davis* case, the Court focused on whether the applicant would *ever* be capable of performing many of the functions required by the profession for which the educational program trains. This suggests the appropriateness of some loosening of the regulatory ban on preadmission inquiry,[37] which would permit colleges to ask whether applicants meet these qualifications. The agency has interpreted that decision to mean that a recipient may obtain information from an applicant concerning his or her capacity to satisfy "essential physical qualifications" but may not ask general questions about disability, such as: "Are there any problems with physical disability that will prohibit you from completing the program?" (CRC Education and Human Development, Inc. 1981:313).

## JUDICIAL INTERPRETATION OF SECTION 504

Section 504 and its implementing regulations have not produced a great deal of litigation focused on substantive issues; and there are only a few cases that involve testing practices. As mentioned above, judicial decisions are divided on the question of whether Section 504 protects against employment discrimination in any but the most limited circumstances, with the result that OCR has instructed its compliance staff not to take action on employment discrimination complaints in the Second, Fourth, and Eighth Circuits.[38] Given this

[36]The 1979 edition of the handbook is being replaced by an updated version, which is scheduled to be released in early 1982. Our discussion is based on a draft of the updated version, which OCR kindly made available to us.

[37]99 S. Ct. 2362 (1979).

[38]The leading cases restricting the force of the regulations in employment discrimination complaints are *Trageser* v. *Libbie Rehabilitation Center, Inc.*, 590 F.2d 87 (4th Cir., 1978); *Carmi* v. *Metropolitan St. Louis Sewer District*, 620 F. 2d 672 (8th Cir., 1980), *U.S.* v. *Cabrini Medical Center*, No. 80-6166 (2nd Cir., Jan. 27, 1981). *But see*, *Hart* v. *County of Alameda Probation Department*, 485 F.Supp. 66 (N.D. La., 1979).

paucity of case law, it is not possible to specify with certainty the obligations imposed by Section 504 on educational institutions and employers who are recipients of federal financial assistance from the Department of Education or the Department of Health and Human Services. Nevertheless, despite the narrowing effect of the *Davis* decision, the body of civil rights case law that provides a context for Section 504 makes it possible to articulate the contours of the emerging law.

## School Testing Cases Under Section 504

The U.S. Supreme Court in *Brown* v. *Board of Education* ruled that the maintenance of dual, segregated school systems denied to black children equal protection of the law and ordered that dual systems be abolished. Dismantling dual systems, however, did not automatically bring about racial integration in the schools. In fact, after *Brown* many formerly segregated school systems introduced testing programs to track students into ability groups, with the effect that patterns of racial segregation continued within a school. As a result, despite the general reluctance of the courts to intervene in matters of education policy, the federal courts have, since the late 1960s, repeatedly struck down the use of ostensibly neutral mechanisms that resulted in perpetuating or recreating segregated systems.[39]

This history provides the general background for the first major testing case brought under Section 504, *Larry P.* v. *Riles*.[40] *Larry P.*, which began in 1972, concerned the use of general aptitude tests as a basis for determining whether black pupils should be placed in special classes for the educable mentally retarded (EMR classes). Thus, the case combined the issues of racial discrimination and discrimination on the basis of (presumed) handicap. The complaint made two principal allegations: first, that the tests in question were racially and culturally biased against black pupils and did not reflect their experience as a class, with the result that some pupils were misclassified and wrongfully removed from the regular course of instruction; and,

[39]See, e.g., *Singleton* v. *Jackson Municipal Separate School System*, 419 F.2d 1211 (1969), rev'd in part on other grounds, 396 U.S. 290 (1970); *Moses* v. *Washington Parish School Board*, 330 F. Supp. 1340 (1971); *Lemon* v. *Bossier Parish School Board*, 444 F.2d 1400 (1971); *United States* v. *Gadsen City School District*, 508 F.2d 1017 (1978).

[40]343 F. Supp. 1036 (1972), 502 F.2d 963 (1974); 495 F. Supp. 926 (1979), 48 *LW* 2298 (1979). In addition to reliance on Section 504, the case alleged violation of other statutory and constitutional provisions, most notably the Equal Protection Clause of the Fourteenth Amendment.

second, that the special education classes were dead-end, nonacademic classes that offered nothing to the pupils placed in them. The case originally concerned placement practices in the San Francisco area, but it ultimately affected the entire state of California.

One of the most interesting things about *Larry P.* was the district court's attention to the U.S. Supreme Court's analysis in *Griggs* that "not only overt discrimination but also practices that are fair in form, but discriminatory in operation" are proscribed (p. 431). Equally important, however, was the court's recognition that the function of public education placed limits on the applicability of those precedents.

*Larry P.* was the first federal case to require scientific validation of tests used for EMR placement.[41] The plaintiffs sought an injunction against the use of the Wechsler Intelligence Scale for Children, the Stanford-Binet, and other intelligence tests administered in the San Francisco United School District until a full trial could be heard. The court issued a preliminary injunction against the use of the tests, reasoning from precedents established in the employment discrimination case law that the use of standardized tests must be shown to be valid for the purpose at hand (in this instance, the identification of mild mental retardation in black children) to avoid the inference of discrimination. Absent such showing, the court said, the use of tests that have adverse impact cannot be considered to be substantially related to a legitimate state purpose and thus constitutes a denial of the equal protection of the law.

By the time the trial on the merits began in 1977, the original complaint had been amended to include alleged violations of three statutes: Section 504 of the Rehabilitation Act of 1973, Title VI of the Civil Rights Act of 1964, and the Education for All Handicapped Children Act of 1975. Ultimately, the evidence supported a decision that both the constitutional and statutory claims had been proved by plaintiffs.

The crucial conceptual question concerned the nature of that empirical showing: What, in the context of educational testing for assignment purposes, takes the place of the job-relatedness doctrine in employment-testing litigation? *Larry P.* does not provide clear guidance. The defendants attempted to establish the predictive validity of the intelligence tests by showing the correlation of those test scores with two criterion measures, namely, achievement test scores and grades. The court rejected this approach to translating

[41]495 F. Supp. 926, 989.

the notion of predicting job performance to the educational context:[42]

> If tests can predict that a person is going to be a poor employee, the employer can legitimately deny that person a job, but if tests suggest that a young child is probably going to be a poor student, the school cannot on that basis alone deny the child the opportunity to improve and develop the academic skills necessary to success in our society. Assignment to EMR classes denies that opportunity through relegation to a markedly inferior, essentially dead-end track.

The argument is that the quality of the academic instruction in the special education classes, which emphasized social adjustment and economic usefulness, would make this a self-fulfilling prophecy.

One weakness of the defendants' line of reasoning lay in their failure to distinguish the role of business from the function of public education in the United States, which the Supreme Court in *Brown* v. *Board* described as "the very foundation of good citizenship."[43] The doctrine of job-relatedness includes the principle of business necessity, by which the courts have recognized that an employer's interest in productivity may outweigh, in limited circumstances, a particular individual's interest in getting a job. In education, there is no other interest competing with the educational needs of each child (except, perhaps, the educational needs of all children that would, according to the 504 regulations, justify the removal of an obstructive child from the classroom[44]). Thus, while validation in the employment context has been understood by the courts to mean showing the relationship of the test to the job (or test scores to job performance), in *Larry P.* it is defined as showing the appropriateness of the test and placement decision to the specific educational needs of the child. The evidence of high correlations between intelligence test scores and school performance did not, in the eyes of the trial judge, justify placing the child in an environment in which the attempt at academic education would, for all practical purposes, cease.[45]

In *Larry P.*, the school officials did not argue strenuously against the allegation of cultural bias; indeed, the opinion remarks that the cultural bias of the tests was hardly disputed in the litigation (p. 959).

[42]495 F. Supp. 926, 969.
[43]347 U.S. 483, 493 (1954).
[44]Section-by-section analysis, 42 *Fed. Reg.* 22691.
[45]The trial judge suggested that construct validation might be a more appropriate strategy than predictive or content validation (fn. 84).

The opinion of the court is largely devoted to the question of what legal consequences flow from a finding of racial bias in the tests.[46] The case might well have developed differently had it turned primarily on the question of bias on the basis of handicap. For example, establishing the prima facie case would have been a different kind of statistical enterprise. But the ruling concerning validation—that it consists in showing the appropriateness of the test and placement decision to the specific educational needs of the child—may have significance for future judicial policy concerning the assessment of handicapped pupils in making placement decisions.

Another case involving the use of intelligence tests for placement of black children in EMR classes, *Parents in Action on Special Education (PASE)* v. *Hannon*,[47] came to quite different conclusions about the adequacy of IQ tests for assessing mental retardation in black children. The plaintiffs in *PASE* charged that the use of racially biased intelligence tests violated the Equal Protection Clause of the Fourteenth Amendment as well as Section 504 of the Rehabilitation Act of 1973, Title VI of the Civil Rights Act of 1964, the Equal Educational Opportunities Act of 1974 (20 USC 1703), and the Education for All Handicapped Children Act. Contrary to the finding in the California case, the trial court in *Parents in Action on Special Education* v. *Hannon* found the Wechsler tests and the Stanford-Binet substantially free of cultural bias. After examining the test questions item by item, the judge decided, on a commonsense basis, that only nine questions were "biased or so subject to suspicion of bias that they should not be used" (slip opinion:98). Because the test scores were interpreted by masters-level school psychologists, many of whom were black, and because test scores were only one of the criteria for the placement decision, the court found it unlikely that those few items would result in misplacement of black children in the Chicago school system. The judge held that the tests, used in this manner, did not discriminate against black children in the Chicago public schools (slip opinion:115).

Although judicial interpretation of the obligations of school officials under Section 504 with regard to testing practices is just beginning, it seems likely that the assessment of handicapped students will continue to be subject to judicial scrutiny, given the special regulatory protections afforded such students. At the very least, school officials

[46]The judgment enjoined California from using any standardized intelligence tests without securing the prior approval of the court.
[47]Civil Number 74 C 3586 (1980).

are on notice that they must address questions of validation and impact. The unquestioned or naive use of intelligence tests or other assessment devices to place children of racial or linguistic minority status in classes for the mentally retarded will not be defensible in court; there is every reason to believe that the courts will afford handicapped students a similar level of concern.

### Postsecondary Admissions

There has not been any litigation concerning postsecondary admissions practices that has focused directly on the use of tests. The few cases to arise have dealt generally with procedural questions, such as the existence of a private right of action under Section 504 (see Paolicelli 1979 and Ray 1979-80). Interpretation of the substantive provisions of Section 504—the meaning of discrimination on the basis of handicap, for example—has just begun to emerge.

The first case to review the scope of Section 504 was *Southeastern Community College* v. *Davis*.[48] In its 1979 decision, the U.S. Supreme Court addressed two important issues: the meaning of the statutory language, "otherwise qualified handicapped individual," and the extent of the modifications an institution must make in its programs to accommodate the handicaps or disabilities of applicants.

The *Davis* case involved the application of Frances Davis, a hearing-impaired licensed practical nurse, to enter the college's associate degree nursing program in order to become a registered nurse. In the course of admissions screening, Davis was examined by an audiologist, who advised the admissions authorities that, while a better hearing aid would enable her to hear sounds, Davis would not be able to understand normal speech unless positioned so that she could lip-read. The college consulted with the director of the State Board of Nursing to determine whether Davis would be eligible for certification if she completed the program. The director recommended against admission on the grounds that Davis would not be able to participate safely in the obligatory clinical training and could not practice after graduation.[49]

Davis filed suit against the college on the grounds that the denial of admission constituted a violation of the Equal Protection and Due

[48]99 S. Ct. 2361 (1979). For discussions of the case, see, Cohen (1980), Hightower (1980), Ray, (1979-80), Cook (1980).
[49]99 S. Ct. n. 69, at 2364-5.

Process Clauses of the Fourteenth Amendment and of Section 504 of the Rehabilitation Act. The district court held that the college's decision not to admit Davis did not violate Section 504; the judge found that while the plaintiff, a handicapped person, was entitled to the protection of Section 504, she was not an "otherwise qualified individual" within the meaning of the statute because the nature of her handicap would not allow her to "fully and effectively participate" in the program.[50] Davis appealed the decision on the basis of the newly issued HEW regulations that defined a qualified handicapped person with respect to postsecondary admissions as "a handicapped person who meets the academic and technical standards requisite to admission or participation in the recipient's education program or activity."[51] In light of those regulations, the Court of Appeals for the Fourth Circuit ruled that the lower court had erred in taking Davis' handicap into consideration, ruling that it should have looked only at her academic and technical qualifications. The court also held that consideration should be given to Davis's claim that Section 504 required the college to modify its nursing program to accommodate her hearing impairment no matter what the cost.[52]

In a unanimous decision, the U.S. Supreme Court reversed the appellate court decision in *Davis*.[53] Writing for the Court, Justice Powell held that Section 504 does not "compel educational institutions to disregard the disabilities of handicapped individuals or to make substantial modifications in their programs to allow disabled persons to participate." The opinion supported the district court's interpretation of "otherwise qualified" to mean "qualified in spite of the handicap"; what the statute prohibits is disqualification of a person based on "unfounded assumptions" about the limitations imposed by a handicap (p. 2366). The Court held further that Section 504 imposes no affirmative obligation on recipients of federal funds to substantially modify existing programs or to lower standards to accommodate a handicapped person (p. 2370), although pointedly stating that the line between a lawful refusal to extend affirmative action and illegal discrimination under Section 504 will not always be clear.

The U.S. Supreme Court decision in *Davis* does not provide detailed guidance as to the distinction between permissible exclusion and

[50]424 F. Supp. 1341, 1345 (E.D.N.C. 1976).
[51]42 *Fed. Reg.* 22678.
[52]574 F.2d 1160-1162.
[53]99 S. Ct. 2361 (1979).

unlawful discrimination under Section 504. It does make clear, however, that the regulatory ban on preadmission inquiry is not applicable to postsecondary programs that require specific physical qualifications and that institutions can take disabilities into account in admitting applicants to such programs. The regulation precluding consideration of handicaps at the admissions stage is, presumably, still enforceable when the applicant's handicap is irrelevant to participation in the program, which might well be the case for most undergraduate courses of study. In the *Davis* case, however, the applicant's hearing disability not only would have prevented her from participating in portions of the clinical practicum (for example, operating-room duty where surgical masks render lip-reading impossible), but also would have posed a potential hazard to her patients once she embarked on a nursing career.

## SUMMARY

Title V of the Rehabilitation Act of 1973 is a civil rights law, akin to the other civil rights statutes passed in the 1960s and 1970s. It is not, however, an affirmative statement of the civil rights of handicapped people; rather, it prohibits discrimination against handicapped people by monitoring the practices of the government, its instrumentalities, and grantees. The protections offered under Title V do not reach to the private sector but only to recipients of federal funds.

The antidiscrimination provisions of Section 504 are further restricted in scope in that they extend only to qualified handicapped individuals. This provision is different from those of all other civil rights statutes, which extend protection to all members of the covered class. The language of Section 504, as well as Congress' failure in the period since 1964 to enact legislation adding discrimination on the basis of handicap to the categories protected against employment discrimination by Title VII, suggests that Congress intended to distinguish between characteristics like race or ethnic origin and having a handicapping condition. Regulatory and judicial construction of Section 504 have recognized that a handicapping condition can, under some circumstances, be a legitimate grounds for exclusion and that distinctions drawn on the basis of handicap do not necessarily reflect prejudiced attitudes. (In future litigation, this may have implications for judicial interpretation of the effects test propounded by the regulations.)

At the same time, Congress and the courts recognize that distinctions drawn on the basis of handicap frequently are the product of prejudice or unwarranted assumptions about the limitations produced by handicapping conditions. The public policy preference for mainstreaming—a theme that pervades the regulations—gives positive expression to the statutory language of nondiscrimination. It is evidence of a federal commitment to the principle that people with handicapping conditions should be afforded opportunities to participate as fully as possible in the society. This policy has brought significant change. Under Section 504 and the Education for All Handicapped Children Act, all children with handicapping conditions are for the first time guaranteed an appropriate education at public expense in the most integrated setting possible. The due process procedures that are the centerpieces of P.L. 94-142 and the Section 504 regulations seek to ensure that educational decisions will be made on the basis of the particular child's needs, not on the basis of unfounded assumptions about the child's performance capabilities.

The meaning of equal opportunity for adults seeking jobs or higher education is not yet as clear as the policy concerning school children, but some general principles have been established. First, the antidiscrimination provisions of Section 504 make it unlawful for recipient institutions to exclude handicapped individuals without making an analysis of the physical requirements of the program and the characteristics of the applicant. When a program of instruction requires particular physical capabilities, the regulatory ban on preadmission inquiries does not apply, at least with respect to those particular physical capabilities. For programs that do not depend on physical characteristics, it is likely that OCR's ban on preadmission inquiry would be sustained, should the agency decide to implement that policy. The panel believes that the policy can reasonably be applied to most academic programs at the undergraduate level, provided that standardized tests that are used as selection aids can be brought to a point where they are as predictive for applicants with handicapping conditions as for the nonhandicapped applicants. Such validation efforts will require an intensive research endeavor. If successful, such research would provide the means for test users to avoid disqualifying an applicant on the basis of unfounded assumptions about the limitations imposed by a handicap.

# 5

# Psychometric Requirements of the Regulations

The regulations implementing Section 504 of the Rehabilitation Act of 1973 specify four requirements regarding testing for admission to postsecondary educational institutions that bear directly on the psychometric characteristics of the tests.[1] An institution subject to the Rehabilitation Act of 1973:

1. may not use a test that has a disproportionate adverse effect on handicapped applicants unless the test has been validated specifically for the purpose in question or unless alternate tests with less adverse effect are not shown to exist [Sec. 104.42(b)(2)];
2. shall assure itself that tests are selected and administered so as to best ensure that the test results reflect the handicapped applicant's "aptitude or achievement level or whatever other factor the test purports to measure, rather than reflecting the applicant's impaired sensory, manual, or speaking skills (except where those skills are the factors that the test purports to measure)" [Sec. 104.42(b)(3)];
3. may not make preadmission inquiries as to whether a person is handicapped [Sec. 104.42(b)(4)]; and
4. "may base prediction equations on first year grades, but shall conduct periodic validity studies against the criterion of overall success

[1]We are not concerned here with the requirements, like those regarding timeliness of test administrations or the accessibility of testing sites, that are not psychometric issues.

in the education program or activity in question in order to monitor the general validity of the test scores" [Sec. 104.42(d)].

The requirements regarding selection for employment are very similar but require that a test be validated against job performance instead of against educational performance.

Since there have been no compliance reviews of these testing requirements and since there is as yet no case law, the authoritative interpretation of these sections of the regulations is still unsettled. Nevertheless, in light of the history of the regulations and the interim policy, some implications seem relatively clear. In operational terms, the regulations seem to require that test developers and users (1) modify tests and test administration procedures for use with handicapped people; (2) construct and administer tests so that they reflect skills independent of disabilities; (3) report scores for handicapped people so that they are indistinguishable from and therefore directly comparable with those for nonhandicapped people; and (4) validate tests used with handicapped people for the purpose at hand. The crucial question is whether there are psychometric techniques that can be used to satisfy these requirements.

This chapter discusses psychometric issues relating to each of these four requirements. Test modifications for handicapped people, which have been made in most tests given to large groups (college applicants or federal civil service examinees, for example), are described in the first section; a review of the evidence relating to the requirement that a test accurately reflect skills independent of a handicap is presented in the second section; validation of tests for handicapped people is discussed in the third section; and issues related to the comparability of tests for handicapped and nonhandicapped people are discussed in the final section.

## MODIFICATIONS OF TESTS FOR HANDICAPPED PEOPLE

While there undoubtedly is room for improvement, more work has gone into modifying tests and test administration procedures than into any other aspect of testing handicapped people. For more than two decades, major national testing programs have made available modified versions of tests for handicapped people. Long before the Section 504 regulations were implemented, the College Entrance Examination Board (now the College Board), the American College Testing Program, the Graduate Record Examination Board, and others provided some options for handicapped examinees that included modified administration procedures, test booklets, and answering procedures. But those efforts, however laudable or well-intentioned, have been far from adequate and have been undertaken by only some test developers. Even today some large testing programs, such as the one administered by the Law School Admission Council, allow only very limited modifications of their tests for handicapped people.

Despite the history of attempts to modify tests for handicapped people, there have been few investigations of the effects of such test accommodations on the resulting scores and on their reliability and validity. Strictly speaking, unless it has been demonstrated that the psychometric properties of a test have not been disturbed by some modification, the claims made for the test by its author or publisher cannot be generalized to the modified version. The major reason given by test developers for not having done systematic studies of modified tests is the relatively small number of handicapped examinees. Test developers have argued that most of the standard methods for investigating reliability and particularly validity cannot be applied to very small samples of people.[2] Studies now being conducted at the Educational Testing Service (for research, not operational purposes) may represent a shift in attitudes, and the panel has learned of very recent research investigations using new techniques for studying small populations.

Especially when studies of the validity of a modified test are not anticipated, that is, when test interpretation will rest largely on uncorroborated generalizations from the standard test, one must be very careful in adapting a test not to make changes that can alter the nature of the task. For example, a test of mechanical ability that involves manipulation of many pieces of apparatus might become, for blind people, a test of tactile acuity (Bauman 1976). Or in a test that presents novel stimuli (for example, raised line drawings), the novelty of the situation might overwhelm an examinee's responses. Although useful guides to modifying tests for administration to handicapped people are available (see, for example, Bolton 1976a,

[2]Testimony of Educational Testing Service (ETS) and American College Testing Program at the panel's open meeting, March 1980; letters to the Office for Civil Rights from John Winterbottom of ETS, dated June 17, 1976; September 10, 1976; November 21, 1977; and January 26, 1978.

Heaton et al. 1980), no guide can obviate the necessity of trying out a modified test on a sample of examinees or of validating the modified version of a test.

### Modifications of Test Administration Procedures

Most modifications in the way a test is administered alter the medium in which the test instructions and questions are presented to the examinees. For visually impaired people, a variety of modifications may be needed. The test booklet may be produced in large print or high-quality regular print, or in braille, or the test may be tape-recorded or read to the examinee by a live reader. These procedures usually require more time for the test administration, so time limits are either extended or waived. The tests so modified are usually administered on an individual basis to provide the needed flexibility in time and to minimize interference of different test administration procedures with one another. Davis and Nolan (1961) found that the oral administration of a verbal achievement test usually results in inflated scores relative to any administration in which the examinee must read (whether regular print, large type, or braille). How serious and pervasive this result may be is unknown.

Deaf people, especially the prelingually deaf, have difficulty in understanding written as well as spoken language; therefore, the intelligibility of the instructions for tests, whether written or spoken, must be considered when tests are modified for the deaf. Modifications of test administration for deaf and hearing-impaired people often include an interpreter who signs or otherwise interprets the test instructions and questions. Most national test programs that use interpreters instruct them in how to administer the test so as to communicate appropriately but without giving clues to correct answers. Additional time to take the test will be needed if the test is signed or interpreted to a deaf person.

If test administration procedures are modified for visually impaired and hearing-impaired people, usually no additional adaptations in those procedures are needed for testing other handicapped individuals. For example, a person without upper limbs who cannot write can use an amanuensis, a person who writes or marks the answers for the test taker. When test modifications are available, examinees with other handicapping conditions select from the available options the one most preferred. A visually impaired examinee should select the test administration procedure that best suits his or her preferred and customary medium; this choice will be especially difficult for people who have recently become impaired.

When examinees cannot record their answers to test questions, the most common procedure is to provide an amanuensis. Other ways of obtaining a response include having the respondent use a tape recorder, a typewriter, or a braillewriter (a machine that types braille). These modifications usually require that a test be administered individually. Some testing programs provide a large-type answer sheet for partially sighted or motor-impaired test takers. Use of a large-type answer sheet does not by itself require an individual administration.

Note-taking and computational aids are sometimes provided for blind examinees because they do not have easy or constant access to the material before them, as do sighted examinees. (When one is searching for a specific piece of information, it is much more difficult and time-consuming to scan braille or a tape recording as compared with print.) Examinees who read braille may benefit from use of note-taking aids such as a braillewriter or a braille slate and stylus, whether they take the test in braille, from a tape recording, or with a reader.

There has been some fear that the use of certain aids, particularly the Cranmer abacus for arithmetic computation, gives blind examinees an advantage over sighted examinees who may use only paper and pencil. Brothers (1972) found that blind eighth-graders who used an abacus were eight months below the sighted norm in arithmetic computation, but that they performed significantly better than their blind peers who used mental computation or a braillewriter. The teaching of mathematics to blind students, while apparently facilitated by the Cranmer abacus, remains a serious concern to educators. In a review of the literature, however, Nester (1974) found that while published research leaves many questions unanswered, it does indicate that the use of the Cranmer abacus does not give a blind test taker an unfair advantage over sighted test takers without a computational aid. The abacus, unlike an electronic calculator, requires of the user a fundamental knowledge of arithmetic operations.

## Alterations in Time for Test Administration

Nearly all national testing programs that provide modified test procedures for handicapped people provide additional time to take the test. The effects of increasing the length of time have not been studied fully, even though time may be an important factor for nonhandicapped test takers. With one possible exception, all of the alternate media used to administer tests to visually impaired people require more time than the regular form. Reading braille and using a cassette recorder or a reader take longer than reading regular print. Reading large type may or may not be more time-consuming, depending on the layout of the material and on the nature and severity of the impairment. It should be noted that the Law School Admission Test allows no extra time for any examinee, a practice that may have particularly severe effects on visually impaired examinees.

In setting time limits for a test for the general population, test developers usually establish a limit within which 75 to 90 percent of the candidates can complete all of the items (see Tinkleman 1971, Toops 1960). Such a procedure could be duplicated for handicapped test takers or for different test modifications, although a large number of trials would be necessary. To obtain such data for a large national testing program, one would have to aggregate examinees over many test administrations in many different locations.

Only a few studies of the time needed by handicapped individuals to complete a modified test are available. For tests for which no studies have been conducted, time limits are either set arbitrarily (usually as a multiple of the standard time) or waived altogether. Studies of the appropriate time limits for modified tests have been undertaken by the U. S. Office of Personnel Management (Nester and Sapinkopf 1981, Sapinkopf 1978). In one study, deaf students first took the Professional and Administrative Career Examination (PACE) with unlimited time. Then the investigators determined the amount of time needed for 90 percent of the test takers to complete each part of the test. Similar procedures were employed in establishing time limits for visually handicapped individuals. Time limits were established separately for each combination of test part and medium of test administration. The results of these studies specifying a time limit for each test part and each medium of test administration, (e.g., braille) or combination of media (e.g., braille and reader) were subsequently incorporated into instructions for test examiners for regular use in administering the test to handicapped people.

Speed tests[3] usually are considered inappropriate for test takers

[3]Individual differences in scores on a pure speed test depend only on speed of response. In a power test, on the other hand, everyone is given enough time to attempt all items, some of which are so difficult that it is highly unlikely that anyone can get a perfect score.

with visual impairments. Typing tests offer a familiar example of a speed test. A study performed in 1958 for the U. S. Civil Service Commission (Shultz and Boynton 1958) found that typing from tape recordings is slower and less accurate than typing from printed copy. On the other hand, allowing blind examinees unlimited time may not always be appropriate. Research by Davis and Nolan (1961) indicates that giving unlimited time and allowing every blind examinee a chance to answer every test item results in inflated test scores.

The majority of the tests considered by this panel are regarded as power tests. Recently, however, questions have arisen as to what extent power tests are actually speeded, and concern has been expressed that speededness might differentially affect the performance of groups of test takers (Donlon 1980a, Donlon 1980b). If it were found that the power tests are more speeded for nonhandicapped examinees than previously thought, there would be reason to question the wisdom (or fairness) of setting time limits for handicapped examinees (particularly those with visual impairments) as a multiple of the time allowed for a standard administration, say 2 or 2½ times the regular time limit. Such an allowance may produce a test that is still speeded for handicapped people and penalizes them unnecessarily. Such a procedure also presumes for example, that, the ratio of the speed of reading braille versus print is the same for all types of material and all levels of difficulty commonly occurring on standardized tests (see Nolan 1962).

A study of nonhandicapped students by Wild and Durso (1979) showed that increasing the time allowed for experimental sections of the Graduate Record Examination (GRE) from 20 to 30 minutes resulted in small but statistically significant score increases. The sizes of the increases were not significantly different for groups defined by ethnicity, age, and sex. Although handicapped test takers were not included in the study, the results are important for that group because they suggest that scores on these experimental subtests of the GRE, developed just like the nonexperimental or "operational" subtests, are significantly affected by speed of response. Thus, one might predict that giving test takers a generous or an unlimited amount of time would significantly increase their scores. The limiting factor of fatigue would, of course, have to be considered if one moved from considering a 10-minute increase (as in the Wild and Durso study) to considering a several-hour increase (as often occurs in practice). The effects of time limits on psychometric properties of tests other than mean scores (especially reliability and validity) must also be considered.

Lengthening the time for administration of a test is only one of several ways in which the testing time for examinees can be altered. Taking more rest periods while holding constant the total length of time for actually taking the test is one such change. Another is a combination of lengthening the test administration time and including more rest periods. Still another is allowing not only a longer time period in which to take a test but also more than one day. Obviously, an unlimited time period during a single day regardless of the time ultimately allowed would not benefit a disabled individual who becomes fatigued in a relatively short period. Considering the negative effects of fatigue, extending time limits well beyond those thought to be defensible for nonhandicapped examinees may put unexpected and unreasonable demands on handicapped examinees.

Although modifications in the time allowed for tests are considered among the appropriate test options, there are few data available to support any conclusions about the effects of modifications in time, number of sittings, or number of recesses on the test results. Furthermore, little is known about how much time people with various handicapping conditions actually need, because records of time actually used are rare, and empirical studies to set time limits are even less frequent. Clearly, more research on time limits for test modifications and for different handicapping conditions is necessary.

### Changes in Test Content

Changes in test content are often required for examinees with visual or hearing impairments. For visually impaired people, items must be examined for possible "visual biases." Test items contain a visual bias if they measure knowledge, skills, or concepts learned primarily through vision or if they use visual stimuli to measure knowledge acquired through other senses. Although either type of visual bias may be detected empirically, the second type may well be easier than the former to identify and correct by simply reading the items, spotting the offenders, and substituting nonvisual stimuli. Since the substitutions may alter other characteristics of the items, the modified items should be tried out before they are used in operational testing situations. Visual biases of the first type may be more difficult to identify and remedy, especially by test developers who are unfamiliar with visual impairments. Examples of information acquired primarily through vision would include questions relating to geology, meteorology, geography, architecture, or geometry or items requiring discrimination of relationships among colors or spatial features.

The most thorough and detailed documentation of modifications in test content is that done on the PACE, administered by the Office of Personnel Management for federal employment. The content of the PACE has been modified for visually and hearing-impaired examinees. For the visually impaired, two item types were deleted—figure analogies and tabular completion—because a suitable method of presenting the content could not be found. Other items were reviewed by panels of experts to identify those with visual biases. Scoring norms were established by administering the modified items to sighted PACE examinees (see Nester 1980, Sapinkopf 1978).

### Changes in the Testing Environment

Many of the modifications in the ways in which tests are administered for handicapped people necessitate that the tests be given individually rather than to groups of respondents. The reasons for having an individual administration include the existence of no practical and convenient way to use a group administration, the desire not to interfere with others in a group taking a test, and other considerations for handicapped examinees, such as wanting to reduce their anxiety over the test. Although the administration of a test on an individual basis is probably the most important modification in the testing environment needed by handicapped examinees, there are some additional alterations that may be required. For example, a change in location will be required if the standard testing site is not accessible to people in wheelchairs. Examinees with certain physical disabilities may be more comfortable with tables or chairs unlike the usual ones; for example, tabletops may need to be bigger or at a different height. Certain lighting conditions may make reading easier for the partially sighted. Sometimes a test may be administered to a person confined to bed, say, a victim of an automobile accident.

The administration of a test to one individual may differ in important ways from the standard group administration. The interaction between the examiner and the examinee may have profound (but usually unknown) effects on the resulting score. Ragosta (1980) studied such interaction and, while she reported many favorable reactions of test takers to test administrators, she also recorded some problems, some of which seemed to stem from inexperience, ignorance, or bias on the part of the test administrator. Some examples of negative comments follow (Ragosta 1980:35-36):

> The teacher (test administrator) was uncomfortable with my disability. He kept asking me questions like . . . did I know what I was there for and did

I realize the importance of the test, etc. I felt he was questioning my mental ability [cerebral palsied student].

I fought to take SATs. They said there was no large print version! A guidance counselor gave the test to me orally; she was aggravated when I had to ask her to repeat. I would like to have taken the test with somebody who believed I would pass [legally blind student].

Writers (amanuenses) sometimes inhibit you because they keep waiting for an answer. Tape recorders might be okay [legally blind student].

When a test administrator walks around, it is hard to hear what he is saying. I try . . . then I read directions again. I lose time [hearing-impaired student].

At present, there are no comprehensive data on the seriousness or pervasiveness of such difficulties. The problems cited above probably deflate the test scores of handicapped people, but without systematic studies there is no way to know the nature and extent of the effects. There are also no data on cases in which test administrators, intentionally or not, give cues to correct answers or otherwise help handicapped examinees.

### The Option of Not Taking a Test

One alternative to modifying a test is to exempt handicapped people from taking the test. When a testing requirement is waived, biographical data, work samples, academic transcripts, and other evidence usually provide a basis on which a candidate's record can be evaluated. Handicapped people, however, particularly those with visual impairments, have argued that exempting them from taking a test places them at a disadvantage compared with other applicants (National Federation of the Blind 1980).[4]

### Costs of Modifying Tests

Since the regulations implementing Section 504 require that tests be appropriately modified for handicapped people, questions of the

[4]Clearly, there are differences of opinion, but most who expressed their views to the panel wanted to improve tests, not to waive them. Nevertheless, in some situations the waiver of a testing requirement may be the fairest and most appropriate action. It should be noted, however, that, for the general population, alternatives to tests, such as those listed above, generally have considerably lower reliability and validity than tests themselves.

costs of such modifications naturally arise. Some test producers protest that the costs are too high. There is no comprehensive information available on this issue, but we present some general estimates of the costs. We note that an appropriate evaluation of the total costs of test modification would require data on the costs of all types of modification for all of the tests used in employment and educational testing. In this section we present only a sketch of such a calculation for educational testing. The cost figures cited in this section were obtained from a private testing organization.

Before proceeding we note two difficulties in calculating costs. First, the expenditures involved in modifying tests represent the true social costs (as typically defined by economists) only if the prices of resources used in test modification adequately reflect their value in alternative uses. Prices will not be accurate reflections of value when markets are not perfectly competitive, and it appears, at least superficially, that the testing industry is not competitive. The number of testing firms is relatively small and the consumers of tests, at least in the educational segment of the industry, are organizationally linked to the producers. The observed data on costs are, therefore, a proxy whose true relationship to social costs is not defined. This caveat applies to all observed costs on testing and not just to the data that we present. The second difficulty in calculating costs lies in determining how much of the costs of modifying tests is attributable to changes required to eliminate test bias relating to handicapping conditions. Consider, for example, a situation in which a printed test is translated into braille. Should one count the expenditures for producing braille tests and of producing and reporting scores as the cost of the modification? Or is it more appropriate to define the cost of modification as the difference between the braille-related costs and those that would have been incurred to test the same number of individuals using standard tests? Either basis of cost calculation could be appropriate depending on the situation.

### *Changes in Content*

Changes in content are required when the substance of a test question relates to information or concepts that certain people cannot experience or perceive because of a handicap. The content of educational admissions tests, however, is most often not modified for handicapped people. Experts review existing standard test forms and choose for modification those with the least potential for bias. No cost estimates are available.

### *Changes in Medium*

Commonly available modifications of admissions tests include large-type, braille, and cassette versions. In 1979-80 the production of braille forms of a widely used test cost roughly $6,800 for 30 copies, or an average cost per test taker of $226. Cassette versions of the test cost $5,600 for 100 copies, or an average cost per test taker of $56. The cost for 200 copies of a large-print version was $4,000, an average cost of $20. The limited number of copies that were produced indicates that a substantial portion of the expenditures are fixed rather than variable costs. The total cost of the large-print version is likely to be approximately constant over a wide range of quantities, since the cost of preparing copy and printing plates is independent of the number of copies produced from those plates. The average cost figures, therefore, are extremely sensitive to the quantity of test instruments produced.

### *Changes in Test Administration*

The primary costs incurred in modifying test administration procedures are the wages paid to test center supervisors and proctors. It was estimated that in 1979-80, the supervision of tests for 500 handicapped people cost $27,000, or an average cost of $54 per test taker. Of this group, 314 took standard versions of the test.

The costs of modifying the testing environment are, at least in terms of current practices, primarily variable in nature. In addition, the heavy reliance on the use of personnel and time indicates that the potential economies of an increase in the number of tests administered is quite small. One would expect, therefore, that total costs are likely to vary rather directly with number of tests administered and that the average total cost per test will be approximately constant over the number of tests administered.

### *Administrative Costs*

Some test modifications require alterations in the method of producing and reporting test scores. In addition, there are a variety of clerical procedures required for the processing of applications for modified tests. In the above example, the costs of producing scores from the 186 modified tests totaled $1,400, averaging approximately $8 per test. An additional $15,600 was reported as the sum of the cost of clerical procedures relating to test registration and score reporting

($11,000) and of the cost of collecting, shipping, and checking test materials ($4,600). The clerical costs were computed from the accounting cost of a special clerical section whose entire function is processing materials for handicapped test takers. Finally there were administrative expenditures for pre-test information booklets in printed and braille form, other information on modified tests, and the costs of "program management." The sum of these costs was $22,200; approximately 55 percent of these costs were for management. The sum of clerical and other administrative costs, therefore, was $37,800, or approximately $76 per person.

Hence, for this test in 1979-80, the average total cost of modifications for handicapping conditions, including all of those mentioned above, was $156 per person, ranging from $130 to $364 per person depending on the type of test modification.

## MEASURES OF ABILITIES INDEPENDENT OF HANDICAPS

The regulations directly state that tests should measure a handicapped person's level of aptitude or achievement and not the impaired functioning unless the latter is what the test purports to measure. This is equivalent to saying that a handicapping condition should have no effect whatsoever on test scores unless the test is explicitly designed to measure an ability directly related to the handicap. In addition, an "Analysis of the Final Regulation," which was published as an appendix to the final regulations, includes the following statement (42: *Fed. Reg.* 22692):

> Section 84.42(b)(3) also requires a recipient to assure itself that admissions tests are selected and administered to applicants with impaired sensory, manual, or speaking skills in such manner as is necessary to avoid unfair distortion of test results. Methods have been developed for testing the aptitude and achievement of persons who are not able to take written tests or even to make the marks required for mechanically scored objective tests; in addition, methods for testing persons with visual or hearing impairment are available. A recipient, under this paragraph, must assure itself that such methods are used with respect to the selection and administration of any admissions tests that it uses.

This explanation logically rests on the assumption that the use of modified tests and test administration procedures is in itself sufficient to ensure that a test will reflect abilities that are unaffected by an examinee's handicap. This assumption is not true; the panel, along with others who are knowledgeable about test development, rejects it as a reasonable or safe working assumption.

Although the goal of constructing measures that are unaffected by a handicapping condition is generally accepted as the ideal, most test developers believe that it is largely unattainable in the near future in many if not most instances. Clearly, there are cases in which a handicapping condition has almost no effect on test performance and, therefore, modifications of the test are not needed. There are also cases in which the modifications that are needed are so straightforward that they can safely be assumed to have no effect on the test scores. However, especially when a handicap is severe and when a test requires high-level cognitive functioning, the effects of the handicap on the test are potentially enormous and extremely difficult if not impossible to eradicate.

In its identification of points in the regulations that the panel believes cannot be supported by current scientific endeavor, the Panel has identified points in psychometric theory that need further development. No test score—for handicapped or nonhandicapped examinees—is a totally pure measure of an ability. Every test score is distorted in some way. Even much of our language regarding tests reveals this phenomenon: test scores reflect, they indicate, they represent. Tests give only indirect pictures of what it is they claim to measure. All measures—physical as well as psychological—are affected in one way or another by the measuring instrument. Psychometricians call this inevitable inaccuracy "measurement error" and estimate it in the process of developing a test. For example, a test of reading ability will be easier for a student who just happens to be interested in and familiar with the subjects in the reading passages. Yet the student's knowledge of those particular subjects has nothing directly to do with his or her reading ability and ideally should not affect scores on the reading test. The estimated measurement error will take into account this and many other (usually unknown) sources of random error in test scores.

Consider another example closer to the panel's focus. Suppose that a group of deaf people is given a test containing passages on American history that are written with a more sophisticated vocabulary and more complicated syntax than required to express the important ideas. For the deaf test takers the test might be a legitimate measure of linguistic fluency in the context of American history, but it is not a suitable measure of knowledge of American history. The well-documented linguistic deficit of deaf people, particularly the prelingually deaf, would prevent them from accurately displaying their knowledge of American history unless the language of the test were simplified. For the deaf examinees in this example, the error in the scores taken as measures of knowledge of American history is likely to be much larger than it would be for nonhandicapped test takers. Some of the error would be random but much would probably be systematic—and it would lower the scores of the deaf people. Additonally, the usual estimates of measurement error do not reflect this or other systematic errors.

Domain-referenced testing provides an example that focuses our attention on the ability that a test is claimed to measure. The initial step in constructing a domain-referenced test is to define the domain, first generally and then in terms of more specific skills or knowledge. (Even this first step is somewhat arbitrary; experts might define domains rather differently.) The next step is to decide how to measure the different skills, what content to include, what levels of difficulty to cover, and how to weight each component in the test. Then the items are written and refined, psychometric properties of the test are determined, and the test is ready to be administered.

Suppose that the finished product is packaged and sold as the Acme Test of Reasoning Ability. The title hardly begins to describe what the test measures. There are many tests of reasoning ability, and they all differ from one another in more or less significant ways. Users of the test would have to delve deeply in the literature (presumably published with the test) on how various concepts were defined, how measures were developed, and what characterized the samples of examinees on whom the test was tried out. Only then would the users begin to understand what scores on the Acme Test of Reasoning Ability actually reflect. Furthermore, the meaning(s) the users attach to scores on the test might change and would almost certainly be enriched with increased familiarity both with the test and with how people with various scores perform in other situations. Some of the users' knowledge would be specific to that test, and some would have derived from experience about that general type of test—a paper-and-pencil, multiple-choice, timed test of reasoning ability.

Measurement issues, already difficult, become much more complicated when the test or the test administration procedures are modified for use with handicapped people. To carry the example further, suppose the test is modified so that it can be given to visually impaired examinees, and assume that the modifications have been expertly executed and that the resulting test is the best that could be devised for the visually impaired. The quality of the modifications notwithstanding, the test users are at a loss as to how to interpret the scores. There are no standards against which to evaluate the scores of the visually impaired. And much of what the users would have learned about the Acme Test must be questioned: Are all of the same subtests used? How heavy was the visual loading of the original test; how much has the content been changed? Are the same cognitive processes used by visually impaired people in answering the test questions? Are the same cognitive processes required of visually impaired people in other situations of interest? Does performance on the test bear the same relationship to other performance for sighted as for visually impaired people? The list of questions is long and has implications far beyond testing. All that is known about perception and cognition could and should be brought to bear.

In summary, the panel believes that psychology and psychometrics are not yet fully capable of ensuring that tests for handicapped people measure skills independent of handicapping conditions. The requirement that they do so, though straightforward in intent, poses serious problems for psychologists who attempt to define various abilities, to measure those abilities, and to describe the underlying cognitive processes. In short, the panel believes that demonstrating that tests can provide measures of abilities independent of handicapping conditions should be regarded as a long-term research goal. The panel believes that full compliance with this requirement is not currently possible; however, compliance with other psychometric requirements of the regulations are not only possible but will lead to tests for handicapped people that can be used fairly and intelligently as predictors of later performance.

## VALIDATION OF TESTS FOR HANDICAPPED PEOPLE

### Educational Testing

The Section 504 regulations require that a test that has a disproportionately adverse effect on handicapped people be validated for the purpose in question and preclude using that test if a test with less adverse effect is shown to exist. The regulations further require that postsecondary educational admissions tests be validated against first-year grades in the educational program and that studies be conducted periodically against the criterion of overall success in the program. Thus, the regulations very clearly emphasize the importance of demonstrating the validity of tests that are used for handicapped people.

Strictly speaking, one should always refer to the validity of a particular use of a test. It is the use and not the test itself that has validity. Validity is not an either/or attribute of a use of a test: it exists in varying degrees in various situations. Conducting validity studies by no means ensures that a particular application of a test is appropriate. The studies help answer such questions as whether the test improves selection, that is, whether students who are selected by means of the test perform better in school than those not so screened. If an admissions test has at least some validity, then students achieving higher test scores should be more likely to achieve higher grades than those with low test scores. Thus, using the test in the admissions process gives a higher probability of selecting students who will succeed in school than not using the test. Certainly, it was the destructive possibility of denying handicapped people opportunities by use of an irrelevant or invalid test that led the drafters of the regulations to stress the importance of validity.

Predictive validity is a measure of the relationship between scores on a test and performance in the situation that the test is intended to predict. In college and professional school admissions, predictive validity studies usually measure the relationship of scores on the admissions test (plus previous grade-point average or other predictors) to first-year grade-point average. In the employment sphere, the prediction equation relates test results (plus other available predictors) to some measure of job success, such as performance appraisal, tangible output, or rate of promotion. Studies of predictive validity can theoretically be performed for any subset of the population, given only sufficient numbers for statistical extrapolation.

Validation studies for the standard forms of admissions tests are conducted separately for each college or university. They may also be conducted separately for each academic department or program, as in the case of the Graduate Record Examination with its advanced tests in 20 disciplines. The validation studies usually are conducted every year as a check on changes in the populations of applicants or matriculants or changes in the grading scales (the well-publicized grade inflation of the late 1960s and 1970s). Therefore, there must be a sufficient number of students entering a given school or program in a given year or in a few successive years if a validation study is to be undertaken. There usually are not enough handicapped students entering one school in any given year to conduct the regular type of validation study.

The administrative arrangement for conducting validation studies is that institutions may elect to subscribe to the validation service offered by the test developers. The subscribers supply students' first-year grades to the testing companies, who perform the data analysis and report the results to the institutions. In the case of undergraduate schools, regression analysis is used to see how well the admissions test scores alone predict freshman grades and also how well high school grade-point averages in conjunction with test scores predict first-year grades. Other predictors, such as variables representing extracurricular activities, can be added to the regression equation; in general, however, the best predictors have been found to be grade-point averages and admissions test scores (Skager 1982).

Neither testing companies nor colleges and universities have routinely conducted either kind of validation study, either against the criterion of first-year grades or against the criterion of success in the program. The testing companies have argued since the drafting of the Section 504 regulations that analogous studies could not be conducted for handicapped students because of the small numbers of such students. Recently, however, research methods that have been developed to study other relatively small groups are being used in small studies of handicapped examinees. The research staff at the Educational Testing Service has developed and used methods of pooling data across institutions or years in order to increase the numbers of minority group members to a level sufficient for statistical study (Braun and Jones 1980, Dempster et al. 1980, and Rubin 1980). They currently are conducting two studies—one of deaf students at the California State University at Northridge, and one of learning-disabled students at Curry College in Massachusetts—and are aggregating the data across several years. Such efforts indicate that validation studies of tests for handicapped people are possible, at least in some settings. The panel looks with optimism on the possibility of pooling data for groups of handicapped students across years and across similar institutions, say, small liberal arts colleges or large state universities.

## Employment Testing

Unfortunately, there is much less hope of applying similar techniques in employment testing of handicapped people. The largest employment testing program in the country is operated by the Office of Personnel Management using the Professional and Administrative Career Examination. Since 1975, when modified versions of the PACE were first made available, approximately 300 blind and 100 deaf people have taken the exam each year (this compares with 100,000 to 150,000 nonhandicapped people per year). OPM has no data on the number of handicapped candidates who are employed, both because their PACE scores are not flagged and because handicapped candidates are not identified on the register of candidates. However, since the PACE covers 118 federal civil service jobs, it is unlikely that there would be enough handicapped people in any given job to conduct validation studies, even if people with certain disabilities tend to be in relatively few of the 118 occupations. As an indicator of the number of deaf people in jobs filled through the PACE, OPM searched the central registry of Schedule A (exempted) appointments and found 11 deaf people in PACE jobs in 1974 in the entire country. (Unfortunately for our purposes, that central registry has been discontinued.) If OPM does not have what could safely be considered a large testing program for handicapped people, there is almost certainly no other employment testing program for handicapped people that could be considered large. In addition, because of the wide variability of jobs—even those that require similar training or seem similar along other dimensions—the problems of pooling jobs for the purpose of validating selection tests are likely to be more severe than in educational settings. Therefore, there is little hope of amassing solid validity data for employment tests of handicapped people except in rare cases. Nevertheless, the panel does not despair of collecting information that will improve employment testing of handicapped people. We see several promising ways of gathering useful data.

The first would be analogous, and as similar as possible, to the methods of performing multijurisdictional validity studies of employment tests in the general population. The principle is endorsed in the *Uniform Guidelines for Employee Selection Procedures* (Equal Employment Opportunity Commission 1978). Highly similar jobs in different places (different businesses or industries or different locations) are pooled for the purpose of validating the single employment test used to select employees for all of the jobs. The procedure requires cooperation among many parties but offers an otherwise nonexistent possibility of validating tests. Of course, care must be taken to ensure the closest possible similarity among situations.

A second possible way of collecting useful data would be similar to a study being undertaken jointly by OPM and the Rehabilitation Research and Training Center at George Washington University. The study began with the identification of handicapped employees throughout the country and the description of accommodations that have been made for them. The study will include a job analysis of the positions held by handicapped employees, a summary of how well the employees are performing, and how they were selected for employment. Thus, in a general sense, one component of the study is a validity study of the employee selection procedures used for handicapped people using the criterion of performance on the job.

## COMPARABILITY OF TESTS FOR HANDICAPPED AND NONHANDICAPPED PEOPLE

The prohibition of preadmission inquiries regarding a handicapping condition, which was added to the regulations following the period of comment, had ramifications that doubtless far exceeded the expectations of the drafters of the provision. This requirement prohibited the usual practice of the testing companies of noting on the score reports to educational institutions that a score resulted from a nonstandard test administration. In most cases, this "flagging" is equivalent to identifying the examinee as handicapped. The abandonment of the practice of flagging was clearly what the drafters had intended because many handicapped people felt that the involuntary disclosure of the fact that they are handicapped was not only a violation of their rights to privacy but an impediment to their opportunity to be considered equally for admission to postsecondary educational institutions.

These considerations notwithstanding, the solution to the problem was not a simple removal of the designation of nonstandard administration on score reports. The testing companies argued that they must be allowed to continue to flag scores resulting from nonstandard administrations: to remove the flag would imply that scores from the modified tests were equivalent to, in fact, indistinguishable from, scores on the standard forms. Yet handicapped examinees' scores have not been shown to be comparable in any sense to those of nonhandicapped people. Hence, universally removing the flags would in many cases work to the disadvantage of handicapped examinees.

In this section we propose that the establishment of a relation between scores from modified tests and the kind of performance in school or employment that serves as the validity criterion for standard tests can, in effect, serve to define comparability of test scores on modified and standard forms. Although this concept derives in straightforward manner from basic psychometric theory, its application is, rather surprisingly, a novel approach to the practical problems of establishing comparability. If all test modifications required by handicapped people could be shown to be strictly comparable with standard tests through traditional equating procedures, then there would be no need for special considerations that attend such modifications. The panel, however, is convinced that traditional approaches cannot be applied to establish comparability of standard and modified forms in all respects, especially with regard to underlying abilities. For this reason we are willing to turn away from accepted procedures and advocate an innovative approach that has not, to the best of our knowledge, been tried on a large scale in operating programs.

When testing companies introduce a new form of an existing test, they use a procedure called "equating" to ensure that the new form will produce scores that can be considered the same as scores on existing forms of the test. Equating is a technical term that describes a process of calibrating two or more alternate forms of the same test that measure the same abilities and are used on the same population of test takers. As Angoff (1971:562-563) notes:

> With equating properly executed it becomes possible to measure growth, to chart trends, and to merge data even when the separate pieces of data derive from different forms of a test with somewhat different item characteristics. It also becomes possible to compare directly the performances of two individuals who have taken different forms of a test. In a high-premium selection program, for example for college admissions or for scholarship awards, it is especially important for reasons of equity alone that no applicant be given special advantage or disadvantage because of the fortuitous administration of a relatively easy or difficult form of the test.

Successful equating lends constancy of meaning to test scores, over time and across applicant groups.

Because such equating has been the usual means of establishing comparability among forms of a test, it is the definition of comparability that test producers have understood the regulations to require. During formal comment on the proposed and draft regulations, they protested the impossibility of complying with such a requirement. One impediment to equating test scores resulting from standard and nonstandard administrations is the largely uncharted effect of variation in the mode of test administration. Psychometricians simply do not now know precisely how scores are affected by translation of a paper-and-pencil test for oral or tactile presentation or by removal of a time limit. In other words, test producers argued that there is insufficient reason to believe that a standard test and its modified counterpart can be considered the same test.

Furthermore, modifications in the medium in which a test is administered have unknown effects on the cognitive processes called on by the various types of test questions. Such effects are extremely difficult if not impossible to measure empirically. Deleting certain types of items from a test—for example, removing cartography questions from orally administered tests—further increases doubt regarding the similarity of a standard and modified test forms. It is, therefore, not clear that the same abilities are being measured.

Finally, because the present strengths of psychometrics are more empirical than theoretical, relatively little is understood about the mental processes underlying test-taking behavior or the specific deficits or the special skills developed by people with handicaps as a result of their visual, aural, or motor impairments. In addition, the techniques most commonly used to equate test forms require that the same population of examinees take at least portions of all forms of the test. When dealing with a population as heterogeneous and necessitating as many special adaptations as handicapped people, this seems almost impossible. In general, then, the test developer cannot consider the handicapped and nonhandicapped populations to be the same in the sense assumed by the technology of equating.

For these reasons, test producers concluded that, despite the policy of the Office for Civil Rights, modified tests could not be considered to produce scores that are strictly equivalent to those produced by standard administrations. After careful consideration of the matter, the panel agrees that it is not now possible to equate tests for handicapped and nonhandicapped people.

There is, however, a second and slightly less restrictive psychometric concept that should be considered in attempts to align more closely test scores for handicapped and nonhandicapped people: the production of "comparable" (in this sense, a technical term) scores. We quote again from Angoff (1971:590):

> Unlike the problem of *equivalent* scores, which is restricted to the case of parallel forms of a test, that is to tests of the same psychological function, the problem of *comparable* scores may be thought of quite simply as the problems of "equating" tests of *different* psychological functions. Ordinarily, two tests are considered to have been made comparable *with respect to a particular group of examinees* if their distributions of scores are identical [emphasis in the original].

As indicated in Angoff's definition, scores usually can be considered comparable only for a specific population taking the test under specific conditions. Comparability can be extended to other groups but only if they are highly similar, with respect to the abilities being measured, to the group on which the comparability was established. The most common procedures for deriving comparability require that the tests be administered to a reference group and that the scores of each test be scaled to have equal means and standard deviations. Obviously, because of the modifications of tests necessary for handicapped people, not all modified forms could be administered to the same group. Even if a way were found to do this, the resulting comparability could not be extended to cover the heterogeneous groups of handicapped people who would eventually take the tests. Thus, the standard technical concept of comparability does not provide a feasible means of establishing the correspondence between standard test forms and those modified for handicapped people.

There is another approach to comparability, however, that is more likely to be attainable if there is full cooperation of test users, test takers, and compliance authorities. The panel considers predictive validity to offer the greatest promise in the relatively large testing programs under investigation. (Small testing programs, particularly employment testing, present special problems.) In this approach, the goal is to make tests for handicapped and nonhandicapped applicants predict equally well the performance of interest. Although the content of tests modified for handicapped people is kept as similar as possible to that for nonhandicapped people, there is no attempt to make the test scores mean exactly the same thing in terms of the abilities being measured. This proposal is discussed more fully in Chapter 6, as it forms the basis for the panel's major policy recommendations, but its psychometric features are discussed here.

Predictive validity gives an estimate of the strength of the association between test scores and a measure of performance on the criterion to be predicted. In college admissions, SAT or ACT scores (usually in conjunction with high school grades) are used to predict first-year college grades. The prediction equation is useful in statistically predicting from test scores and high school grades how well college applicants are expected to perform in the freshman year of college, based on experience with many previous applicants. Colleges and universities typically participate in validation studies performed by the testing companies and review the results of the studies for their own campuses. Thus, over time, admissions officers accumulate knowledge, based on empirical experience at their schools, about the meaning and predictive significance of test scores and patterns of scores and grades. The predictive validation technique works fairly well for the general population, although there are always individual deviations (some of them large), and suspicion occasionally arises that the particular interpretation of test scores is inappropriate for an entire group of applicants—in our case, people with handicapping conditions. In that instance, more refined studies of the special group are in order.

The panel believes there is sufficient reason to posit the predictive validity approach to defining comparability as the most fruitful path toward a reasonable solution to the current problems in testing handicapped people. The first step in the proposed plan is research to answer questions of whether the approach, which is technically possible, will yield satisfactory score transformations and, secondly, whether the prediction equations will be sufficiently accurate. Put another way, the basic question is whether, with existing scores, one prediction equation is suitable for all students, including students with a specific handicap taking a particular modified form of a test. If not, the question becomes one of what adjustments in the prediction equations are needed for the handicapped people, and whether the adjustments can be accomplished by a transformation of the score scale for the modified test forms. Answers to these queries can be obtained through empirical investigation. Furthermore, the necessary data already exist; they need to be compiled and analyzed. The studies necessary to determine the feasibility of making the scores on modified forms comparable to those on standard forms through predictive validation would be possible if there is cooperation among test users, test publishers, handicapped students, and the Office for Civil Rights.

The technology needed to determine the predictive validity of tests for handicapped people in large testing programs is currently available. The procedures routinely used to validate tests for the general population could be modified to avoid the problem of the small numbers of handicapped students by pooling (grouping together) students at several similar schools or students who entered a given institution in different years. Given the prediction equations at a number of colleges and universities based on all students and scores for students with a particular handicap who took a particular modification of the test, predicted and actual criterion scores can be obtained. For example, students who took the large-type version of the ACT and enrolled in large state universities in the Midwest could be grouped together and compared with a sample of their nonhandicapped classmates. Criterion scores at each school could be standardized so they could be compared across schools, and the discrepancies between predicted and actual criterion scores could then be pooled across institutions. Similar techniques could be used to aggregate across years at a given school. Distributions of discrepancies between predicted and actual criterion scores for handicapped students could then be analyzed and compared with the corresponding distributions for the general population. The comparison of the distribution of prediction errors for the handicapped and nonhandicapped groups would tell whether prediction for the two (or more) groups was comparable or whether there were systematic differences between the groups.

The approach could be improved by the use of Bayesian techniques (see Lindley 1970, Novick et al. 1972) or empirical-Bayes techniques (see Braun and Jones 1980, Rubin 1980). The Bayesian and empirical-Bayes techniques may offer substantial advantages in terms of estimation because of the small number of handicapped students in most institutions. But the basic concept is the same. If there is a consistent tendency for predicted grades to be lower (or higher) than actual grades for members of a special group, then either different prediction systems are needed or predictor scores for the special group need to be rescaled by a transformation equation that will eliminate the systematic tendency for predicted scores to be too low or too high.

The types of outcomes that might be anticipated and the associated problems in meeting the federal regulations can be considered without delving into the technical details of estimation (or, for that matter, identifying the estimation techniques to be used). It should be noted, however, that the answer regarding comparability or the particular score transformation to be used may not be the same for every special group or every modification. The possibility of this complication can be seen more fully when we examine the general prediction equation. Let

$Y_{ij}$ = the criterion score for person $i$ at institution $j$,
$T_{ij}$ = the test score for person $i$ at institution $j$,
$X_{ij}$ = the score on the nontest predictor for person $i$ at institution $j$,
$E_{ij}$ = the error of prediction for person $i$ at institution $j$.

The basic linear model for a nonhandicapped person taking the standard form of the test may then be written as

$$Y_{ij} = a_j + b_j T_{ij} + c_j X_{ij} + E_{ij}, \quad (1)$$

where $a$, $b$, and $c$ are regression coefficients. Parallel equations could be constructed for handicapped applicants taking nonstandard forms of the test as

$$Y_{ijk} = a_j + b_j T_{ijk} + c_j X_{ijk} + E_{ijk}, \qquad (2)$$

where $k$ designates each combination of handicapping condition and modified form of a test.

Values for test scores and the nontest predictor, presumably high school grade-point average, would be entered in the first equation for nonhandicapped students and into the second equation for groups of handicapped students at selected colleges. Predicted first-year grades would be calculated separately for groups and then compared with actual first-year grades.

Thus, at a given institution (or cluster of institutions) there would be one equation for the nonhandicapped students, (1), and one for each major combination of handicapping condition and test modification, (2). One pair of assumptions to be tested is whether the same prediction equation works equally well for people with the same handicapping condition who take different modified forms and whether one equation serves people with different handicapping conditions who take the same form.

The regression coefficients and error terms would be compared for the different groups. Ideally, of course, the regression coefficients would be the same in both equations, the distribution of error terms ($E_{ij}$) would be the same for handicapped people as for the rest of the population, and the equations would be the same at all institutions. This would be equivalent to saying that special adjustments for the scores of handicapped people are unnecessary at all institutions and that the prediction is as accurate for all handicapped groups as for the general population; that is, that the same regression equation works equally well for handicapped and nonhandicapped examinees. This would mean that a person would not need to be identified as handicapped and that the predictor scores would not have to be adjusted depending on handicapped status. Under those conditions the scores would be comparable for purposes of this prediction, and special flagging of scores would be unnecessary.

The major concern would be with the error terms. Again, ideally, the prediction errors for the nonhandicapped and the handicapped would have the same distribution, which would indicate that prediction using the modified test forms and high school grades was as accurate for handicapped people as for the general population at those schools. If, on the other hand, predictions based on a modified form tended to have substantially larger errors of estimate, then the question of flagging would again need to be addressed. The best solution to this problem, of course, would be to find an improved test modification that yielded equally accurate predictions to those of the standard form.

A second concern would be with the comparison of the regression coefficients for the nonhandicapped and the handicapped equations. Ideally, the same equation would work equally well for both groups; that is, test scores and high school grades would be weighted equally in the two prediction equations, which would imply that transformations of the test scores would not be necessary for handicapped people. If any of the regression coefficients differs from equation (1) to (2), there would then be a need for either separate prediction equations for modified forms at various schools or for an adjustment of the test scores for the modified form. The first of these possibilities, separate prediction equations at different schools, is technically easier, but major changes would be required on the part of test users and publishers for this solution to satisfy the requirements of the regulations. In order to avoid identifying handicapped students, scores would have to be reported in terms of predicted grades at selected institutions. Test scores, per se, would not be reported for any applicant. Though technically feasible, this would indeed be a major shift—one that would require agreement among a diverse array of institutions and test takers. It would also prevent alternative uses of test scores. For these reasons the panel does not endorse this option.

The second alternative, transforming modified form test scores, is the clearly preferable alternative, but a technically satisfactory solution may or may not exist. The goal would be to find a transformation of test scores, $T_{ijk}$, for the modified form such that, after the transformation, the regression cofficients in equations (1) and (2) are equal. This means that test scores would be weighted equally for handicapped and nonhandicapped applicants, as would high school grades. Furthermore, the desired transformation would be the same at all institutions. It is possible to imagine situations in which this goal could be readily achieved, but its feasibility can be determined only through the analysis of empirical results. It is possible that the goal could be achieved to a satisfactory degree for some handicaps and modified forms but not others.

Until the validation research we have outlined is completed, there is no way of knowing whether the goal of equivalent prediction for handicapped and nonhandicapped people can be attained in the near future. If it appears that the goal will not be reached for some time, then it will be necessary to weigh the relative advantages of temporarily accepting differences in precision of prediction while avoiding preadmission identification of a handicap versus flagging scores or removing the test requirement. There seems to be no simple resolution of this potential dilemma, only the hope that research will identify test modifications that avoid it.

# 6

# Recommended Policies and Procedures

The Panel on Testing of Handicapped People was charged with the task of studying the psychometric, social, economic, legal, and ethical issues surrounding the use of standardized tests in making decisions about handicapped people, with particular reference to postsecondary admissions. The panel's foremost conclusion is that the technical problems of developing and validating tests that accommodate specific handicaps, while very difficult, are not insurmountable.

In the first part of this chapter we outline a plan of action that offers promise of a solution to the problem of producing test scores for handicapped applicants that can be used in the same way as scores for the general population. The proposed solution is, we believe, the single most important product of the panel and will, if acted on responsibly by all concerned parties, succeed in eliminating the most serious problems currently associated with establishing nondiscriminatory testing practices for handicapped people. That section, on the issues of validity and comparability, is divided into three subsections: (1) the regulations and the problem of comparability, (2) flagging, and (3) small testing programs. The panel's conclusions and recommendations are presented at the end of each subsection.

The panel has also reached a number of other conclusions regarding the ways in which tests are developed for, administered to, and used to make decisions about people with handicapping conditions. The second part of this chapter presents those additional conclusions and recommendations, which address issues other than the central policy questions that constituted our major charge. The second part of the chapter, which presents issues of test administration, is also divided into three subsections, each with its own conclusions and recommendations.

In Chapter 7, we suggest research directions that, over the longer term, can be expected to illuminate the underlying mental processes tapped by various test tasks and thus provide better insight into the nature of the differences in cognitive or expressive functioning related to deafness, blindness, or other handicapping conditions.

## THE ISSUES OF VALIDITY AND COMPARABILITY

Tests can, and sometimes do, open the way to new opportunities for handicapped people by allowing them a chance to demonstrate their abilities; but tests can also function as barriers to the fullest possible participation of handicapped people in American society. For tests to serve the interests of people with handicaps more consistently than they have in the past, a major cooperative effort will be required. In order to carry out its policy recommendations, the panel calls on government officials, testing companies, large institutional test users, and handicapped test takers to join together in a program of test development and validation research that offers the promise of ensuring handicapped applicants equal opportunity in the selection process. The participation of each is crucial to the success of the plan specified below.

### Section 504 and the Problem of Comparability

The fundamental intent of Section 504 of the Rehabilitation Act of 1973 is to eliminate unnecessary barriers, including potentially discriminatory testing practices, to the full participation of handicapped people in the life of the nation. Administrative interpretation of Section 504 has focused on two situations in which tests are commonly used in making decisions about people: testing for admission to postsecondary educational institutions and testing for selection and promotion in employment settings.

As detailed in Chapter 5, the regulations implementing Section 504 seem to require that test developers and users modify tests and test administration procedures for use with handicapped people, construct and administer tests in such a manner that they reflect skills independent of handicapping conditions, report scores for handicapped people in a manner such that they are indistinguishable from those for nonhandicapped people, and validate tests for handicapped people for the purpose at hand. In the subsection of the regulations dealing with employment testing, the requirement that a test be shown to be job-related is substituted for the requirement that it be validated against educational performance.

These requirements derive logically from two assumptions: first, that handicapped people can be tested in a way that will not reflect the effects of their handicap; and second, that the resulting test scores will be comparable in some sense to those of the general population. The panel considers the first assumption a long-term research goal, not a present actuality. With regard to the second assumption—with due respect to the discipline of psychometrics and to the good intentions of the compliance authorities—we conclude that the requirement that test results must reflect the handicapped applicant's aptitude or achievement level rather than the applicant's impaired sensory, manual, or speaking skills is largely beyond the present competence of psychometrics. Compliance authorities should treat the second requirement as a goal of science and social policy rather than as a requirement of the law that can be currently implemented.

The panel spent much time deliberating various definitions of comparability that would satisfy the requirement of the regulation that test scores of handicapped applicants not be differentiated from those of other test takers while at the same time keeping within the bounds of current psychometric learning, and we propose a new approach to this issue. The regulations do not explicitly state that tests or test scores for handicapped people must be made comparable to those for nonhandicapped people, but that is clearly the implication of the regulations (see Chapter 5). The regulations' prohibition of the identification of test scores that result from nonstandard administrations to handicapped individuals (flagging) assumes that test scores for handicapped people can be made comparable to (in fact, indistinguishable from) those for nonhandicapped people. If tests that have been modified as required could be shown to be strictly comparable to standard tests through traditional procedures of demonstrating comparability, there would be no need for special considerations of modified tests. Those procedures are not, however, applicable to tests modified for handicapped people.

After careful consideration, the panel concluded that it is not now possible to achieve the kind of comparability based on traditional equating procedures. Instead, the panel has concluded that predictive validation, that is, the establishing of a relation between scores from modified tests and the kind of performance in school or employment that serves as the validity criterion for standard tests, can and should be used to define comparability of modified and standard forms. Although using predictive validity to define the comparability of different forms of a test derives in straightforward manner from basic psychometric theory, it is, rather surprisingly, a novel approach to the practical problems of establishing comparability. The panel is convinced that traditional approaches cannot be applied to establish comparability of standard and modified forms in all respects, especially with regard to underlying abilities. For this reason we recommend turning away from accepted procedures and advocate an innovative approach that has not, to the best of our knowledge, been tried on a large scale in operating programs.

We recommend that, in the four-year period after implementation of the panel's recommendations, sponsors of the large testing programs develop modified tests to accommodate most kinds of sensory and motor handicaps and conduct predictive validity studies in order to ascertain whether the modified tests have a predictive power near that of the standard tests used with the general population. Theoretically, this is an attainable form of comparability, but empirical validity studies will have to be conducted in order to determine the actual feasibility of the approach. At the end of the research and development period, it should be possible to determine whether modified and standard forms of a test actually have comparable predictive power. If the studies proceed smoothly, it may also be possible to report the results of standard and modified tests on a single scale, because the tests will have equivalent predictive power. The existence of a single scale would totally obviate flagging. If during the research and development period one or more modified forms are found to predict the criterion measure much less well than the standard form, then it may still be possible to refine each modified form in order to improve its predictive validity. (See Chapter 5 for definitions of validity and for technical discussion of the feasibility of this proposal and of score transformation.)

The major technical problem with doing validation research on modified tests in the past has been the inadequacy of sample size, but that problem can be obviated by pooling data gathered in several years or at large numbers of similar educational institutions. The Office for Civil Rights can play an important role in facilitating this process by encouraging the National Center for Education Statistics and the Committee on National Statistics of the National Research Council to gather demographic statistics on the handicapped student population.

We recommend that work be concentrated first on the large testing programs so that the costs can be spread across a sizable applicant population and so be kept within reasonable bounds. Most of the large testing programs have been offering some modified forms for years, and the panel was informed that a good deal of data exists at colleges and universities that could provide the initial steps in a systematic research effort. Thus, there should be no need for for a lengthy lead-in period. We therefore recommend that work commence as soon as possible and that the validation studies be completed within four years of the implementation of these recommendations by the Office for Civil Rights.

The labels "large" and "small" testing programs are used as an abbreviated way to distinguish between those programs in which validation research is believed to have a greater or smaller probability of being feasible. The distinction is not perfectly clear, however, and is not just a matter of size. In general, the greater the experience with a testing program, the better the validation study is likely to be. The experience with a program can be measured in several ways, including total number of administrations, number of years used, extensiveness and quality of research on the test, and number of settings (for example, number of colleges or employers). A "small" program would be one that is relatively new, seldom used, and from which the examinees go into a variety of schools or jobs. Without question, the Scholastic Aptitude Test and the American College Testing Program's assessment can be considered "large testing programs," although some combinations of test modification and handicapping condition may be troublesome for even these tests. In addition, most modifications of the Graduate Record Examination Aptitude Tests, and the Graduate Management Admission Test (although modifications of the GMAT first became available in 1979-80) can be validated for handicapped people. It may well be that certain modifications of other tests can also be validated for handicapped examinees. We believe that work should begin with the large testing programs mentioned above so that procedures can be refined and applied to other situations and so that—with great care—findings can be generalized.

*Conclusion* The existing research on the validity of tests and test modifications used with handicapped people in postsecondary admissions and employment selection is in most cases insufficient to judge adequately a given test's validity. Most postsecondary admissions tests are modified and administered to handicapped people without empirical evidence of the appropriateness of the modifications. In addition, the modified forms are not developed empirically or used on a trial basis before they are administered for real decision making.

*Conclusion* It is not now possible to establish the comparability of modified and standard tests by the formal equating procedures that are used to establish the equivalence of alternate forms of a test used with nonhandicapped people.

*Conclusion* Empirical validation of the predictive power of modified tests is theoretically attainable and would seem to satisfy the statutory requirement that handicapped individuals receive equal treatment in postsecondary admissions and employment selection.

*Conclusion* Evenhanded treatment of handicapped and nonhandicapped applicants would be best achieved by requiring that the predictive validity of a modified test be equivalent (within a given range) to that for the original test. In that situation, scores on the modified test could be used for prediction in the same way, and with the same degree of confidence, as scores on the standard test.

*Conclusion* Given the existence of equivalent predictive validities for standard and modified tests, there would be no technical bar to translating the scores from all of the tests to a common scale.

*Conclusion* The main technical problem in establishing the predictive validity of modified tests, the inadequacy of sample size, can be overcome by pooling data from several institutions or from several years.

*Conclusion* The practicality of undertaking predictive validity research is clear in the case of the large testing programs. Many postsecondary admissions tests are in this category, although it may be difficult to get a sufficient sample population for every category of handicap on tests like the Graduate Record Examination Advanced Tests, which cover 20 disciplines.

*Recommendation 1* The Panel recommends that the Office for Civil Rights require that postsecondary educational institutions subject to Section 504 of the Rehabilitation Act of 1973, in their role as members of the corporations that sponsor the large testing programs, instruct the testing companies to begin at the earliest opportunity to develop modified tests to meet the needs of individuals with sensory and motor handicaps and to perform predictive validation studies on these tests. The validity studies should be completed and reported within four years of the implementation of this panel's recommendations by the Office for Civil Rights.

*Recommendation 2* To ensure the success of these validation efforts, the Office for Civil Rights should do everything in its power to encourage handicapped students to participate in the studies (after admission). Such encouragement might include making information about the purposes of the validation program available to the major organizations representing the handicapped and to those who counsel handicapped people, and undertaking other public education activities.

*Recommendation 3* Validation studies should be performed separately for each type of test modification. In some cases it may also be necessary to validate a particular modification for people with different types or degrees of handicap. For example, in the version of a test presented orally or on tape, people with a learning disability may have a pattern of responses and a relationship between test and criterion that are distinct from people with a visual impairment.

*Recommendation 4* Test developers should, as the predictive validation proceeds, develop separate scales for each test, both standard and modified. When the modified tests have been brought to a condition of equivalent predictive power with the test for the general population, the scores can be translated to a common scale before reporting. At this point, all reasons for flagging will have been eliminated.

*Recommendation 5* The panel recommends that the requirement in the regulations to use only validated tests for handicapped people be waived during the four-year research period, provided that a user of modified tests with unknown validity for the appropriate handicapped group may use only those tests for which producers certify that research on validation of the type here described is under way. The Office for Civil Rights should establish provisions for monitoring and periodic reporting by test developers to show adherence to the recommended policies regarding validation studies.

*Recommendation 6* The panel recommends that after the four-year research period no test user covered by the regulation may use a modified form of a test whose validity with respect to relevant performance is unknown or for which the necessary refinements in the modified forms have not been made.

*Recommendation 7* The panel recommends that at the close of the four-year research period a working group be assembled to examine the validity evidence submitted by the testing companies and other investigators. The tasks of the group should include (1) determination of the usefulness of modifications for various handicapped groups, that is, demonstration of reasonably equivalent degrees of predictive validity as compared with the validity of the standard forms for the general population, and (2) determination of specific consequences in those cases in which the predictive validities are not found to lie within acceptable limits for a modified form or a particular handicapped group.

Clearly, if the validity of a modified form approximates that of the standard form, the working group will recommend acceptance and use of the modified form. If the validity of another form is slightly less than acceptable, there may be reason to believe that with a reasonable amount of further effort the form can be improved and the predictive validity thereby increased (for example, by using a better reader for a cassette version, or a simpler answer sheet, or a clearer presentation of math items for the visually impaired). If the validity of a modified form is markedly lower than is acceptable, the working group must decide whether further work on the form is likely to be fruitful or whether that form should be dropped. The working group should look for patterns across tests, for example, finding for all tests studied that no adjustment is needed for a given modification or handicapping condition. In drawing generalizations, caution must be exercised to ensure close similarity of the tests, the abilities being measured, and the performance being predicted. The panel recommends that the rights of the test takers to accurate assessment should be given highest priority, with somewhat lower priority being given to prohibition of preselection inquiry. The panel further recommends that individual applicants should be given the right to decide for themselves whether or not they choose to take forms of the test that have not been found technically adequate.

## Flagging

One of the most difficult and controversial aspects of the federal attempt to ensure equal treatment of handicapped people in selection situations has been the flagging of test scores to indicate a nonstandard administration. The evidence, limited though it may be, indicates that handicapped test takers as a group tend to score markedly lower on such tests as the college admissions tests than their nonhandicapped peers. In light of this evidence, test developers and others reasoned that, as a group, handicapped applicants would be penalized more if their scores were not flagged than if they were. Hence, testing companies currently publish statements alerting decision makers to weigh more heavily other sources of information about an applicant whose test score is flagged.

Test developers, psychologists, and educators suspect that some of that difference in test scores may result from inadequacies in the modified tests, while some may result from poorer educational opportunities, more limited experience than the average test taker, or limitations produced by the handicapping condition. In the absence of systematic validation studies, it is impossible to estimate how much of the score difference is error and how much reflects lower performance probabilities. It was, no doubt, the strength of this concern that led the Office for Civil Rights to hold in abeyance since early in 1978 the part of the regulations that bans preadmission inquiry through an informal agreement known as the "interim policy." Although the regulations remain on the books as the standard for testing people with handicapping conditions, OCR's interim policy acknowledges that more research into the validity of the modified tests is necessary before full compliance can be realized.

The panel has listened closely to the representatives of handicapped people. Many have expressed the opinion that the existence of an interim policy, particularly one as tentative and unofficial as the understanding currently *in situ*, has blunted the intent of Section 504. Contrary to the lengthy process of comment and discussion that preceded final publication of the regulation in 1977, they point out, the interim policy was established at the initiative of the Office for Civil Rights alone. The population that the rules were designed to protect—handicapped test takers—had no voice in the establishment of this crucial waiver of a portion of the regulations.

At the same time, there is no consensus within the handicapped community on the merits of identifying oneself as handicapped during the admissions process. The panel has heard strong statements on both sides of the issue and finds merit in each position. There is strong agreement, however, on two points: (1) the quasi-official interim policy must be rescinded as soon as possible; and (2) to require an individual to take an examination with unknown validity and meaning is to nullify that person's effort.

We endorse both points and take them as the basis for our

recommended plan of action. To the degree that it is successful, an intensive research effort to establish the predictive validity of modified admissions tests will ultimately obviate the necessity for any flagging of test scores derived from nonstandard administrations. In the meantime we strongly urge that the client boards and testing companies adopt a policy of allowing each applicant who has taken a modified test to decide whether or not the user institution should be alerted to that fact. Presumably, many who achieve high scores will opt for anonymity; others with high scores may feel that openness about their handicapping condition gives them added advantage; those whose scores imply below-average performance will want their test scores flagged in order to have other factors weighed more heavily in the selection decision.

The *quid pro quo*, of course, is that after being admitted, every handicapped student must be strongly encouraged to participate in the validation studies.

*Conclusion* The research literature shows that the oft-held assumption that the identification of an applicant as handicapped always works to his or her disadvantage is not accurate. In fact, identification sometimes works to the advantage of the applicant with a handicapping condition (see Chapter 1 and Appendix A).

*Recommendation 8* Considering the diversity of situations and the varied perceived effects of identification of a person as handicapped, the panel recommends no general prohibition or allowance of flagging. The panel recommends that in the period before the validation studies have been completed, the locus of control over the flagging of scores to be used for educational admissions should be shifted from the test developer to the handicapped person. The gains in privacy and control to the handicapped applicant outweigh any disadvantage associated with the temporary divergence from customary practice. Moreover, equity considerations suggest that the gain for handicapped individuals outweighs the possible disadvantage for the nonhandicapped, who would have no corresponding choice. However, this recommendation requires that applicants be carefully counseled concerning both the merits and the disadvantages of identifying a handicapping condition. The decision to alert admissions officers to the presence of a handicap that may adversely affect test scores should be separate from and independent of the test taker's decision about voluntary participation in validation research.

## Small Testing Programs

Most of the discussion above has been developed with postsecondary admissions tests in mind. Although there is no theoretical reason why the conclusions and recommendations drawn with that focus should not also be applicable in the employment sphere, most employers and licensing and certification agencies, among others, have relatively small testing programs. The issues in validating tests administered to small numbers of people—handicapped and nonhandicapped—are somewhat different from those for large testing programs, even where the samples of handicapped people can be considered relatively small. In small programs there are different economic and technical considerations, most of which emanate from the fact that there is not a large base of experience from the testing of the general population to provide support for the testing of the handicapped. The technical problems with empirical validation with small samples are particularly severe because some sources of variability may be unknown. Some large employers, including the federal government, could draw on large enough samples of handicapped applicants to do predictive validation studies. There is also some possibility that multijurisdictional validation efforts could solve the problems of sample size for certain kinds of jobs and certain kinds of handicapping conditions.

Nevertheless, predictive studies in employment will be far more difficult to institute and organize than in the educational context. It seems likely that most employers will have to depend on the experience that will be gleaned in other settings in the coming years and in the meantime continue with the alternate assessment procedures, such as interviews, work samples, and probationary periods, among others (described in Chapter 3).

*Conclusion* Small testing programs, including most employment testing, present great problems. It may often be impractical to do empirical studies in the employment sphere, although the concept of multijurisdictional studies offers some hope for a means of conducting validation research. Absence of validated employment testing, especially for entry-level jobs, may be particularly problematic for some handicapped people because there is less likely to be supporting evidence that an employer could use in place of or in addition to a test score.

*Recommendation 9* The panel recommends that research on the predictive validity of tests for the handicapped be undertaken in the employment sphere as well as in education, even though most private employers have small testing programs. Although the research is likely to take longer and to be less rigorous than that for large programs, there are some techniques that offer promise of solutions. Pooling of data across institutions and across years may provide solutions to problems in some situations; current multijurisdictional validation of employment tests may offer techniques that could be adapted for use with handicapped applicants in some job categories or in some educational settings. These and other potentially beneficial techniques should be explored by those with small testing programs. Large employers with large testing programs, such as the federal government, should proceed immediately with the kinds of validation research outlined above for large educational testers.

*Recommendation 10* The panel recommends that the Office for Civil Rights encourage the use of multiple sources of information by employers in their selection of qualified handicapped applicants. Sources of information, which supplement or substitute for test scores, include letters of recommendation, personal interviews, job samples, and probationary periods of employment. Encouragement to use multiple sources will be most critical for entry-level jobs where it also may be most difficult to find several relevant sources.

## ISSUES OF TEST ADMINISTRATION

Emanating from the panel's study are other conclusions and recommendations that supplement or support the major policy recommendations on validity and comparability.

### Modifying Tests For Handicapped People

The panel has been in an especially fortunate position to view the policies regarding modifications of tests for handicapped people held by a wide variety of organizations. Because of its high visibility (from notices in professional journals and newsletters and from publicity related to the panel's open meeting in March 1980), the panel has received requests for guidance from people responsible for large and small testing programs as well as from those concerned with testing in classrooms. From its vantage point the panel has observed that the practices and the levels of sophistication vary widely among the groups who have assumed or who have been given the responsibility for accommodating the needs of handicapped people in their testing programs.

*Conclusion* Although it is true that modifications of some tests have been available for 20 years or longer, methods for accommodating the needs of handicapped people on standardized tests are far from systematic or universally known. The factors to be considered are numerous and often much more subtle or complicated than many people recognize. The panel has been impressed by the determination, thoroughness, and sensitivity of some and appalled by the ignorance and insensitivity of others who are responsible for testing handicapped people. Among at least some of them, however, there appears to be a desire to learn how to modify tests appropriately.

*Recommendation 11* The panel recommends wider publicity and distribution of information on how to modify tests and test administration procedures for use with handicapped people. One of the handiest and most helpful references is the *Guide for Administering Examinations to Handicapped Individuals for Employment Purposes* (Heaton et al. 1980). Although this guide may not give sufficient detail for all users, it may serve as a useful model for similar documents concerning other types of tests.

*Recommendation 12* One commonly employed technique, that is, the use of groups of expert handicapped people to review modified tests, is endorsed by this panel. No one knows as well as a knowledgeable and sensitive blind person, for example, what difficulties other blind people are likely to encounter on a particular test.

*Recommendation 13* We underscore here the necessity of research on the effects of modifications on test scores and on the effects of handicapping conditions on the cognitive processes underlying test performance. Obviously, modifying tests and test administration procedures is but one step in accommodating handicapped people in the testing situation. Knowing what the resulting scores signify is of the utmost importance and can be determined only after a considerable amount of carefully planned, executed, and analyzed research.

## Demand For Modified Test Forms

The data from the two largest developers of educational tests clearly indicate an increasing number of administrations of modified tests over the last five or so years. The increases are probably caused by increased numbers of handicapped people completing high school and applying to some type of postsecondary school as well as by handicapped people's increased awareness of the availability of the modified forms.

*Conclusion* The increases in the number of handicapped people taking standardized tests (whether modified or not) are important for several reasons. First, they indicate that more handicapped individuals are participating more fully in American society. Second, they underscore the necessity of making modified forms available; the demand is growing too fast to be ignored. Third, the increasing numbers offer greater hope for timely and rigorous validation of the tests administered to handicapped people.

*Conclusion* The cited increases notwithstanding, there have been a number of complaints of inadequate or inaccurate information regarding the availability of the modified forms. Systematic data on the magnitude of the problem do not exist, but the panel believes the complaints should be considered seriously. Lack of information about modified forms of tests may discourage some handicapped people from attempting or accomplishing some important and satisfying endeavors.

*Recommendation 14* High school counselors should assume responsibility for informing handicapped students of the availability of modified forms of college admissions and other relevant tests. Counselors should help individual students select the most appropriate modification and assist them in any other way possible, for example, in requesting the modified form and in understanding the implications of flagging or not flagging a test score.

## Special Problems With Certain Tests

A few tests or types of tests have come to the Panel's attention as posing special problems for handicapped people.

### *Minimum Competency Tests*

As the number of handicapped students completing high school grows, there is increased need to examine state and local policies regarding minimum competency testing programs. There are two broad areas of concern directly relevant to the panel's charge: the availability of modified forms of the tests and the awarding of diplomas contingent on passing the minimum competency test.

*Conclusion* The fairness of minimum competency testing programs, particularly those that make the awarding of a diploma contingent on passing the test, may be critical for many handicapped people who complete high school. Full consideration of the needs of handicapped students is essential if they are not to be summarily denied high school diplomas. Where diplomas are required for further education or for employment the impact of minimum competency programs is especially acute.

*Recommendation 15* The Office for Civil Rights should study the effects of minimum competency testing programs on handicapped people. State and local policies should be reviewed to ensure that only validated tests are used for handicapped people, that modified forms are readily available, and that scoring procedures are demonstrably nondiscriminatory. Special attention should be given to policies regarding the awarding of diplomas based on scores on minimum competency tests.

### *The Law School Admission Test*

The panel has heard more criticism of the LSAT than of any other single test or testing program. Criticisms focus on the policy of allowing no extra time in the administration of the LSAT, a policy set presumably to approximate compliance with the Section 504 regulations.

*Conclusion* The panel believes that the restrictive policy of the Law School Admission Council regarding accommodations on the LSAT for handicapped people is discriminatory and detrimental to potential law school applicants with handicapping conditions.

*Recommendation 16* The panel recommends that the Law School Admission Council review its policy in light of this panel's central policy recommendation. We encourage that more modifications of the test and its administration procedures be supplied and that validation studies be conducted, as described earlier in this chapter.

*Certification and Licensing*

Inquiries by the panel revealed that relatively few handicapped people have requested modifications in certification or licensing examinations. Still there is some reason to suspect that handicapped people are discouraged from pursuits that would lead to attainment of a professional certificate or license long before they approach the testing situation. Since the panel has had little hard evidence concerning certification and licensing, we draw no firm conclusions regarding the presence or absence of discrimination. Nevertheless, the panel believes these credentials may become increasingly important as more handicapped people complete education and training programs and prepare to enter the labor force.

*Recommendation 17* Because of the dearth of sound evidence and the potential importance of professional credentials for handicapped people, the panel recommends that the Office for Civil Rights perform a modest but nonetheless important investigation to determine whether there are, as some suspect, serious problems for handicapped people in obtaining occupational certificates and licenses due to requirements for achieving a score on a standardized test.

## FUTURE DIRECTIONS

We do not pretend that improvement and validation of modified tests for handicapped people will be an easy or automatic process. The implementation of our recommended plan of action for test validation will be difficult. It may be necessary, for example, to validate a given modified test form for a number of kinds or degrees of handicap. A test designed for the deaf will, no doubt, demonstrate different predictive power for those who have been deaf since birth and those who experienced later onset. For that reason we have suggested a time period that is long enough to allow for the completion of the validation studies; however, we want to express our sense of the urgency of the situation. Four years is adequate time only if work is begun immediately and if sufficient resources are dedicated to the endeavors. For several of the postsecondary admissions tests, data have already been accumulating for several years. Those data should be retrieved and analyzed without delay.

We would also caution that the program we are recommending will not solve all of the problems that handicapped applicants have with test performance. It is the totality of one's education, training, and experience that is brought to a standardized test, and many handicapped people have grown up in relatively deprived or atypical circumstances. These deficits can only be remedied by better schooling and a more accessible environment throughout the maturational years.

What the program can do is to assure that at the moment of competition, the handicapped applicant is assessed as accurately as any other applicant. In other words, the program cannot make up for things not learned or abilities not developed, but it can ensure that the probability of successful performance in a college program (or on the job) is adequately predicted. Without such a program of validation research, the use of tests risks great injustice.

The Office for Civil Rights cannot, of course, mandate the success of the validation effort, but it can facilitate it. It can and should require that the necessary research be conducted within four years after its implementation of this panel's recommendations. This requirement is well within the power of OCR because of existing enforcement and institutional arrangements. OCR currently has the authority to find colleges or universities out of compliance with the Section 504 regulations. It is those same schools that have power over the testing companies through their membership in the governing bodies such as The College Board. Thus, if OCR implements the panel's central policy recommendation and if the testing companies do not perform the required research, the colleges will be found out of compliance for using tests that are not being validated for handicapped people.

We believe that the plan outlined above offers the best possible synthesis of fairness considerations and technical capabilities for the foreseeable future. The proposed solution, however, has all the limitations of any approach that is largely atheoretical. Predictive validity does not explain why some people will probably succeed and some fail, and it does not describe the abilities that are being measured. It describes the statistical relationship between test scores and the performance to be predicted. Therefore, we also strongly urge the gradual accumulation of research on cognitive abilities to greatly enhance information obtained through validation strategies that are based solely on statistical relationships. In psychometrics there is a revitalized interest in construct validity, that is, in theories of what each kind of item measures. This line of research seems particularly important in understanding the abilities of people who have handicapping conditions and of finding the most productive accommodations, not just in test format, but of pedagogical methods, restructuring of job tasks, and so on. The Office of Personnel Management has made some important beginnings with its modifications of the PACE (although that examination is now to be phased out for reasons unrelated to its use with handicapped people).

It is important to emphasize that this is the work of decades. But it is work that should begin now and with the encouragement of federal funding agencies, such as the National Institute on Handicapped Research and other parts of the Department of Education.

# 7
# Recommended Research

Almost since the promulgation of the Section 504 regulations, it has been clear that there exists insufficient information to allow for the demonstrably valid testing of handicapped people, as required in the regulations. Information on standardized and modified tests taken by handicapped people, that is, data on their reliability and validity, and on the effects of modifying test administration procedures, is essential to the fulfillment of the spirit of the Rehabilitation Act of 1973. In other words, full compliance with the Section 504 regulations will be possible only after further research has been completed. Therefore, in order that colleges and universities would not be found out of compliance until the needed research could be planned and executed, the Office for Civil Rights formulated and instituted the interim policy. The task of specifying the research that would provide the necessary information about tests and their use for people with handicapping conditions was explicitly included in the charge to the Panel on Testing of Handicapped People. Therefore, the panel has incorporated research items that deal specifically with characteristics of tests as administered to handicapped people in both its research and policy recommendations.

As the panel's work progressed, it became apparent that too little was known not only about the tests administered to handicapped people to determine their validity, but also about the effects of existing testing practices on the performance of handicapped people. The panel, therefore, has specified in its research agenda studies to produce the desired information on how test scores are used and how they affect the lives of people with handicapping conditions. Several topics, all having significant implications for policy, are included under this broad heading. The first is the validity of tests administered to people with handicapping conditions. The second is information on the experiences of handicapped people as they encounter tests: for example, how often they are tested, what kinds of tests they take, what information they obtain from counselors, and how they perceive tests and testing personnel. The third is the decision-making process: how test scores and other information are used to make selection decisions regarding handicapped people and what will be the effects on these practices of different flagging policies and of additional information on test validity. Such studies offer the added advantage that they will provide data on which to evaluate the effects of modifications in the policies recommended by the panel.

At the outset, the panel was hindered in its attempts to define the scope of the problems involved in testing of handicapped people and to place them in perspective. The hindrance took the form of unreliable, inconsistent, or uninterpretable data on handicapped people in the United States and on their experience in taking tests and in entering the mainstream of education and work. As a consequence, the panel also recommends a fourth topic of research: the improvement and expansion of demographic data on people with handicapping conditions, particularly those who have the potential to enter the mainstream of American life. Some of the research recommended in this area is only indirectly related to the panel's study and, therefore, is given lower priority, even though it is of primary interest to others. Within each of the four main sections of the research agenda, those topics for proposed studies that the panel voted to give highest priority are marked with an asterisk (*) and are placed first within their respective sections.

## THE VALIDITY OF TESTS FOR HANDICAPPED PEOPLE

Information on the validity of tests administered to handicapped people is most urgently needed so that progress toward compliance with the Section 504 regulations can be made. It is for good reason that validity is mentioned most prominently in the regulations. Lacking knowledge of the validity of a test, that is, of some indication of how well a test measures what it purports to measure, one is prevented from using the test results with confidence. Although some handicapped individuals can take standardized tests under the standard conditions and be reasonably certain that their abilities are being reflected accurately, others require modifications in the test or testing procedures that cast doubt on the accuracy and meaning of the measures. The effects of most modifications are unknown, and the panel strongly urges research to begin charting the effects, especially on the validity of the instruments.

## *Nonstandard Testing Procedures and Validity

What are the effects of modifying tests and test administration procedures on the distributions of test scores, test reliability, test validity, and subjective reports of examinees, such as ease of comprehension of test instructions and questions, perceived time pressures, and feelings of fatigue?

Very little is known about the effects of various deviations from standard test administration procedures. Even changes for nonhandicapped examinees, such as varying time limits or rest periods, have been insufficiently studied. More pertinent to the panel's study, the effects of changes in the standard test administration procedures (such as large type, tape recorders, amanuenses, and others) are virtually unknown. Of central concern is the effect of these changes on the validity of the test. If it could be shown that all of the modifications made for handicapped people in a given test produced scores that predicted future performance as well as scores on the regular version of the test, then nearly all doubt about the appropriateness of the test would disappear. Without that information, however, the person trying to use the scores does not know their meaning and has no guidelines for legitimate interpretations.

Studies on this topic would focus on the effects of test modifications on objective measures, such as changes in the distribution of test scores (means and standard deviations), test reliability, test validity, and subjective reports of the examinees (for example, ease of comprehension of instructions and test questions, perceived time pressures, and feelings of fatigue). Such studies must include as much information as possible on the characteristics of the various modifications and on their relation to one another and to the standard forms. Information can be accumulated to build a store of knowledge on what modified tests seem to measure for people with different handicapping conditions and whether the abilities measured appear to differ over various modifications.

Admittedly, some of the research will present subtle and complicated problems in experimental design. Research on the effects of changes in the medium of presentation (for example, braille versus different sizes of print versus aural presentation) will probably require the use of very carefully matched samples, because few people would be equally facile in several modes of presentation and because they probably could not take the same test several times for the purpose of comparing media. Some of the problems might be overcome through the use of experimental designs, perhaps involving balanced presentations of different test forms or perhaps through training of nonhandicapped experimental subjects in the use of alternate media (for example, cassettes). Although ethical considerations will prohibit most experimentation in actual test situations, other types of research present fewer difficulties and could even be performed using non-handicapped examinees. For example, some research on speed of responding as it affects test scores and on the effects of various time limits and rest periods could be done with nonhandicapped people. Because of the methodological difficulties inherent in much of the work suggested in this research, it will be especially important that researchers exercise extreme care and that they be especially observant to note when procedures do and do not work. It may be that some of the most valuable findings will be more qualitative or subjective than quantitative or objective.

### *Validation Techniques for Use on Small Samples of Examinees

What methods are currently available for measuring test reliability and validity with small or heterogeneous samples? What are the advantages and disadvantages of the methods, including pooling data across samples?

The panel's policy recommendations deal extensively with validation research and rely heavily on pooling data from several samples as a workable technique. Nevertheless, we acknowledge that the technique is not yet fully developed and also that there are situations in which pooling may be of limited value. Therefore, we recommend that the limits of the applicability of pooling be explored, that other techniques be sought, and that the practical implications of reduced certainty in the validity of tests be investigated. We suggest two tasks: a review of the current techniques of measuring test reliability and validity, and the development and trial of methods of estimating test reliability and validity for small samples. The first task should be conducted by or in close cooperation with the test development companies and should emphasize any techniques that offer promise for either small or heterogeneous samples. The second task calls for the development of practical ways to prepare data for pooling, for example, standardizing grades across schools or programs or years. Other techniques, such as matching handicapped and nonhandicapped students or employers, should also be explored.

## Uncertainty in the Validity of Tests for Small Samples of Examinees

How accurate is the information regarding validity that is obtained by pooling data across small samples relative to that obtained by using large samples? What are the effects on decision making of varying degrees of certainty regarding test validity?

Psychometricians and test developers have traditionally relied on large samples of examinees on which to norm tests and to measure their reliability and validity. Emphasis on people with handicapping conditions, however, has confirmed what has been learned in work with minority groups: practical techniques for developing and validating tests used with small samples must be refined. Fortunately, as noted in Chapter 5, new techniques for pooling data across institutions and years have been developed for minority groups and offer promise for work with handicapped examinees.

The main advantage of using large samples is that they increase the researcher's confidence in the results. A test developed on a sample of 50 people may have the same validity coefficient for predicting job success as a test developed on a sample of 1,000, but the larger sample produces more reliable statistics—that is, estimates that vary less from sample to sample. However, increasing sample size is only one statistical method for reducing uncertainty; pooling results from small samples over time or across situations is another. There should be an investigation of the effects of pooling techniques on the accuracy of information about tests, especially their predictive validity.

Furthermore, rather little is known about how information regarding error in test scores or in predictions based on test scores is used by decision makers. Therefore, there should be an exploration of the ways in which information on the uncertainty in test scores or in test validity is used by decision makers. This task could be accomplished by reviewing measures of reliability and validity of a sample of tests and surveying a sample of people who use those tests to determine if there is a relationship between the uncertainty of the scores and their predictive power, on the one hand, and the ways the scores are used, on the other.

## HANDICAPPED PEOPLE AND THE TESTING SITUATION

Even though this panel has amassed information on the testing of handicapped people from many sources, there remain important areas in which little information is available. Five research topics are suggested below.

### *Types of Modifications

What are the characteristics, particularly regarding handicapping conditions, of handicapped people who request test modifications, in comparison with those who take standard administrations, in comparison with those who request test waivers, and in comparison with those who choose not to participate in activities requiring tests?

The panel has compiled the available data on the frequency of use of various modifications of several educational, employment, and certification or licensing tests. However, the picture presented by these data is far from complete. In many cases the type or severity of the handicapping condition of the people requesting each modification is not known; it is not known how many handicapped people took the test in the standard form or requested a waiver; and it is not known how many other eligible handicapped people do not—for a variety of reasons—request modified tests. The panel suggests that such information be collected from examinees in the future because of its utility in at least two regards: first, the information could be used to help future handicapped examinees decide what modifications would be most appropriate; second, the information would be essential in validity studies.

### *Alternatives and Supplements to Standardized Paper-and-Pencil Tests

What procedures that may be used as alternatives or supplements to standardized paper-and-pencil tests offer special promise of application for people with handicapping conditions?

Although test scores are but one part of the information used to make decisions about people, there have been many criticisms of standardized testing and many calls for alternatives. There has not been much evidence of success in finding practical and valid alternatives, however, even for the nonhandicapped population. The need for such alternatives and supplements may be seen as even greater for the handicapped population since the meaning of scores on many tests is called into question by the modification of testing procedures.

The panel therefore recommends research on the means of assessing the abilities of handicapped people other than with standardized paper-and-pencil tests. In the educational sphere, in addition to teachers' ratings, the use of a questionnaire on a student's accomplishments may have promise. The Graduate Record Examination Board has begun work on something similar for its general student population. Performance tests, long used by rehabilitation agencies, may provide an alternative to paper-and-pencil tests in the employment sphere. Assessment centers, which are becoming popular in selecting business executives, cost from $300 to between $3,000 and $4,000 per person and may require several days to administer, but they may be useful in selecting high-level professionals with handicapping conditions.

Studies of such methods should assess their practicality—the ease with which they can be applied to handicapped people—as well as their demands on time and money. Studies should also attempt to determine the potential for systematic discrimination against handicapped people and should compare that risk with the potential or known bias of standardized paper-and-pencil tests. The validity of alternative methods of assessment should also be examined if collection of the necessary data is feasible. Failing an actual evaluation of the validity of the techniques, the practicality of compiling quantitative data necessary for measures of validity should be examined. Reasonable but nonquantitative or nonobjective means of judging the relative quality of the alternative measures should be explored.

## Attitudes of Testing Personnel Toward Handicapped People

What are the effects of attitudes toward handicapped people held by testing personnel on the test scores of handicapped individuals and on the uses of those scores?

It is widely reported that nonhandicapped individuals have a variety of attitudes toward handicapped people, many of them inaccurate or discriminatory. Some research shows that certain people react realistically toward blind people whom they know but are afraid of or hostile toward the blind as a group. Nonhandicapped people may assume handicapped people generally to be incompetent, although in some instances they are believed to possess superior abilities. (A review of the research literature on labeling of handicapped people appears in Appendix A.)

The panel has particular interest in the attitudes of personnel who interact with handicapped people with regard to tests—counselors, examiners, readers, amanuenses, and those who use test scores in making decisions. The panel recommends that studies of the attitudes of testing personnel in a variety of settings be conducted.

Data for the studies could be drawn from samples of four groups: (1) people who administer tests to handicapped examinees for educational, employment, and licensing purposes; (2) people who assist handicapped examinees with the tests, that is, read for them, sign for them, and so on; (3) people who score the tests or evaluate the scores; and (4) people who make decisions on the basis of test scores. For purposes of clarification and corroboration, data should be gathered in a variety of ways, such as attitude questionnaires and interviews with testing personnel as well as interviews with handicapped examinees. The goals of the studies should be to estimate the nature and extent of the effect of the attitudes of testing personnel on the test performance of handicapped people and on the use of those scores and to guide the development of strategies for eliminating, mitigating, or offsetting these effects.

### Requesting Test Modifications

What information do handicapped individuals who may need to request a modified test currently have, and what do they need to make the best informed decisions?

Handicapped examinees currently make a decision regarding tests that their nonhandicapped peers are not asked to make: which modification of a test offers the most advantageous testing arrangement. There is some fear that test takers with handicapping conditions may not have sufficient information from test publishers or counselors to choose most wisely among the alternatives available. People with mild handicapping conditions may have a very difficult choice to make: whether to take the standard administration, which may be more troublesome but will be reported without a special identifier, or to take a modified form, which may be somewhat easier but will for most tests result in a flagged score and greatly reduced interpretability. People recently disabled may also have an extremely difficult choice because they may not yet have acquired a facility for any modified form; they are likely to find both choosing the form and actually taking the test troublesome. The pervasiveness and severity of the problems associated with choosing one type of test administration over others are unknown and could be investigated by surveying handicapped examinees. Questions relating to knowledge about and attitudes toward test modifications could be answered in a small study or could be incorporated into a larger study.

## Coaching and Experience in Taking Tests

What are the effects on later test performance of handicapped people's experiences with tests, including the experiences cumulated over the years in school as well as the specific training in test coaching courses?

Evidence—both experimental and anecdotal—suggests that if one's experience in taking tests is limited, then test performance may be artificially suppressed by lack of familiarity with common testing procedures and test-taking strategies. Results of studies of coaching and the experience of adults taking tests long after they have completed their schooling (when they are unfamiliar with tests and tend to score lower than one might predict) support this finding. Furthermore, for handicapped students the tests they take in elementary and secondary schools may bear little resemblance to modifications of standardized tests for college admission. Therefore, the panel recommends conducting studies to determine if handicapped people's experience with standardized tests seriously disadvantages them.

Two general types of studies are suggested: experimental studies of the effects for handicapped examinees of coaching, that is, special training in strategies to use in taking tests; and nonexperimental studies (probably using carefully matched samples) of handicapped students with varying degrees of experience with standardized tests. Studies of the second type may be helpful in shaping policies regarding the exemption of handicapped people from testing requirements. Studies of coaching would help in measuring the efficacy of offering coaching courses for handicapped people, either courses essentially the same as those for nonhandicapped people or courses with special instruction on how to handle modified test forms. One must be clear in generalizing from either type of study to distinguish between intensive training in test-taking skills and long-term exposure to tests.

## Longitudinal Studies through Transition Stages

What information and advice do handicapped people receive, what strategies do they use, and what problems do they face as they encounter tests at points of transition in their lives?

Tests are used to influence decisions at important transition points in people's lives. Those transition points may be especially critical for people who are trying to overcome disadvantages in order to participate fully in American society, including some handicapped people. At times when they may need special support, handicapped people may receive inaccurate information or inappropriate counseling. What problems do handicapped people face, what advice do they receive, and what strategies do they use as they prepare to move from high school to college, or from school to work, or from sheltered workshops to regular jobs, or from life with families to life on their own? How well do various techniques in counseling and rehabilitation serve the needs of handicapped people in transition?

To answer these and similar questions, the panel recommends longitudinal research following a sample of handicapped people from high school through their early to middle twenties. Data should be collected and analyzed on a wide variety of topics, including any difficulties that occur in testing situations; the relationships of test scores to other variables (school experience and performance, teachers' ratings, socioeconomic variables, and others); the consequences of labeling on a person's expectations and performance; and the consequences of labeling on decisions made about an individual. Data should include perceptions of the handicapped people, their parents, teachers, employers, and counselors as well as more objective measures, such as test scores, grades, and other measures of aptitude or performance. Sample design should be given especially careful consideration to balance the desire to have a homogeneous sample for ease of management and a heterogeneous sample for ease of generalizability.

## HANDICAPPED PEOPLE AND THE DECISION-MAKING PROCESS

More important than the test scores themselves are the ways in which they are used to influence decisions about people. The use of the scores is especially critical for handicapped people since they are seldom normed and are often flagged as a signal that they cannot be interpreted in the same ways as scores that result from the standard administration of a test.

## *Role of Test Scores in the Decision-Making Process

How are test scores actually used in making decisions regarding handicapped people for education, employment, rehabilitation, and certification or licensing purposes?

The information the panel has uncovered on how various institutions (schools, employers, rehabilitation agencies, and certification or licensing agencies) use tests for handicapped people is somewhat fragmented, and the information available in employment settings is especially sketchy. Since more complete information would be helpful, we recommend surveys of key personnel in schools, employment settings, rehabilitation agencies, and certification or licensing agencies. Information regarding employment selection and placement is especially difficult to obtain because of the small numbers of handicapped applicants and employees and because of the lack of large-scale tests or systematic selection procedures. However, that information is critical in identifying and overcoming barriers to the employment of qualified people with handicapping conditions. The surveys should describe current policies and compare any policies that are different for handicapped and nonhandicapped people. They should seek to distinguish between policies for handicapped people that seem fair and effective and those that do not. Such surveys should also estimate the prevalence of different policies and compare the stated objectives of the policies with what is actually achieved. The surveys should be conducted so that results can be reported separately for various types of institutions or organizations: large state universities compared with small liberal arts colleges, various types of business or industries, private compared with public rehabilitation agencies, and so on. Such work should be linked to studies of the effects of testing (or of various selection procedures and policies), and every effort should be made to determine what procedures are actually used, not just purported to be used.

## Flagged Scores

How are flagged test scores actually used in making decisions about handicapped applicants?

When admissions tests for postsecondary schools are taken under nonstandard conditions, the score reports to the schools make note of that fact and thereby notify the admissions officers that the applicants are probably handicapped. Yet preadmission inquiry regarding handicapping conditions is prohibited in the federal regulations on the assumption that the information would be used to applicants' disadvantage more often than to their advantage. Some admissions officials argue, however, that the flags on the test scores are used to the advantage of handicapped applicants: if the flagged score is high and other material corroborates it, the student is admitted; if the flagged score is low, it is ignored and other information is used to decide about admitting the applicant. A survey of actual practice might corroborate this view or reveal different uses, or, at the very least, variations in the use of flagged scores. Furthermore, it is not known how often a flagged test score is the only indication in an applicant's portfolio that he or she is handicapped. Such information could be revealed by the applicant's enrollment in a special school, program, or classes; in letters of recommendation; in certain extracurricular activities; or by the candidate's voluntary statement.

While there has been research on the effects of labeling a person as handicapped, the sum of evidence yields contradictory conclusions. Additional knowledge would greatly aid in formulating policy. Therefore, the panel recommends research to describe the current use of flagged scores. A sample of individual cases should be followed through the admissions process to attempt to ascertain the effect of flags on the interpretation of scores and on the weight of the scores in the decision-making process. Admittedly, this kind of study is difficult to conduct because of necessary assurances of confidentiality, and the results will be suspect if the admissions officers know explicitly about the goals of the study. Therefore, the study design is critical, and the study may need to be supplemented with an experiment in which admissions officers make decisions regarding hypothetical handicapped and nonhandicapped candidates, with control variables relating to their qualifications. The panel acknowledges that the difficulties may lead to results that are less than completely satisfactory but believes this topic is important enough to warrant study.

### Models for the Decision-Making Process

What decision rules and models are used in determining whether handicapped individuals should be admitted to schools, or employed, or awarded certificates and licenses? What are the implications of models used in various institutions for the counseling of handicapped individuals?

Given the current situation in which test scores for handicapped people have unknown validity and are flagged, the most equitable and efficient way to use the scores seems elusive. Presuming that some scores will continue to be flagged until validation research is complete, thoughtful attention should be given to the identification of decision-making strategies that are the most equitable for all applicants and the most efficient for the institutions or organizations. The panel has been told that there exist informal, mostly nonquantitative rules of thumb used by school admissions officers, and there are certainly analogies in settings outside education. The panel urges a study of formal and informal decision rules, examining the ramifications for the applicants, for the decision makers, and for the institutions. Once the models, using the term loosely, are described, they could be tested with retrospective or prospective studies. Attention should be given, in the reporting of the study, to the need to counsel handicapped applicants on the probable effects of requesting that test scores be reported with or without flags. Researchers should also be sensitive to the possibility of generalizing from situations with relatively abundant data (some forms of postsecondary education) to others with scarce data (most notably, employment).

## DEMOGRAPHIC DATA ON HANDICAPPED PEOPLE

The first question raised by the panel in beginning its study concerned the number of people with various handicapping conditions who might be able to enter the mainstream of American life. The panel wanted to gain a sense of the size, complexity, and severity of the problem under investigation. The question divided itself into three components: (1) How many Americans in various age groups have handicaps of differing types and severity? (2) How many people with each handicapping condition are employed or in postsecondary schools, and how many apply for positions but are rejected? (3) How frequently do handicapped people take tests, and how often are the tests an important factor in their acceptance or rejection? We found much less information to answer these questions than we had expected. Hence, this fourth and final section of the panel's research agenda concerns the demography of the population of people with handicapping conditions who may be in school or in the labor force. (The panel's charge did not cover handicapped people who are institutionalized or who are not attempting to enroll in school or to be employed.) While we believe these demographic studies are important and of interest to a broad constituency, they are somewhat peripheral to our work, and we therefore give them lower priority than studies more directly related to testing.

## Incidence of Handicapping Conditions

What are the existing sources of data on handicapped people, and how can they be made compatible? How can definitions of handicapping conditions used for a variety of purposes by different groups be made comparable?

Nearly every piece of federal legislation and every agency or organization dealing with handicapped people uses a different definition of handicapping condition or handicapped person. One reason for the differences stems from the particular mission or concern of a particular act or agency. It would be naive to expect an agency concerned about the placement of elementary school students in educational programs to define its population of interest in a way perfectly compatible with that of an organization concerned with the employment of adults. A second reason for the differences is that, for the many types of disability, the severity of an impairment is described in different ways. For example, hearing impairments are scaled in relation to unimpaired auditory acuity and may be related to a specific range of pitch. Blindness is scaled very differently, however, and there are several markedly different types of visual impairment (for example, total blindness, perception of light only, and restriction of visual field) that are not amenable to clear and concise comparison. For motor handicaps, there is no widely accepted scale of severity. The lack of a common scale makes many potentially valuable comparisons across handicaps difficult if not impossible.

Since classification schemes differ, and estimates vary widely, even when definitions seem comparable, we urge that steps be taken to make the various definitions of handicapping conditions as comparable as is practical. One possible way to do this would be to hold a conference with appropriate representatives from the National Health Survey, the Social Security Administration, other relevant agencies, and professional and advocacy associations along with people experienced in the statistical aspects of demography. The topics to be covered should include:

1. Summaries of sources of data on handicapped people. The summaries could be organized by type of disability, type of source (for example, public or private sector), or use of the data (for example, administrative or research).

2. Characteristics of each data source. Attention should be given to how to combine data from various sources that have different purposes, use different definitions of disabilities, and employ different methods of data collection.

3. Additional analyses of existing data. Is there additional information that could be obtained from existing data sets? In particular, can finer tabulations be made for type and severity of handicapping condition? Is there information relating to particular concerns of the panel and the Office for Civil Rights (for example, testing, education, and employment) that can be obtained from existing sources?

4. Data for the future. What data collection efforts are anticipated for the future? How can shortcomings of existing data sets be overcome? What are the most important questions to be answered by analysis of the data? What efforts should receive highest priority? How should various efforts be coordinated? How convincing are the arguments for maintaining different definitions of handicapping conditions in different surveys? The results of such a conference would be useful to both researchers and policy makers in the private sector and in government. Such a conference should increase the likelihood that unnecessary duplication of effort is reduced, that the data collected by diverse sources would be compatible, and that the data would be collected and analyzed in the most useful and comprehensible fashion.

## Social Indicators Regarding Handicapped People

How can one describe the social and economic characteristics of the lives of people with handicapping conditions?

There are a number of signs that the lives of handicapped people are changing markedly with regard to education, work, and independent living arrangements. For policy and administrative purposes it is important to have accurate and current information about social and economic characteristics of the lives of these people. Therefore, the panel recommends that social indicators regarding handicapped people be compiled.

The book *Social Indicators III* (U.S. Department of Commerce 1980), produced by the Bureau of the Census, should serve as a model for work on the handicapped population. The new work (whether a separate volume or part of a more general publication) should present data on social, economic, educational, and health characteristics of handicapped people. The quality of data from different sources should be indicated as they are compiled and published. Data that relate social, educational, health, and employment factors should be located (or collected), analyzed, and presented.

As the existing data are compiled, consideration should be given to other questions to be asked and other data to be collected. In addition, the desirability of producing such a compilation periodically and charting changes or trends should be assessed. It is likely that the Office of Federal Statistical Policy and Standards in the U.S. Department of Commerce could offer valuable assistance in planning or executing this project.

## Epidemiology of the Handicapped Population

How can one describe the incidence and distribution of various handicapping conditions across population groups defined by age, sex, racial or ethnic membership, social and economic characteristics, and the like. What are the known causes of various conditions? What are the projected needs of these groups?

Providing services to meet the diverse needs of handicapped people could be planned more effectively if information about the incidence and distribution of various handicapping conditions were known. Since certain groups, say children affected *in utero* by their mothers' rubella, commonly have a unique set of needs, knowing the incidence of rubella among pregnant women in various cohorts would make it relatively easy to predict the future structure and probable needs of a segment of the population. To follow this example further, schools for the deaf could plan more effectively and testing organizations could predict the demand for certain types of modifications if information on rubella were known. Therefore, studies of the epidemiology of disabilities would be useful for a wide range of situations. The major topics that should be investigated are the incidence, distribution, and likely or known causes of various disabilities and the educational, medical, and social needs of people with various disabilities.

People with multiple handicaps often have special needs or a combination of needs that may not be readily met in existing administrative arrangements for providing services. In addition, one handicap may be masked by or may masquerade as another, creating the possibility that some needs are not met. To allow for better informed planning in the short and long run, the panel also recommends that research be conducted to provide useful estimates of the size of groups with multiple handicaps and to describe their needs at various points in the life cycle.

### Effects of Handicapping Conditions

What are the direct and the indirect effects on a person's experiences of having a handicapping condition?

It is commonly recognized that handicapping conditions have both direct and indirect effects on a person's experiences. For example, the parents of a handicapped child may unnecessarily restrict the child's experiences, thus compounding the disabling effects of the primary handicapping condition. In order to determine appropriate and effective means of remediation and to prevent future problems, it is important to separate the direct from the indirect effects of handicapping conditions. As a first step, researchers should determine whether available data sources can be analyzed to help separate the various effects for different handicapping conditions.

# References


American Association of Collegiate Registrars and Admissions Officers, and the College Board (1980) *Undergraduate Admissions: The Realities of Institutional Policies, Practices, and Procedures*. New York: College Entrance Examination Board.

American College Testing Program (1973) *Assessing Students on the Way to College: Technical Report for the ACT Assessment Program*, Vol. 1. Iowa City, Iowa: American College Testing Program.

American Psychiatric Association (1980) *Diagnostic and Statistical Manual*, 3rd ed. Washington, D.C.: American Psychiatric Association.

American Psychological Association, American Educational Research Association, and National Council on Measurement in Education (1974) *Standards for Educational and Psychological Tests*. Washington, D.C.: American Psychological Association.

Anastasi, A. (1976) *Psychological Testing*, 4th ed. New York: Macmillan.

Anderson, B. L. (1982) Test use today in elementary and secondary schools. In A. Wigdor and W. Garner, eds., *Ability Testing: Uses, Consequences and Controversies*, Part II. Report of the Committee on Ability Testing. Washington, D.C.: National Academy Press.

And in Britain. . . . (1979) *Public Interest* 57:117-118.

Anderson, R. J., and Sisco, F. H. (1977) *Standardization of the WISC-R Performance Scale for Deaf Children*. Series T, No. 1. Washington, D.C.: Office of Demographic Studies, Gallaudet College.

Angoff, W. H. (1971) Scales, norms, and equivalent scores. Pp. 508-600 in R. L. Thorndike, ed., *Educational Measurement*. Washington, D.C.: American Council on Education.

Backman, M. E. (1977) *The Development of Micro-TOWER: A Battery of Standardized Work Samples for Assessing Vocational Aptitudes*. New York: ICD Rehabilitation and Research Center.

Barron, S. (1980) Testimony submitted to open meeting of Panel on Testing of Handicapped People, March 14-15, National Research Council, Washington, D.C.

Bauman, M. K. (1976) Psychological evaluation of the blind client. Pp. 249-268 in B. Bolton, ed., *Handbook of Measurement and Evaluation in Rehabilitation.* Baltimore, Md.: University Park Press.

Bolton, B., ed. (1976a) *Handbook of Measurement and Evaluation in Rehabilitation.* Baltimore, Md.: University Park Press.

Bolton, B., ed. (1976b) *Psychology of Deafness for Rehabilitation Counselors.* Baltimore, Md.: University Park Press.

Bolton, B., and Cook, D. W., eds. (1980) *Rehabilitation Client Assessment.* Baltimore, Md.: University Park Press.

Brand, R. C., and Claborn, W. L. (1976) Two studies in comparative stigma: employer attitudes and practices toward rehabilitated convicts, mental and tuberculosis patients. *Community Mental Health Journal* 12:168-175.

Braun, H. I., and Jones, D. H. (1980) Graduate Management Admissions Test Prediction Bias Study. Graduate Management Admissions Council and the Educational Testing Service, Princeton, N.J.

Brothers, R. J. (1972) Arithmetic computation by the blind: a look at current achievement. *Education of the Visually Handicapped* 4:1-8.

Brown, R. (1965) *Social Psychology.* New York: Free Press.

Burns, R. L. (1970) *Graduate Admissions and Fellowship Selection Policies and Procedures,* Part 1 and Part 2. Princeton, N.J.: The Graduate Record Examination Board and Educational Testing Service.

Caputo, D. V., Goldstein, K. M., and Taub, H. B. (1981) Neonatal compromise and later psychological development: a ten-year longitudinal study. Pp. 353-386 in S. L. Friedman and M. Sigman, eds., *Preterm Birth and Psychological Development.* New York: Academic Press.

Carnes, G. D. (1979) *European Rehabilitation Service Providers and Programs.* East Lansing, Mich.: Michigan State University.

Cohen, M. (1980) Discrimination on the basis of handicap: the status of Section 504 of the Rehabilitation Act of 1973. *Iowa Law Review* 65 (January):446-467.

Colenbrander, A. (1977) Dimensions of visual performance. *Transactions of the American Academy of Ophthalmology and Otolaryngology* 83:332-337.

Cook, T., and Laski, F. (1980) Beyond *Davis*: equality of opportunity for higher education for disabled students under the Rehabilitation Act of 1973. *Harvard Civil Rights/Civil Liberties Law Review* 15(Fall):415-473.

Cooper, J. (1979) Report of the Special Advisory Panel on Technical Standards for Medical School Admission. Internal memorandum 79-4, January 25, 1979. Association of American Medical Colleges, Washington, D.C.

Cooperative Institutional Research Program of the University of California, Los Angeles, and American Council on Education (1980) *The American Freshman: National Norms for Fall 1979.* Cooperative Institutional Research Program, Graduate School of Education, University of California, Los Angeles.

CRC Education and Human Development, Inc. (1981) Update of *Handbook for the Implementation of Section 504 of the Rehabilitation Act of 1973.* Draft Final Handbook Revisions. February 6. Prepared under contract no. HEW-100-80-0010 for the Office for Civil Rights, U.S. Department of Education, Washington, D.C.

Cronbach, L. J. (1970) *Essentials of Psychological Testing,* 3rd ed. New York: Harper and Row.

Davis, C. J., and Nolan, C. Y. (1961) A comparison of the oral and written methods of administering achievement tests. *International Journal for the Education of the Blind* 10:80-82.

Davis, H., and Silverman, S., eds. (1978) *Hearing and Deafness*, 4th ed. New York: Holt, Rinehart, and Winston.

Dearman, N., and Plisko, V. (1980) *The Condition of Education, 1980 Edition* (p. 6). Washington, D.C.: National Center for Education Statistics.

Dempster, A. P., Rubin, D. B., and Tsutakawa, R. K. (1980) *Estimation in Covariance Components Models*. Princeton, N.J.: Educational Testing Service.

DiFrancesca, S. (1972) *Academic Achievement Test Results of a National Testing Program for Hearing Impaired Students, United States: Spring 1971*. Series D, No. 1. Washington, D.C.: Office of Demographic Studies, Gallaudet College.

Donlon, T. F. (1980a) An Annotated Bibliography of Studies of Test Speededness. GRE Board Research Report GREB No. 76-9R. Educational Testing Service, Princeton, N.J.

Donlon, T. F. (1980b) An Exploratory Study of the Implications of Test Speededness. GRE Board Professional Report GREB No. 76-9P. Educational Testing Service, Princeton, N.J.

Droege, R. C., and Mugaas, H. D. (1976) The USES testing program. In B. Bolton, ed., *Handbook of Measurement and Evaluation in Rehabilitation*. Baltimore, Md.: University Park Press.

Engebretson, M. F. (1979) Note: administrative action to end discrimination based on handicap: HEW's Section 504 regulation. *Harvard Journal on Legislation* 16(Winter):59-89.

Equal Employment Opportunity Commission, Civil Service Commission, U.S. Department of Labor, and U.S. Department of Justice (1978) Uniform guidelines on employee selection procedures. *Federal Register* 43(166):38290-38315.

Farina, A., and Felner, R. D. (1973) Employment interviewer reactions to former mental patients. *Journal of Consulting and Clinical Psychology* 41:363-372.

Farina, A., and Rina, K. (1965) The influence of perceived mental illness on interpersonal relations. *Journal of Abnormal Psychology* 70:47-51.

Federal Trade Commission, (1978) The Effects of Coaching on Standardized Admission examinations. Staff memorandum of the Boston Regional Office of the Federal Trade Commission. Boston Regional Office, Federal Trade Commission, Boston, Mass.

Federal Trade Commission (1979) Effects of Coaching on Standardized Admission Examinations: Revised Statistical Analyses of Data Gathered by Boston Regional Office of the Federal Trade Commission. Bureau of Consumer Protection, Federal Trade Commission, Washington, D.C.

Friedman, T., and Williams, E. (1982) Current uses of tests for employment. In A. Wigdor and W. Garner, eds., *Ability Testing: Uses, Consequences, and Controversies*, Part II. Report of the Committee on Ability Testing. Washington, D.C.: National Academy Press.

Furth, H. (1966) A comparison of reading test norms of deaf and hearing children. *American Annals of the Deaf* 111:461-462.

Gordon, T. L. (1979) Study of U.S. medical school applicants, 1977-78. *Journal of Medical Education* 54(9):677-702.

Gorth, W. P., and Perkins, M. R. (1979) *A Study of Minimum Competency Testing Programs*. Washington, D.C.: National Institute of Education.

Gottwald, H. (1970) *Public Awareness About Mental Retardation*. Research Monograph. Reston, Va.: Council for Exceptional Children.

Gowman, A. (1957) *The War Blind in American Social Structure*. New York: American Foundation for the Blind.

Greenberg, B. L., and Greenberg, S. H. (1971) The measurement of college potential in the hearing impaired. *American Annals of the Deaf* (116):372-381.

Grossman, H., ed. (1973) *Manual on Terminology and Classification in Mental Retardation, 1973 Revision*. Washington, D.C.: American Association on Mental Deficiency.

Grossman, H., ed. (1977) *Manual on Terminology and Classification in Mental Retardation: 1977 Revision*. Washington, D.C.: American Association on Mental Deficiency.

Guskin, S. L. (1963) Dimensions of judged similarity among deviant types. *American Journal of Mental Deficiency* 68:218-224.

Guskin, S. L. (1963) Measuring the strength of the stereotype of the mental defective. *American Journal of Mental Deficiency* 67:569-575.

Guskin, S. L. (1978) Theoretical and empirical strategies for the study of the labeling of mentally retarded persons. Pp. 127-158 in N. R. Ellis, ed., *International Review of Research in Mental Retardation*, Vol. 9. New York: Academic Press.

Haney, W., and Madaus, G. (1978) Making sense of the competency testing movement. *Harvard Educational Review* 48(4):462-484.

Hatfield, E. (1975) Why are they blind? *The Sight-Saving Review* 45(1):3-22.

Heaton, S. M., Nelson, A. V., and Nester, M. A. (1980) *Guide for Administering Examinations to Handicapped Individuals for Employment Purposes*. Personnel Research and Development Center. PRR 80-16. Washington, D.C.: U.S. Office of Personnel Management.

Heller, K.A., Holtzman, W.H., and Messick, S., eds. (1982) *Placing Children in Special Education: A Strategy for Equity*. Washington, D.C.: National Academy Press.

Hightower, L. (1980) Rehabilitation Act of 1973—application to postsecondary educational programs: *Southeastern Community College* v. *Davis*. *Southern California Law Review* 31(January):394-408.

Himes, J. S. (1950) Some concepts of blindness in American culture. *Social Casework* 31(December):1-7.

Hobbs, N. ed. (1976) *Issues in the Classification of Children, Volumes 1 and 2*. San Francisco, Calif.: Jossey-Bass.

Hobbs, N. (1978) *The Futures of Children: Categories, Lables, and their Consequences*. San Francisco, Calif.: Jossey-Bass.

Hoemann, H. W. (1972) Communication accuracy in sign-language interpretation of a group test. *Journal of Rehabilitation of the Deaf* 5:40-43.

Jain, H. C. (1979) *Disadvantaged Groups on the Labour Market and Measures to Assist Them*. Paris: Organization for Economic Cooperation and Development.

Johnson, R., and Heal, L. W. (1976) Private employment agency responses to the physically handicapped applicant in a wheelchair. *Journal of Applied Rehabilitation Counseling* 7:12-21.

Jones, D., and Ragosta, M. (198l) Validity studies of the SAT for the deaf. Draft report. Educational Testing Service Princeton, N.J.

Jones, R. L. (1980) *Attitudes and Attitude Change in Special Education*. National Support Systems Project. Minneapolis, Minn.: University of Minnesota.

Karchmer, M., and Trybus, R. (1977) *Who Are the Deaf Children in "Mainstream" Programs?* Research bulletin R-4. Washington, D.C.: Office of Demographic Studies, Gallaudet College.

Kirchner, C., and Peterson, R. (1979a) Statistical briefs: the latest data on visual disability from NCHS. *Journal of Visual Impairment and Blindness* 73(April):151-153.

Kirchner, C., and Peterson, R. (1979b) Statistical brief #5—employment: selected characteristics. *Journal of Visual Impairment and Blindness* 73(June):239-242.

Kleck, R. (1968) Physical stigma and nonverbal cues emitted in face-to-face interactions. *Human Relations* 21:19-28.

Kleck, R. (1969) Physical stigma and task-oriented interactions. *Human Relations* 22:53-60.

Kleck, R. (1975) Issues in social effectiveness: the case of the mentally retarded. Pp. 181-195 in M. J. Bejab, ed., *The Mentally Retarded and Society: A Social Science Perspective*. Baltimore, Md.: University Park Press.

Kleck, R., et al. (1966) The effects of physical deviance upon face-to-face interaction. *Human Relations* 19:425-436.

Koestler, F. (1976) *The Unseen Minority*. New York: McKay.

Lambert, N., and Sandoval, J. (1980) The prevalence of learning disabilities in a sample of children considered hyperactive. *Journal of Abnormal Child Psychology* 8:33-50.

Lemert, E. M. (1951) *Social Pathology: A Systematic Approach to the Theory of Socio-Pathic Behavior*. New York: McGraw-Hill.

Levine, E. S. (1960) *The Psychology of Deafness, Techniques of Appraisal for Rehabilitation*. New York: Columbia University Press.

Levitin, T. E. (1975) Deviants as active participants in the labeling process: the visibly handicapped. *Social Problems* 22(April):548-557.

Lindley, D. V. (1970) A Bayesian solution for some educational prediction problems. Educational Testing Service Research Bulletin #70-33. Princeton, N.J.: Educational Testing Service.

Linn, R. L. (1982) Ability testing: individual differences, prediction and differential prediction. In A. Wigdor and W. Garner, eds., *Ability Testing: Uses, Consequences, and Controversies*, Part II. Report of the Committee on Ability Testing. Washington, D.C.: National Academy Press.

Lloyd, J. (1979) Ascertaining the reading skills of atypical learners. In D. Sabatino and T. Miller, eds, *Describing Learner Characteristics of Handicapped Children and Youth*. New York: Grune and Stratton.

Lord, F. M. (1977) Practical applications of item characteristic curve theory. *Journal of Educational Measurement* 14(2):117-138.

Lord, F. M., and Novick, M. R. (1968) *Statistical Theories of Mental Test Scores*. Reading, Mass.: Addison-Wesley.

Lowenfeld, B., ed. (1973) *The Visually Handicapped Child in School*. New York: John Day.

Lukoff, I. F., and Whiteman, M. (1963) *Attitudes and Blindness*. Lexington, Mass.: Nolan Norton Company.

Madaus, G. F., and McDonagh, J. T. (1979) Minimal Competency Testing: Unexamined Assumptions and Unexplored Negative Outcomes. Paper presented at 9th annual conference on large-scale assessment, National Assessment of Educational Progress, Denver, Colo., June 11-14, 1979.

Maxey, J., and Levitz, R. (1980) ACT Services for the Handicapped. Paper presented at meeting of American Association of Collegiate Registrars and Admissions Officers, New Orleans, La.

McClung, M. (1977) Competency testing: potential for discrimination. *Clearinghouse Review* 2:439-448.

McCrone, W., and Chambers, J. (1977) A national pilot study of psychological evaluation services to deaf vocational rehabilitation clients. *Journal of Rehabilitation of the Deaf* 2:1-4.

Messick, S. (1980) *The Effectiveness of Coaching for the SAT: Review and Reanalysis of Research from the Fifties to the FTC*. Princeton, N.J.: Educational Testing Service.

Miller, S. (1979) Career education: lifelong planning for the handicapped. In D. Sabatino and T. Miller, eds., *Describing Learner Characteristics of Handicapped Children and Youth*. New York: Grune and Stratton.

Miner, M. (1976) *Selection Procedures and Personnel Records.* Personnel Policies Forum Survey No. 114. Washington, D.C.: Bureau of National Affairs.

Minskoff, J. (1973) Differential approaches to prevalence estimates of learning disabilities. In F. de la Cruz, B. Fox, and R. Robert, eds., *Minimal Brain Dysfunction.* New York: New York Academy of Sciences.

Mykelbust, H. R. (1964) *The Psychology of Deafness. Sensory Deprivation, Learning, and Adjustment,* 2nd ed. New York: Grune and Stratton.

Nagi, S. (1979) The concept and measurement of disability. Chap. 1 in E. D. Berkowitz, ed., *Disability Policies and Government Programs.* New York: Praeger Publishers.

National Association of State Directors of Special Education, and North Carolina Department of Public Instruction, Division of Exceptional Children (1979) *Competency Testing, Special Education and the Awarding of Diplomas: A Report of Survey Information.* Washington, D.C.: National Association of State Directors of Special Education.

National Center for Education Statistics (1978) *Fall Enrollment in Colleges and Universities, 1978 (Preliminary Estimates).* Cited in Wulfsberg, R., and Peterson, R. (no date) *The Impact of Section 504 of the Rehabilitation Act of 1973 on American Colleges and Universities.* Washington, D.C.: National Center for Education Statistics.

National Federation of the Blind (1980) Testimony presented at open meeting of Panel on Testing of Handicapped People, March 1980, National Academy of Sciences.

Nester, M. A. (1974) *Use of the Cranmer Abacus by Blind Persons.* U.S. Civil Service Commission, Personnel Research and Development Center. PS74-2. Washington, D.C.: U.S. Civil Service Commission.

Nester, M. A. (1980) Testing Handicapped Persons for Employment. Paper presented at meeting of American Psychological Association, Montreal, September 1980.

Nester, M. A., and Sapinkopf, R. (1981) *Statistical Characteristics of the Written Test for the Professional and Administrative Career Examination (PACE) for Deaf Applicants.* U.S. Office of Personnel Management, Personnel Research and Development Center. Washington, D.C.: U.S. Office of Personnel Management.

Nolan, C. Y. (1962) Evaluating the scholastic achievement of visually handicapped children. *Exceptional Children* 28:493-496.

Nolan, C. Y. (1964) Research in teaching mathematics to blind children. *International Journal for the Education of the Blind* 13:97-100.

Nolan, C. Y., and Ashcroft, S. C. (1959) The Stanford Achievement Arithmetic Computation Tests: a study of an experimental adaptation for braille administration. *International Journal for the Education of the Blind* 8:89-92.

Novick, M. R., Jackson, P. H., Thayer, D. T., and Cole, N. S. (1972) Estimating multiple regressions in m-groups: a cross-validation study. *British Journal of Mathematical and Statistical Psychology* 25:33-50.

Organization for Economic Cooperation and Development (1979) *Policies for Apprenticeship.* Paris: Organization for Economic Cooperation and Development.

Osguthorpe, R. T., Long, G. L., and Ellsworth, R. G. (no date) The Effects of Reviewing Class Notes for Deaf and Hearing Students. National Technical Institute for the Deaf, Rochester, N.Y.

Paolicelli, D. (1979) Employment discrimination against the handicapped: can *Tragesar* repeal the private right of action? *NYU Law Review* 54(December):1173-1198.

Pipho, C. (1979) Updates of the Survey of State Activity in Minimal Competency Testing. Education Commission of the States, Denver, Colo.

Pottinger, P., Weisfeld, N., Tochen, D., Cohen, P., and Schaalman, M. (1980) Competence assessment for occupational certification. In *The Assessment of Occupational*

*Competence.* Prepared for the National Institute of Education, Contract NIE 400-78-0028. Available from ERIC Clearinghouse, #(CH):CE027162.

Prentice-Hall, Inc. (1975) *P-H Survey: Employee Testing and Selection Procedures—Where Are They Headed?* Englewood Cliffs, N.J.: Prentice-Hall, Inc.

President's Committee on Employment of the Handicapped (no date) Employer of the Year Questionnaire. Washington, D.C.

President's Committee on Employment of the Handicapped (1971) *American Profile: What States Are Doing (and Can Do) To Hire the Handicapped.* Washington, D.C.

President's Committee on Employment of the Handicapped (1980) Incentives in Germany. *Disabled USA* 3(9):25.

Ragosta, M. (1980) *Handicapped Students and the SAT.* College Board Research and Development Reports RDR 80-81, No. 1. Princeton, N.J.: Educational Testing Service.

Rasch, G. (1960) *Probabalistic Models for Some Intelligence and Attainment Tests.* Copenhagen: Danish Institute for Educational Research.

Ray, N. (1979-80) Note: legislation by implication: the exercise of legislative authority under the 1978 amendments to Section 504 of the Rehabilitation Act of 1973. *Kentucky Law Journal* 68:141-183.

Richardson, W., and Higgins, A. (1965) *The Handicapped Children of Alamance County, North Carolina.* Wilmington, Del.: The Nemours Foundation.

Robinson, H. B., and Robinson, N. M. (1976) *The Mentally Retarded Child: A Psychological Approach,* 2nd ed. New York: McGraw-Hill.

Rosenberg, B. (1977) *The Development of TOWER: A World Standard for Vocational Evaluation of the Handicapped.* New York: ICD Rehabilitation and Research Center.

Rosewater, A. (1979) Minimum Competency Testing Programs and Handicapped Students: Perspectives on Policy and Practice. Unpublished manuscript, George Washington University Institute for Educational Leadership, Washington, D.C.

Rubin, D. B. (1980) Using empirical Bayes techniques in the Law School Validity Studies. *Journal of the American Statistical Association* 75(372):801-816.

Sameroff, A., and Chandler, M. (1975) Reproductive risk and the continuum of caretaking casualty. In F. Horowitz, ed., *Review of Child Development Research,* Vol. IV. Chicago: University of Chicago Press.

Sapinkopf, R. (1978) *Statistical Characteristics of the Written Test for the Professional and Administrative Career Examination (PACE) for Visually Handicapped Applicants.* U.S. Civil Service Commission, Personnel Research and Development Center TM 78-1. Washington, D.C.: U.S. Civil Service Commission.

Schein, J., and Delk, M. (1974) *The Deaf Population of the United States.* Silver Spring, Md.: National Association of the Deaf.

Schein, J. D., Delk, M. T., and Hooker, S. (1980) Overcoming barriers to the full employment of deaf persons in federal government. *Journal of Rehabilitation of the Deaf* 13(3):15-25.

Schrader, W. B. (1971) The predictive validity of College Board admission tests. In W. H. Angoff, ed., *The College Board Admissions Testing Program: A Technical Report on Research and Development Activities Relating to the Scholastic Aptitude Test and Achievement Tests.* New York: College Entrance Examination Board.

Schrader, W. B. (1976) Summary of law school validity studies, 1948-1975. In Law School Admission Council, *Annual Council Report.* Washington, D.C.: Law School Admission Council.

Shears, L. M., and Jensen, C. J. (1969) Social acceptability of anomalous persons. *Exceptional Children* 36:91-96.

Shultz, M., and Boynton, M. (1958) Typing tests: visual copy vs. recordings. *Public Personnel Review* 19:24-27.

Siegel, L. J., and Senne, J. J. (1981) *Juvenile Delinquency: Theory, Practice, and Law*. St. Paul, Minn.: West Publishing Company.

Skager, R. (1982) On the use and importance of tests of ability in admission to postsecondary education. In A. Wigdor and W. Garner, eds., *Ability Testing: Uses, Consequences, and Controversies*, Part II. Report of the Committee on Ability Testing. Washington, D.C.: National Academy Press.

Spear, J., and Schoepke, J. (1979) Psychologists and Rehabilitation: Mandates and Current Training Practices. Unpublished manuscript. University of Missouri, Columbia.

Stunkel, E. R. (1957) The performance of deaf and hearing college students on verbal and non-verbal intelligence tests. *American Annals of the Deaf* 102:342-355.

Thomae-Forgues, M., and Erdmann, J. (1980) Datagram: MCAT scores and academic records of natural science and humanities majors applying to medical school, 1978-79. *Journal of Medical Education* 55(11):971-972.

Thorndike, R. L., and Hagen, E. (1977) *Measurement and Evaluation in Psychology and Education*, 4th ed. New York: Wiley.

Tinkleman, S. N. (1971) Planning the objective test. Pp. 46-80 in R. L. Thorndike, ed., *Educational Measurement*. Washington, D.C.: American Council on Education.

Toops, H. A. (1960) A comparison, by work limit and time limit, of item analysis indices for practical test construction. *Educational and Psychological Measurement* 20:251-260.

Trybus, R., and Karchmer, M. (1977) School achievement scores of hearing impaired children: national data on achievement status and growth patterns. *American Annals of the Deaf* 122:62-69.

U.S. Department of Commerce (1980) *Social Indicators III: Selected Data on Social Conditions and Trends in the United States*. Bureau of the Census. Washington, D.C.: Government Printing Office.

U.S. Department of Education (1980) *The Condition of Education*. National Center for Education Statistics. NCES80-400. Washington, D.C.: Department of Education.

U.S. Department of Health, Education, and Welfare (1975) *The Condition of Education: A Statistical Report on the Condition of American Education, 1975*. GPO #017-080-01391-6. National Center for Education Statistics, Education Division. Washington, D.C.: Government Printing Office.

U.S. Department of Health, Education, and Welfare (1978) Survey of income and education, spring 1976, preliminary data compiled by the National Center for Education Statistics. P. 38 in M. Golladay and J. Noell, eds., *The Condition of Education, l978 Edition, Statistical Report*. GPO #017-080-01822-5 National Center for Education Statistics, Washington, D. C.

U.S. Office of Personnel Management (1980) *Statistical Profile of Handicapped Federal Civilian Employees*. OPM Document 128-06-6. Washington, D.C: Office of Personnel Management.

U.S. Office of Personnel Management and Council of State Governments (1979) *Analysis of Baseline Data: Survey on Personnel Practices for States, Counties, Cities*. Washington, D.C.: Government Printing Office.

Venti, S., and Wise, D. (1980) Test Scores, Educational Opportunities, and Individual Choice. Discussion paper series, John Fitzgerald Kennedy School of Government. Cambridge, Mass.: Harvard University.

Vernon, Mc. (1968) Fifty years of research on the intelligence of deaf and hard-of-hearing children: a review of literature and discussion of implications. *Journal of Rehabilitation of the Deaf* I(4):1-12.

Wainer, H., and Wright, B. D. (1980) Robust estimation of ability in the Rasch model. *Psychometrika* 45(3):373-391.

Walter, G. (1970) Some observations about deaf and hearing students at RIT (Rochester Institute of Technology). Pp. 290-296 in Convention of American Instructors of the Deaf. *Report of the Proceedings of the 44th Meeting of the Convention of American Instructors of the Deaf*. Senate Document 91-59. 91st Congress, 2nd Session. Washington, D.C.: Government Printing Office.

Walter, G. (1977) *A Technique for Measuring Vocabulary Knowledge*. Rochester, N.Y.: National Technical Institute for the Deaf.

Wepman, J., Cruickshank, W., Deutsch, C., Morency, A., and Strother, C. (1976) Learning disabilities. Pp. 300-317 in N. Hobbs, ed., *Issues in the Classification of Children,* Vol. I. San Francisco, Calif.: Jossey-Bass Publishers.

Wigdor, A. (1982) Psychological testing and the law of employment discrimination. In A. Wigdor and W. Garner, eds., *Ability Testing: Uses, Consequences, and Controversies,* Part II. Report of the Committee on Ability Testing. Washington, D.C.: National Academy Press.

Wild, C., and Durso, R. (1979) *Effect of Increased Test-Taking Time on Test Scores by Ethnic Group, Age, and Sex*. GRE Board Research Report GREB No. 76-6R. Princeton, N.J.: Educational Testing Service.

Willingham, W. W. (1974) Predicting success in graduate education. *Science* 183:273-278.

Wolfe, J. (1973-74) Disability is no handicap for duPont. *The Alliance Review* (Winter).

Woodward, C. V. (1957) *The Strange Career of Jim Crow*, rev. ed. New York:Oxford University Press.

Wright, B. D. (1977) Solving measurement problems with the Rasch model. *Journal of Educational Measurement* 14(2):97-116.

Yuker, H. E., Block, O. R., and Young, J. H. (1970) *The Measurement of Attitudes Toward Disabled Persons*. Albertson, New York: INA Mend Institute.

APPENDIX **A**

# The Effects of Knowing Someone is Handicapped on Decision Making: A Review of the Literature*

SAMUEL L. GUSKIN

Federal law and our beliefs in equal opportunity require that decisions on educational admissions and employee selection be unbiased. People with handicapping conditions must not be denied admission to schools or employment positions because they are members of a particular group or class. One way to enforce this principle is to deny access to information on group membership to decision makers. This approach may be feasible when decisions are made largely on the basis of established credentials that provide objective data, such as test scores, high school grades, employment experience, and educational background. In these cases, such potentially biasing information as age, sex, race, disability, and religion can be deleted from application forms. This solution to the problem assumes that, if decision makers know the particular characteristic of a person, in our case, that a person has a handicapping condition, then the decision will be biased against the person. This paper reviews the published literature relating to that hypothesized biasing effect.

What kind of theory and research is relevant to this problem? Sociological and social psychological writers and investigators have been interested in such topics as bias, prejudice, and stereotypes for over 50 years (see, for example, Rice 1926). In more recent work

*This literature review was drawn from a larger paper by the author commissioned by the Panel on Testing of Handicapped People.

over the past 15 years, psychologists and educators have become interested in the effects of expectations in the laboratory (Rosenthal 1976) and in the school (Dusek 1975), sociologists have been examining the consequences of labeling someone as deviant (Schurr 1971), and personnel selection researchers have become concerned with interviewer bias against women and minority group members (Arvey 1979a,b). There is also a considerable body of literature on bias in testing (Jensen 1980) and in selective admissions in higher education (Carnegie Council on Policy Studies in Higher Education 1977). Finally, in the past few years cognitive psychologists have provided new approaches to deal with the classification and integration of information that bears directly on how stereotypes about groups are formulated and what their consequences are (Hamilton 1979). Because of the scope and size of the potentially relevant works, this review is highly selective and draws most heavily on those studies deemed most critical.

In addition to the larger body of relevant work outlined above, research and theory dealing specifically with reactions to the handicapped are accumulating (Bartel and Guskin 1980). Topics include attitudes and stereotypes (Gottlieb 1975a,b, Jones 1980, Yuker et al. 1970), reactions to integration (Semmel et al. 1979), labeling and bias (Guskin 1978, MacMillan et al. 1974, Rains et al. 1975), and the presumed negative consequences of knowing that individuals are handicapped (Hobbs 1975 a,b).

## FOCUSING ON THE DECISION-MAKING PROCESS

As Arvey (1979b) has pointed out, stereotypes may influence a decision in three ways: (1) their general negative effect may lead directly to rejection; (2) the content of the group stereotype may be inconsistent with the occupational stereotype or job expectations; (3) the stereotype may lead the decision maker to use a different set of criteria or standards in evaluating the applicant. To illustrate each of these influences, (1) attitudes toward the mentally ill may be very negative, leading to few job offers; (2) expectations regarding the mentally retarded may lead employers to select them for unskilled but not skilled jobs; (3) the blind applicant for college who has high school diploma but was in the bottom half of the class may be admitted to college because even this marginal performance is seen as a sign that the individual is highly motivated and intelligent whereas a sighted person with the same credentials would be judged inadequate.

As Arvey (1979b) points out, interviewers may also become biased as a result of differential behavior on the part of the interviewee that leads to discomfort or misinterpretations by the interviewer. Thus, interviewers may experience tension in interviewing a candidate with a speech defect and therefore may attribute poor social or intellectual skills to the applicant. In the case in which decisions are based on written documents rather than interviews, the same phenomenon may appear in letters of reference from those with only superficial contacts with the applicant, whose discomfort is conveyed in the letter.

We have seen, then, how information about handicaps may lead to negative outcomes and also how positive effects may be obtained. What evidence is there that these actually occur?

## EMPIRICAL FINDINGS ON THE EFFECTS OF KNOWING SOMEONE IS HANDICAPPED

### Stereotypes and Attitudes About the Handicapped

In this type of study, interviews, questionnaires, or other paper-and-pencil instruments are employed to obtain answers to such questions as: What do you think a typical mentally ill person would be like? How willing would you be to have each of the following people as a roommate: epileptic, amputee, athlete, delinquent? . . . Would you be willing to employ a disabled worker? In all of these cases, the respondent is given almost no information about the person except the handicap, and even that information is usually a popular label rather than a clear picture of the handicapping condition. In addition, these studies usually involve a forced choice situation. That is, the person may choose which answer to give but may not indicate that he feels he had inadequate information to make a judgment. Under these conditions, it is not surprising that reactions to the handicapped are less favorable than to the nonhandicapped and that there is a hierarchy of preferences for handicaps (Yuker et al. 1970, Jones 1980).

We may illustrate a study of stereotypes by examining some of the findings of Gottwald's (1970) national public opinion survey on public information about mental retardation. On one part of the survey, respondents were asked to describe a "mentally retarded" person and a "normal" person on a series of 16 bipolar adjective scales. The retarded person was seen more negatively than the normal person on each of the 16 scales. The largest differences were on insane-sane, useless-useful, sick-healthy, and ignorant-educated. The smallest differences were on the adjective pairs ugly-beautiful, cruel-kind, dishonest-honest, immoral-moral and unhappy-happy. These results are consistent with earlier data on smaller and less representative samples (e.g., Guskin 1963a,b), which have also found that mental retardation is associated by others with incompetence and mental illness and is seen as very different from delinquency.

An illustration of an attitude study that provides evidence on a hierarchy of handicaps is found in an investigation by Shears and Jensema (1969), who first asked 94 normal adults to rank 10 "anomalies" in terms of perceived severity and then had them indicate their degree of acceptance of each condition on a series of situations varying in "social distance" from "would marry" to "would live in the same country." In both severity and willingness to accept people with the condition, the most positive reactions were to the amputee, blind, and wheelchair conditions; intermediate reactions were to the harelip, stutterer, and deaf-mute conditions; there was a more negative reaction to the cerebral palsied; and the most unfavorable reactions were to the mentally ill, retarded, and homosexual conditions. The most relevant findings for this paper are those that indicate how willing respondents would be to work with each type of person. Approximately 90 percent say they would work with those who were amputees, in wheelchairs, or blind; most would work with those with a harelip (80%), stutterers (74%) or deaf-mutes (67%); only half would work with the cerebral palsied; and far fewer would work with the mentally ill (37%), retarded (30%), or homosexual (27%).

A variant of this approach that is more relvant to the issue at hand is the investigation of employers' ratings of employment acceptability. Rickard and colleagues (1963) studied 105 personnel directors and school administrators and reported that former tuberculosis patients were preferred, followed by wheelchair handicapped, then deaf people; epileptics were the least preferred. A similar study (Nikoloff 1962) asked 197 principals to evaluate the employability of handicapped people as teachers. Blind or deaf people were judged to be less employable than those with a speech handicap, who were in turn less employable than those with an artificial leg or crutch.

## The Influence of Handicap Labels on Evaluation of Individuals

The second category of studies attempts to test explicitly the assumption that stereotypes and attitudes do in fact affect the way we react to others. Subjects are asked to make ratings after they are presented information about an individual with or without indicating that the individual is handicapped. The other information may be presented in a verbal sketch (e.g., Guskin 1963b, Jaffe 1966, Cook and Wollersheim 1976, Herson 1974, Kirk 1974) or videotape (Budoff and Siperstein 1978, Gottlieb 1974, 1975a, Guskin 1962b, Loman and Larkin 1976, Seitz and Gesky 1977). The videotape may be of a trained nonhandicapped actor (e.g., Gottlieb 1974, 1975a) or of the unrehearsed behavior of a handicapped individual (e.g., Guskin 1962a,b). Furthermore, the sketches or tapes may be structured or selected to vary systematically with the behavior of the individual.

Two investigations by Gottlieb (1974, 1975a) illustrate this paradigm. In the first study (Gottlieb 1974), elementary school children judged a child observed on a videotape as performing either competently or incompetently on a spelling task. The observed child was described either as a fifth-grade pupil or as being enrolled in a special class for retarded children. The observed child was actually the same on both tapes and had been instructed to perform competently for the "competent" segment. The study was carried out in two schools, one middle-class and one lower-class. The label did *not* have an effect on either school, and only in the middle-class school did the competence manipulation result in differential judgments.

In the second investigation (Gottlieb 1975a), the design was similar but the videotapes varied in aggressive behavior. The same child was shown either playing quietly with clay at his desk or "acting out" with it: throwing the clay on the floor, stomping on it, banging it with his fist. This time the retarded label and the aggressiveness—and the interaction of the two variables—had significant effects on children's judgments: when the observed aggressiveness and retarded label were combined, the judgments (ratings and social distance measures) were substantially more negative than could be predicted from the separate effects of each variable. One interpretation of these findings is that judges tend to "normalize" when the data is not fully convincing, interpreting the verbal or behavioral information as possibly normal. However, the combination of the two negative pieces of information pushes the judge over the threshold for perceiving the child as deviant.

Gottlieb's two studies (1974, 1975a) illustrate the diversity of findings of studies in this area. Handicapping information may lead to more negative evaluations, but the effect is highly dependent on other information presented about the individual. Positive information will tend to neutralize the stereotype while negative information may be accentuated by the stereotype. Of course, if the other information is unambiguously negative, the stereotype may even result in more favorable judgments (Golin 1970).

## Judgments of Resumes

One highly relevant variant of the above approach presents subjects with simulated job resumes with or without labeling information and instructs them to rate the suitability of the applicant for employment and/or an appropriate salary offer. Studies using this method to examine bias resulting from race, sex, or age information as well as handicaps are summarized by Arvey (1979b). Studies using this paradigm with handicap labels have been reported by Krefting and Brief (1977), Rose and Brief (1979), and Shaw (1972).

The Shaw (1972) study was designed to examine the differential effects of negative stereotypes on evaluation of candidates for different occupations. The stereotyping information was either gender (male or female), state of financial and domestic affairs (married or divorced and having personal financial problems), or physical health (no problem specified or 4-F, a withered arm, and weak vision requiring glasses). Subjects were 132 college recruiters, roughly half of whom were seeking science and engineering graduates and half seeking management trainees. They were given resumes with photographs, and half were randomly given variants of the resumes that included one of the three types of stereotyping information. Since the major interest of the author was in the difference between the two occupations in the stereotyping effect, they never did test the biasing effect itself but only the occupational impact on the effect. There was no differential effect of occupation when the candidate had a physical health problem. However, the author presented descriptive data and noted that the health problem led to more positive ratings on an adjective check list than did the control condition. The differences were smaller and less consistent when subjects were asked to make ratings relative to hiring the candidate, but there was clearly no trend to reject the handicapped applicant.

Krefting and Brief (1977) examined the effects of applicant disability and work experience on judgments of a set of application materials by 145 college students. The position applied for was a typist's position, and all of the information provided was positive in tone, indicating the candidate was qualified. Under the disability condition, the applicant was indicated to be confined to a wheelchair due to an automobile accident. A physician's report stated that the applicant "is a paraplegic confined to a wheelchair, but her condition has been stable for over four years. She has adjusted well to her condition and lets it interfere as little as possible with her activities." Disability information did have a negative effect on rated potential for promotion (and on rated health), but it had a positive effect on ratings of work motivation and potential for staying. It had no effect on other evaluation criteria (for example, ability, potential for quality output, potential for quantity output, potential for absenteeism, potential for tardiness, potential for getting along with others). On overall rating of the applicant, no main effect of disability was found, but there was significant interaction between disability and experiences. While the disabled applicant without experience was preferred to the inexperienced nondisabled, when both applicants were experienced, the nondisabled was preferred. (Another way of describing the finding is that among the disabled, the inexperienced applicant was somewhat preferred; for the nondisabled, the experienced applicant was highly preferred.) This result was contrary to the authors' expectations that there would be a generally negative reaction to the disabled but that this would be counteracted by experience. A related interaction that may explain the overall ratings is that on potential for staying. For the nondisabled, those with experience are seen as more likely to stay than the inexperienced; for the disabled, the inexperienced are seen as more likely to stay.

Rose and Brief (1979) compared the effects of two types of disability (epileptic and amputee) on evaluations of candidates for jobs varying in degree of public contact and degree of supervisory responsibility. As in the previous study, the applicant was described as highly qualified in the simulated application materials and the disability was described as under control and not influencing job performance. Ratings were made on a series of employment-related scales by 211 advanced business administration students, and a judgment was made about whether the applicant should be hired. The effects of the disability were examined on 11 measures. The only negative effect of disability was a lower salary rating for the amputee than for the epileptic or nondisabled. Positive effects of disability were found when comparing the epileptic condition with the control on satisfactory relationship with clients and customers and working well with other employees. The authors point out that their positive findings may be limited to the case where clients are described as highly qualified.

These findings on judgments of resumes are even less supportive of a negative stereotyping effect of handicap information than the studies involving verbal descriptions or videotapes. Perhaps the incorporation in the resume studies of information describing positive qualities that are directly relevant to employment leads to a discounting of negative stereotypes.

### Field Experiments Examining the Effects of Handicap Information

A few investigations go beyond the simulation of decision making to observe what behavior occurs when handicap information is provided or withheld in a naturalistic environment. In a series of studies, Kleck has examined the effect of a simulated disability (amputee in wheelchair) on the way others interact both verbally and nonverbally with the person (Kleck 1975).

In one investigation (Kleck et al. 1966) in which the "amputee" was an interviewer, it was found that there was greater physiological arousal (GSR) when interacting with the amputee than when interacting with a nondisabled interviewer; shorter answers were given to questions from the amputee than from the nondisabled; and the person interviewed expressed more frequent conformity to the interviewer's presumed beliefs when the latter was an amputee. The results suggest greater anxiety or tension and less "naturalness" when interacting with a disabled person.

In a second study, Kleck (1968) filmed the behavior of the subject being interviewed and had him rate the interviewer. Kleck found more favorable impressions of the disabled interviewer than the nondisabled, less movement in the presence of the disabled, and less variation in focus of visual attention when being interviewed by the amputee. As in the earlier study, opinions were distorted in the direction of that of the amputee. These findings also imply less freedom or more tension when interacting with the disabled.

In a third study (Kleck 1969), the nondisabled person was asked to train two other people in Origami (oriental paper folding) after being trained herself. One of the people she trained was an "amputee"; both were confederates of the experimenter. The training sessions were monitored by a hidden television camera. Kleck measured the distance between the trainer and her student and found that the average distance was less with the "normal" than the "disabled" person. This effect occurred, however, only in the first teaching session, not the second. Similarly, a difference in impressions, which favored the amputee, occurred only after the first and not the second session. Finally, disabled learners in both sessions were rated as more interested and motivated in the learning task. As in the first two investigations, verbal statements by the nondisabled seemed to be biased in favor of the disabled but nonverbal measures suggested less comfort with the disabled. The third study adds the suggestive finding that some of the differences diminish after a period of time.

A series of studies by Jones (1968) examined the influence of the presence of a simulated "blind" person on the performance of other people on a learning task. While there was no observable influence on the learning task, subjects said their performance was impaired as a result of interaction with the blind person.

Farina and his associates have conducted a related series of investigations. Farina and Ring (1965) examined the influence of interaction with a presumed mentally ill person on performance on a cooperative game. Both people were naive subjects but none, one, or both were privately informed that the other was mentally ill. It was found that perceiving the coworker as mentally ill enhanced performance. However, when the coworker was perceived as mentally ill, subjects preferred to work alone; they also tended to blame the mentally ill partner for inadequacies in their joint performance. The results make clear that discomfort may accompany improved performance under certain conditions.

Although a number of studies have manipulated information in teaching situations, modeled on the well-known and highly criticized expectancy study by Rosenthal and Jacobson (1968), the emphasis in these studies has generally been on measuring outcomes for learners, and the findings have usually been disappointing (Dusek 1975). Furthermore, few of these studies have involved the handicapped, and even fewer have manipulated information about the handicap (as opposed to information about general potential).

Guskin (1978) summarized the expectancy findings as they relate to mental retardation. It appears that while real differences in ability can influence the behavior of those who interact with the retarded, it is more difficult to demonstrate effects of artificially induced beliefs about competence level on interaction. One exception to the generally negative findings on this topic is provided by Farina and colleagues (1976). College students were asked to participate in an experiment at a state training school, supposedly to determine what kind of students worked best with what kind of residents. Students were told they would meet someone who was either mentally retarded, mentally ill, or normal. The person they actually met was a confederate of the experimenter. The interaction was a pair of learning tasks, in the first of which the student was to administer shocks when the learner made errors. The major behavioral measures were the magnitude and the duration of shocks administered. (These were not actually received by the confederates.) It was found that mentally retarded confederates were administered *less* intense shocks and of *less* duration than either the "mentally ill" or "normal" confederates. There was also a significant interaction between the confederate and the label. One of the four confederates was administered longer shocks as the mentally retarded than in both of the other conditions.

Thus the behavioral findings of this study indicate that the mentally retarded label can have a differential effect on the performance of others and that the effect appears to be supportive, at least in this type of learning situation where less may be expected of the retarded. The differential effects of the characteristics of particular "retarded" individuals on others' reactions is also of interest, since some retarded individuals may actually elicit more punitive responses as a result of the label. Overall, then, these interaction experiments suggest highly varied outcomes of thinking someone is handicapped, depending on whether what is measured is nonverbal or verbal or task performance and on the interactive demands of the situation.

### Reactions to Interaction with Handicapped Job Applicants

In an extension of their studies of reactions to mentally ill people, Farina and his associates have carried out a series of investigations of workers' evaluations of former mental patients following job interviews. In each study, workers were told that management was exploring the use of fellow workers to carry out job interviews and evaluate candidates and was also interested in the job potential of former mental patients. Before each interview, the worker was told that the applicant either was or was not a former mental patient. The applicant was the same for all interviews in each substudy and varied from study to study in gender. The type of worker—including hospital workers, department store employees, and university physical plant employees—varied from study to study, but all were considered to fall within the lower socioeconomic classes. In addition to varying the information about hospitalization for mental illness, the interviews also varied in the behavior displayed by the applicant. For half of the interviewers in each study, the applicant portrayed calm, relaxed behavior; for the other half, the applicant portrayed nervous, tense behavior. In all of the studies, this behavioral difference resulted in significant effects in that the more nervous applicant was seen much less favorably. The findings were much less consistent for the information about mental illness. Generally, male workers rejected former mental patients and women accepted them, and male former patients were more rejected than females. Since the earlier studies involved same-sex applicants and interviewers (Farina et al. 1973), subsequent investigations (Farina and Hagelauer 1975, Farina et. al. 1978) examined variations in both applicant and interviewer sex. It was found that women accepted both male and female former mental patients but that men reacted differently, depending on the applicant's gender, showing very weak biasing effects for women but dramatically negative reactions to male former mental patients.

One of the limitations of the above series of studies is that these interviewers were not normally involved in making personnel decisions. In another study (Farina and Felner 1973), a confederate of the experimenters obtained 32 job interviews in manufacturing firms, indicating in half of these that he had been in mental hospital for the previous nine months and in the other half that he had been traveling for the same period of time. The interviews were surreptitiously recorded and subsequently analyzed for probability of getting a job and interviewer friendliness. The actual number of jobs offered either immediately or subsequently by telephone was two for the former patient condition and four for the control condition. Obviously, the numbers are too small to demonstrate significant effects. However, on the rated probability of getting a job and friendliness of interviewer, the former mental patient was rated significantly lower than the control.

Johnson and Heal (1976) had an applicant approach 50 employment agencies looking for a job as a receptionist-typist. She appeared for half of the interviews in a wheelchair. She was offered fewer future job interviews when handicapped and was generally discouraged by the interviewers.

Unlike the previous studies, each of which had a single person as the applicant in all job interviews, Brand and Claiborn (1976) had six trained college students apply for a total of 36 advertised retail sales jobs, presenting themselves as former convicts, former mental patients, or former tuberculosis patients. Although the presented work history was marginal, approximately two thirds of the applicants were offered positions regardless of the stigmatizing conditions. No significant differences appeared among the three conditions. The authors attributed the findings to the verbal and social skills of the applicants in the interview situation.

Taking together the three studies of actual job interviews and studies of worker interviews of former mental patients, it appears that handicap information may bias some kinds of interviewers against certain types of applicants, but that this negative effect is by no means inevitable.

## SUMMARY AND DISCUSSION OF EMPIRICAL STUDIES

What can we make of the diverse set of findings reported and their inconsistency with the commonly described bias against handicapped people? First, the studies indicate that when people know only the handicap, they react negatively to it, and the strength of the reaction varies greatly by the nature and severity of the handicap.

Second, information about handicap may influence judgments of a hypothetical person presented in verbal sketches or of an observed individual presented on videotape. Although negative effects have been demonstrated, they are highly dependent on the particular features of the person that are not related to the handicap. In many instances no differences are found, and occasionally positive effects of handicap labels are obtained. In the special case in which the information was presented as a set of application materials for a job, three studies found either a slight positive effect or mixed positive and negative effects, depending on the applicant's experience, the specific disability, and the particular judgment being made.

Finally, where investigators have examined what happens in situations in which other people interact with the handicapped individual, interpersonal behavior appears to be influenced by the handicap, showing that the other person is uncomfortable and attributes the discomfort to the handicapped person. Behaviors, however, may be protective rather than negative. In those investigations in which the interaction involves a handicapped job applicant, findings are mixed, depending on the sex of the applicant and the interviewer as well as other unspecified factors.

Can we say any more than "it depends—that handicapping information may or may not influence decisions but that we cannot predict its effect in any specific situation because there are too many other variables that may influence the effect?" Why are these findings not fully supportive of reports of widespread difficulty experienced by handicapped people in obtaining jobs (e.g., Nagi et al. 1972)?

One clue comes from Farina's series of studies in which the job applicant's nervousness was manipulated for half of the candidates who were controls and half of those who were supposedly former mental patients. Nervousness consistently resulted in rejection, although the label had mixed effects. Apparently, when applicants demonstrate confidence and social skills in the interview, this often overcomes any resistance that might be established by the handicap. Similarly, in the studies by Gottlieb (1974, 1975a,b), and Yoshida and Meyers (1975), competence was recognized and the label "mentally retarded" was ignored. It may be that handicapped applicants are less likely to present themselves in a way that establishes their competence, in other words, more like the nervous candidate in Farina's studies. Another study by Farina and his associates (1971) demonstrates that mental patients were more likely to be tense and perform poorly in a situation in which they thought the other person knew they were mentally ill. It may be that a lack of confidence and competence in job interviews is also common among nonhandicapped individuals with a recent history of unemployment.

Another possible explanation is that most of the handicapped people seeking jobs are men, and most employment interviewers are men—conditions that Farina's studies suggest are least favorable for handicapped people. In addition, many of the less severely handicapped people may not have observable handicaps and may choose to "pass" as nonhandicapped, thereby depressing the "success rate" for research purposes and also giving employers no reason to change their perceptions of handicapped people.

How relevant are these findings to formal decision making, where the candidate is not met and the applicant is judged largely on the basis of objective data, such as test scores? First, most of the experimental studies do not involve interaction with the candidate but require judges to rate or make decisions on the basis of verbal descriptions or resumes, and, therefore, seem relevant. Second, ratings based on interviews may have the same status before the law as do test scores (Arvey, 1979a,b) and their appropriateness may be challenged if they result in disproportionate rejection of applicants who are handicapped, and if they cannot be demonstrated to be otherwise valid.

It should be noted that very little, if any, bias was found in the studies that used resumes. The characterization of the applicant in the materials was positive in each study, and in none of the studies did the decision maker assume that the judgment would lead to actual employment or rejection of an applicant. This may limit the applicability of the findings to the "real world" of formal decision making.

## CONCLUSIONS

1. Knowledge that someone is handicapped, in the absence of other exposure to or information about the person, is likely to lead

to less positive evaluations than if the person did not have a handicapping condition.

2. These evaluations will vary with the severity and nature of the handicap.

3. When other information is known about a person, knowledge of a handicap will have less impact than when other information is absent.

4. Depending on the nature of both the other information and the handicapping knowledge, the effects of the latter may be nil, small or large, positive or negative.

a. Where the other information is positive and inconsistent with a stereotype (e.g., a blind high school senior in the upper half of his regular high school class), the handicap will not result in a more negative evaluation and may, by its contrast with the stereotype, lead to a more positive evaluation than for a nonhandicapped person with the same "other" characteristics.

b. Where the other information is ambiguous or somewhat negative, the handicap information may either accentuate the negative evaluations or decrease them (e.g., a below-average SAT score may be seen as accountable by the special difficulty faced by a blind student taking an oral or braille version of the test).

5. Empirical data on these effects (in #4) are limited both in number and in representativeness of natural conditions. Most relevant studies are simulations using college students and paper-and-pencil measures.

6. Formal decisions in "real life" are more heavily constrained by other factors, such as the proportion of all applicants who can be (or must be) hired and formal decision rules about minimal academic records and requirements and minimal test scores.

7. Decisions about handicapped people are also influenced by the desire to be fair, to be consistent with regulations, and to appear just and equitable.

8. Although the avoidance of negative bias is, of course, the primary concern, positive discrimination in admissions or employment may have even more serious negative consequences for handicapped people if they are placed in a situation in which they are likely to fail.

## REFERENCES

Arvey, R. D. (1979a) *Fairness in Selecting Employees.* Reading, Mass.: Addison-Wesley.

Arvey, R. D. (1979b) Unfair discrimination in the employment interview. *Psychological Bulletin* 86:736-765.

Bartel, N. R., and Guskin, S. L. (1980) A handicap as a social phenomenon. In W. Cruickshank, ed., *Psychology of Exceptional Children*, 4th ed. Englewood Cliffs, N.J.: Prentice-Hall.

Brand, R. C., and Claiborn, W. L. (1976) Two studies in comparative stigma: Employer attitudes and practices toward rehabilitated convicts, mental and tuberculosis patients. *Community Mental Health Journal* 12:168-175.

Budoff, M., and Siperstein, G. N. (1978) Low income children's attitudes toward mentally retarded children: Effects of labeling and academic behavior. *American Journal of Mental Deficiency* 82:474-479.

Carnegie Council on Policy Studies in Higher Education (1977) *Selective Admissions in Higher Education*. San Francisco, Calif.: Jossey-Bass.

Cook, J. W., and Wollersheim, J. P. (1976) The effects of labeling of special education students on the perceptions of contact versus noncontact peers. *Journal of Special Education* 10:187-198.

Dusek, J. B. (1975) Do teachers bias children's learning? *Review of Educational Research* 45:661-684.

Farina, A., and Felner, R. D. (1973) Employment interviewer reactions to former mental patients. *Journal of Abnormal Psychology* 82:268-272.

Farina, A., Felner, R. D., and Boudreau, L. A. (1973) Reactions of workers to male and female mental patient job applicants. *Journal of Consulting and Clinical Psychology* 41:363-372.

Farina, A., Gliha, D., Boudreau, L. A., Allen, J. B., and Sherman, M. (1971) Mental illness and the impact of believing others know about it. *Journal of Abnormal Psychology* 77:1-5.

Farina, A., and Hagelauer, H. D. (1975) Sex and mental illness: The generosity of females. *Journal of Consulting and Clinical Psychology* 43:122.

Farina, A., Murray, P. J., and Groh, T. (1978) Sex and worker acceptance of a former mental patient. *Journal of Consulting and Clinical Psychology* 46:887-891.

Farina, A., and Ring, K. (1965) The influence of perceived mental illness on interpersonal relations. *Journal of Abnormal Psychology* 70:47-51.

Farina, A., Thaw, J., Felner, R. D., and Hust, B. E. (1976) Some interpersonal consequences of being mentally ill or mentally retarded. *American Journal of Mental Deficiency* 80:414-422.

Golin, A. K. (1970) Stimulus variables in the measurement of attitudes towards disability. *Rehabilitation Counseling Bulletin* 14:20-26.

Gottlieb, J. (1974) Attitudes toward retarded children: Effects of labeling and academic performance. *American Journal of Mental Deficiency* 79:268-273.

Gottlieb, J. (1975a) Attitudes toward retarded children: Effects of labeling and behavioral aggressiveness. *Journal of Educational Psychology* 67:581-585.

Gottlieb, J. (1975b) Public, peer and professional attitudes toward mentally retarded persons. Pp. 99-125 in M. J. Begab and S. A. Richardson, eds., *The Mentally Retarded and Society: A Social Science Perspective*, Baltimore, Md.: University Park Press.

Gottwald, H. (1970) Public awareness about mental retardation. Research Monograph. Reston, Va.: Council for Exceptional Children.

Guskin, S. L. (1962a) The influence of labeling upon the perception of subnormality in mentally defective children. *American Journal of Mental Deficiency* 67:402-406.

Guskin, S. L. (1962b) The perception of subnormality in mentally defective children. *American Journal of Mental Deficiency* 67:53-60.

Guskin, S. L. (1963a) Dimensions of judged similarity among deviant types. *American Journal of Mental Deficiency* 68:218-224.

Guskin, S. L. (1963b) Measuring the strength of the stereotype of the mental defective. *American Journal of Mental Deficiency* 67:569-575.

Guskin, S. L. (1978) Theoretical and empirical strategies for the study of the labeling of mentally retarded persons. Pp. 127-158 in N. R. Ellis, ed., *International Review of Research in Mental Retardation*, Vol. 9. New York: Academic Press.

Hamilton, D. L. (1979) A cognitive-attributional analysis of stereotyping. Pp. 53-84 in L. Berkowitz, ed., *Advances in Experimental Social Psychology*, Vol. 12. New York: Academic Press.

Herson, P. F. (1974) Biasing effects of diagnostic labels and sex of pupil on teachers' views of pupils' mental health. *Journal of Educational Psychology* 66:117-122.

Hobbs, N., ed. (1975a) *Issues in the Classification of Children*, Vol. 1,2. San Francisco, Calif.: Jossey-Bass.

Hobbs, N. (1975b) *The Futures of Children: Categories, Labels, and Their Consequences*. San Francisco, Calif.: Jossey-Bass.

Jaffe, J. (1966) Attitudes of adolescents toward the mentally retarded. *American Journal of Mental Deficiency* 70:907-912.

Jensen, A. R. (1980) *Bias in Mental Testing*. New York: Free Press.

Johnson, R., and Heal, L. W. (1976) Private employment agency responses to the physically handicapped applicant in a wheelchair. *Journal of Applied Rehabilitation Counseling* 7:12-21.

Jones, R. L. (1968) Cognitive functioning in the presence of the disabled. Paper presented at the meeting of the American Psychological Association.

Jones, R. L. (1980) *Attitudes and Attitude Change in Special Education*. Minneapolis, Minn.: University of Minnesota National Support Systems Project.

Kirk, S. A. (1974) The impact of labeling on rejection of the mentally ill: An experimental study. *Journal of Health and Social Behavior* 15:108-117.

Kleck, R. (1968) Physical stigma and nonverbal cues emitted in face-to-face interactions. *Human Relations* 21:19-28.

Kleck, R. (1969) Physical stigma and task-oriented interactions. *Human Relations* 22:53-60.Kleck, R. (1975) Issues in social effectiveness: The case of the mentally retarded. Pp. 181-195 in M. J. Begab and S. A. Richardson, *The Mentally Retarded and Society: A Social Science Perspective*. Baltimore; Md.: University Park Press.

Kleck, R., Ono, H., and Hastorf, A. H. (1966) The effects of physical deviance upon face-to-face interaction. *Human Relations* 19:425-436.

Krefting, L. A., and Brief, A. P. (1977) The impact of applicant disability on evaluative judgments in the selection process. *Academy of Management Journal* 19:675-680.

Loman, L. A., and Larkin, W. E. (1976) Rejection of the mentally ill: An experiment in labeling. *Sociological Quarterly* 17:555-560.

MacMillan, D. L., Jones, R. L., and Aloia, G. F. (1974) The mentally retarded label: A theoretical analysis and review of research. *American Journal of Mental Deficiency* 79:241-261.

Nagi, S., McBroom, W. H., and Colletts, J. (1972) Work employment and the disabled. *American Journal of Economics and Society* 31:20-34.

Nickoloff, O. M., II. (1962) Attitudes of public school principals toward employment of teachers with certain physical disabilities. *Rehabilitation Literature* 23(11):344-345.

Rains, P. M., Kitsuse, J. I., Duster, T., and Freidson, E. (1975) The labeling approach to deviance. Pp. 88-100 in N. Hobbs, ed., *Issues in the Classification of Children*, Vol. 1. San Francisco, Calif.: Jossey-Bass.

Rice, S. A. (1926) Stereotypes: A source of error in judging human character. *Journal of Personnel Research* 5:268-276.

Rickard, T. E., Triandis, H. C., and Patterson, C. H. (1963) Indices of employer prejudice toward disabled applicants. *Journal of Applied Psychology* 47:52-55.

Rose, G. L., and Brief, A. P. (1979) Effects of handicap and job characteristics on selection evaluations. *Personnel Psychology* 32:385-392.

Rosenthal, R. (1976) *Experimenter Effects in Behavioral Research,* Enlarged Edition. New York: Irvington.

Rosenthal, R., and Jacobson, L. (1968) *Pygmalion in the Classroom.* New York: Holt, Rinehart, and Winston.

Schurr, E. M. (1971) *Labeling Deviant Behavior: Its Sociological Implications.* Englewood Cliffs, N.J.: Prentice-Hall.

Seitz, S., and Gesky, D. (1977) Mother's and graduate trainee's judgments of children: Some effects of labeling. *American Journal of Mental Deficiency* 81:362-370.

Semmel, M. I., Gottlieb, J., and Robinson, N. M. (1979) Mainstreaming: Perspectives on educating handicapped children in the public schools. Pp. 223-279 in D. C. Berliner, ed., *Review of Research in Education,* Vol. 7. Washington, D.C.: American Educational Research Association.

Shaw, E. A. (1972) Differential impact of negative stereotyping in employee selection. *Personnel Selection* 25:333-338.

Shears, L. M., and Jensema, C. J. (1969) Social acceptability of anomalous persons. *Exceptional Children* 36:91-96.

Yoshida, R. K., and Meyers, C. E. (1975) Effects of labeling as educable mentally retarded on teachers' expectancies for change in a student's performance. *Journal of Educational Psychology* 67:521-527.

Yuker, H. E., Block, O. R., and Young, J. H. (1970) *The Measurement of Attitudes Toward Disabled Persons.* Albertson, N.Y.: INA Mend Institute.

APPENDIX **B**

# Testing of Handicapped People: Summary Proceedings of an Open Meeting, March 14-15, 1980

The Panel on Testing of Handicapped People held an open meeting as part of its study of current practices in the testing and assessment of people with various handicapping conditions, the nature of the selection process as encountered by handicapped individuals who seek employment or educational opportunities, and the extent to which handicapped people are participating in our schools and work force. The panel conducted the meeting to provide interested groups and individuals the opportunity to present their views and supply pertinent data. The meeting was held on March 14-15, 1980, at the National Academy of Sciences.

Participants were asked to submit written testimony prior to the meeting and were urged to share with the panel copies of any studies on the assessment and selection of people with various handicaps, the participation of handicapped people in education and employment, and alternatives to conventional testing that are especially suitable for handicapped people. A list of people and organizations invited to contribute to the meeting is attached; those who spoke at the meeting or submitted material are so designated.

## TEST DEVELOPERS

Several test developers, both profit-making and nonprofit organizations, presented material to the panel. The U.S. Office of Personnel Management (OPM) also presented information on test development, but since their procedures have unique characteristics, they will be discussed separately. The major test developers are best known for their tests used for educational selection and placement; however, two of the three organizations also develop tests for employment selection as well as certification and licensure.

The American College Testing Program (ACT) reports that in each of several recent years 11,000 of their 1,000,000 test takers say they will require some accommodation (presumably because of a handicapping condition) on the college campus, but only 1,000 take the ACT in modified form. The Educational Testing Service (ETS) reports that in 1978-79 about 2,500 of their 1,000,000 test takers took the Scholastic Aptitude Test (SAT) in modified form. ETS has no record of those handicapped examinees who take the SAT under standard conditions. While the Psychological Corporation publishes tests used in educational, medical, and employment settings, their test of major interest to the panel is the Miller Analogies Test, which is used along with other information to make decisions regarding admissions to graduate schools. The Psychological Corporation has no available data on the numbers of handicapped people who take that test. In their score reports to test users, all three test developers note those scores that resulted from a nonstandard administration of a test.

The major activity of test developers in accommodating the needs of handicapped examinees is modifying the test administration procedures, with some attention being given to culling out (or modifying) test items that are inappropriate for a given handicapping condition. Modifications of testing procedures include extended time limits, printing of the test in large type or braille, recording of the test on cassettes, printing of large answer sheets, and provision for the use of a reader or an amanuensis. Some tests administered to the deaf may have reduced emphasis on verbal ability. Not all altered formats or procedures are available for all testing programs. The selection of which to make available appears to depend on the judged appropriateness of the modifications for the particular test and predicted activity as well as on economic considerations. Good adaptations require keen awareness of ramifications of a variety of handicapping conditions as well as considerable sophistication in test development.

Only one of the three private test developers who testified had at that time conducted validation studies for handicapped examinees alone. ACT has studied the performance of handicapped students who took the ACT on a national test date, that is, who took the test without modification. (Since that time ETS has also undertaken studies of the predictive validity of the SAT for some handicapped students.) ACT found the test predicted first-year college grades as well for those handicapped examinees as for the nonhandicapped; however, this study leaves unanswered the question of how well various modifications of a test predict later performance. Test developers say they have conducted no such studies because of the small numbers of students with the same handicap entering the same institution in the same year. ACT reports that only 13 colleges requiring the ACT had enrolled 75 or more handicapped students in a recent three-year period. ETS has suggested a strategy that may allow for the pooling of students in different schools for the purpose of conducting predictive validity studies. ETS has also suggested that studies of construct validity might be possible where studies of predictive validity are precluded by small sample sizes. There have been no studies to estimate the magnitude of score differences expected as a result of different test administration procedures.

## FEDERAL GOVERNMENT

The Office of Personnel Management (OPM) reported on the changes in test administration methods and test content to accommodate handicapped people in the Professional and Administrative Career Examination (PACE). OPM offers considerable flexibility in test administration methods to handicapped examinees. Time limits have been set empirically for each test part and each type of modification. OPM has done extensive work in changing the content of a test to measure the intended abilities. Their work falls into four categories: (1) deleting single items and substituting more appropriate items to measure the same ability, (2) modifying items to better measure the intended ability, (3) deleting all items of one type and substituting another item type to measure the ability, and (4) deleting all items to test an ability and therefore not measuring that ability.

In modifying its tests OPM uses experts who are knowledgeable about specific handicaps, as do other test developers. OPM also compiles and uses considerable information on the psychometric characteristics of its items and tests. Tests for handicapped competitors are statistically "equated" with those for nonhandicapped competitors; that is, they are made to have approximately the same mean, standard deviation, and distribution of scores. OPM uses measures of construct validity rather than predictive validity, thereby being able to estimate the validity of a test as modified in a particular way. Scores obtained by handicapped people are not flagged but are used in the same manner as those of nonhandicapped competitors.

Representatives from the Bureau of Education for the Handicapped (BEH) outlined its role in administering P.L. 94-142, the Education for All Handicapped Children Act, with particular emphasis on aspects relating to assessment of handicapped children. BEH has funded several research projects on testing of handicapped people and is concerned with issues such as the following: How can existing tests be modified for appropriate use with the handicapped? What interpretations of results of modified tests are warranted? How can handicapped people be treated fairly in minimum competency testing programs, especially when graduation from high school is made contingent on passing the tests? In the fall of 1980 BEH will collect data on the extent to which handicapped children experience testing in the schools. The panel expressed interest in seeing a report of those data.

Representatives from the Veterans Administration (VA) focused on the positive aspects of psychological testing, stating that tests offer a compassionate, objective, and precise means of evaluating people's performance. The VA provides vocational counseling to its clients to assist them in achieving independence and efficiency. Representatives of the VA noted that norms based solely on handicapped examinees may not be appropriate when handicapped people are competing with nonhandicapped. Tests were not seen as barriers to appropriate job placement, although it was noted that this belief was based on experience rather than data. It was stressed, however, that tests can be dangerous unless used appropriately by personnel who are well-trained with respect to both testing and dealing with handicapped people.

The spokesperson from the National Institute on Handicapped Research (NIHR) described the new organization, its probable future activities, and those of its predecessors, especially the Rehabilitation Services Administration (RSA). Since the early 1960s RSA has funded research relating to the development of tests but not the validation or use of tests. NIHR is interested in statistical data on handicapped people and will be responsible for collecting the information in a central location.

## EDUCATORS

Several educators, or people from organizations representing educators or educational institutions, testified in the open meeting. The

National Education Association (NEA) expressed its concern about implementation of the Education for All Handicapped Children Act (P.L. 94-142), an act the NEA endorses. The NEA is principally concerned with the use of tests in formulating students' individualized educational programs (IEP). They believe that teachers and others should be adequately trained to administer and interpret tests in order to formulate satisfactorily a student's IEP. The NEA opposes the use of equivalency examinations in lieu of traditional criteria for awarding a high school diploma. The NEA believes that handicapped students should not be denied the right to take tests and that reduced standards of educational achievement should not be applied to handicapped students. However, the NEA seriously questions the value of using standardized tests at all.

A spokesperson from the American Association of Collegiate Registrars and Admissions Officers (AACRAO) described the difficulties in trying to deal fairly with handicapped people who apply for admission to college. It was reported that it is common, but not universal, practice to note when low scores are associated with a nonstandard administration of a college entrance test so that special consideration can be given the handicapped applicant. There is said to be considerable confusion among admissions officers, however, over the meaning of scores resulting from nonstandard test administrations. It is also possible that an admissions officer will fail to notice that a particular score has been flagged. In a survey by AACRAO of 60 public and private four-year schools in 11 states, no school reported changing its admissions policies because of the implementation of the Section 504 regulations. AACRAO recommends continuing to collect and analyze data to judge the validity of the tests as given to handicapped people. It was reported that schools do not usually reject students solely because of low test scores.

A representative from the Center for Unique Learners, which offers assessment services to multiply handicapped students at Gallaudet College, spoke to the panel. She stressed that one of the main problems is in the human interaction in the testing situation: that it is important to distinguish between an examinee's failure to understand a question and his or her failure to know the answer, and that it is also important for a test administrator to be supportive, to give a handicapped examinee a sense of accomplishment.

The Association on Handicapped Student Service Programs in Post-Secondary Education submitted written testimony to the panel. Briefly, the association endorses the use of data such as grades and extracurricular activities to supplement test results as well as research to increase the accuracy of assessment of handicapped people.

**EMPLOYERS**

Human Resources Center of Albertson, New York, submitted a written statement to the panel. The statement outlined some of the testing problems faced in the rehabilitation of people with disabilities. Flexibility in testing, the use of local norms, and a close link with the local business community were stressed as important to the success of the rehabilitation system.

The Metropolitan New York Chapter of the National Rehabilitation Association issued a brief written statement outlining its concerns with discriminatory testing procedures.

A representative of the Animal Husbandry Division, Department of Animal Medicine, Uniformed Services University of the Health Sciences spoke at the meeting. He outlined concerns relating to appropriate training and testing of hearing-impaired personnel. He recounted that the deaf people in his training program were trained and tested fairly only when a sign interpreter was provided.

Representatives from the New York State Office of Vocational Rehabilitation (OVR) were present at the meeting. They stressed the need for psychologists involved in the testing of handicapped people to shed their biases and preconceived notions about what handicapped people can do and to become familiar with rehabilitation practices for modifying jobs or training handicapped people to perform certain jobs. The main problem is perceived to be the improper use of tests, stemming from inadequate training of those who administer tests, not the tests per se. The New York OVR has anecdotal, but not systematic, evidence to support this view. They believe that the current safeguards against discriminatory testing of handicapped people are inadequate in part because handicapped people may not be aware of their rights and the sanctions available to them and because employers may not know exactly what constitutes compliance with the federal regulations.

An unscheduled speaker represented Youthwork, Inc., a firm under contract with the U.S. Department of Labor doing CETA (Comprehensive Employment and Training Act) demonstration projects with economically disadvantaged, minority, and handicapped young people. Youthwork, Inc., is interested in learning how to modify tests appropriately for handicapped people and is willing to share with the panel information it has on the experiences of handicapped youth in its programs.

## GROUPS REPRESENTING HANDICAPPED PEOPLE

The statement of the American Foundation for the Blind discussed problems associated with testing visually impaired people, such as deciding which norm groups to use for comparative purposes, determining the extent to which a low score is attributable to impaired visual functioning rather than lack of ability, the effect of the amount of vision on the testing process, and the advisability of using certain test modifications and aids. It was noted that blind people are divided in their attitudes toward special tests and separate norms.

Testimony from the National Federation of the Blind cited numerous examples of discrimination against blind people, some involving the use of tests. The representative stressed that blind people want to be treated equally, that is, the same as nonhandicapped people. They seek equality of opportunity and view testing as a right that should not be denied blind people. For example, they want the right to take the LSAT to compete for admission to law school. Furthermore, many think the flagging of a score as resulting from a nonstandard administration is prejudicial and confusing to those who try to interpret the test score. They want tests that are the same as those for sighted people and that can be interpreted in the same way. The National Federation of the Blind offers its help to those who work with the blind and try to understand their special situations, including those who construct or modify tests for the blind.

The spokesperson for the National Association of the Deaf contended that no test currently in use is valid for the deaf and that tests should be given in the examinee's language, which for many deaf people is American Sign Language. Pending the development of tests that are fair and valid for deaf individuals, they should not be tested. Deaf people should be involved in future test development and modification. Cases of discrimination against deaf people in public and private employment were described.

The Alexander Graham Bell Association of the Deaf advocates aural-oral communication of deaf people to facilitate their participation in society. It was noted that audiometric tests are often used to place hearing-impaired children in educational programs and that the decision to keep a hearing-impaired child out of the regular classroom may work to his or her disadvantage. Audiometric tests are necessary for hearing-impaired students, but they should be supplemented with other tests. Since hearing-impaired children learn language at a different rate from hearing children, tests involving their linguistic ability will not show the same stability as those of hearing children. Tests are viewed as providing useful information, and the notation of a nonstandard administration as necessary and desirable.

Representatives from the United Cerebral Palsy Association (UCPA) testified that their organization supports the notion that tests should be modified so as to assess a person's abilities rather than his or her sensory or motor impairment. The UCPA further advocates the use of other information, such as developmental history, observation, and nonstandardized tests, to supplement test results in making decisions about individuals. The UCPA recommends that a professional or consumer who is knowledgeable about necessary accommodations be consulted when a person with cerebral palsy is tested. They recommend the use of item analyses to investigate the reasons for low scores of handicapped people. The UCPA representatives see educational mainstreaming as a positive goal. They suggest that handicapped people receive training in test-taking skills and strategies.

The representatives from the Association for Children with Learning Disabilities (ACLD) highlighted some of the areas of disability to be considered in testing learning-disabled children. Learning disability is defined as a discrepancy between mental ability and one or more of the following areas of behavior: auditory receptive language, auditory expressive language, reading, written language, mathematics, nonverbal skills, perceptual-motor functions, attention, social perception, logical thinking, problem solving, and others. The definition is applied independent of achievement level; that is, a generally intelligent person may have a learning disability in a specific area. It is important to use a test of mental ability that yields scores for verbal and nonverbal functioning. A comprehensive test battery should tap many of the functions listed above in order to pinpoint the problem area. Test modifications need to be determined on an individual basis. ACLD estimates that at least 3 or 4 percent of the school population has a learning disability, but others estimate that figure to be as high as 17 percent.

## PROFESSIONAL ORGANIZATIONS AND RESEARCHERS

Two groups within the American Psychological Association (APA) were represented at the meeting: the Division of Industrial and Organizational Psychology (Division 14) and the Task Force on

Psychology and the Handicapped of the Board on Social and Ethical Responsibility.

The representative of the task force outlined issues of concern to psychologists, particularly the establishment and use of appropriate norms and the limited information on the validity of tests administered to handicapped people. The APA supported P.L. 94-142 but is concerned about proper implementation of the act, in particular, the appropriate use of tests with handicapped children. It was noted that most textbooks on testing say little if anything about testing handicapped people, and that textbooks on the disabled rarely say much about testing. The APA encourages the panel to help in its efforts to ensure adequate training of people who test handicapped individuals. The task force encourages the use of behavioral assessments, such as the work sample, in place of the usual standardized tests, even though developing and using them can be very expensive.

In 1975 the Division of Industrial and Organizational Psychology published principles for the validation and use of personnel selection procedures, but concerns regarding handicapped people were not specifically mentioned. That publication is currently being revised and will be shared with the panel when it has cleared review. Employers must deal with complicated and perhaps conflicting federal requirements with regard to recruitment and selection, including the regulations regarding handicapped people. Industrial psychologists have serious doubts as to whether compliance with the regulations concerning testing of the handicapped is possible. In response to a question, the representative speculated that courts may accept evidence of validity (such as content validity) other than predictive or criterion-related validity if the study, especially the job analysis, is well done. He predicted that in the future more tests will be used in employment selection and that they will be better than those currently used.

The representative from the American Association for the Advancement of Science (AAAS) described the work of the AAAS with handicapped scientists over the last five and a half years. The AAAS has studied the barriers faced by scientists in their education and careers. The American Council on Education (ACE) has initiated project HEATH (Higher Education and the Handicapped) to give technical assistance to 3,000 colleges and universities regarding compliance with the Section 504 regulations. The representative sees testing as a major source of discrimination against handicapped people but believes that nondiscriminatory tests should be made available to handicapped people, who may want to demonstrate their abilities via test results.

The AAAS representative said that the executive director of the American Association of Collegiate Registrars amd Admissions Officers had reported informally that a study by that organization showed that admissions officers pay little attention to the test scores of handicapped applicants unless the score is high but consider other indicators of performance. If that is true, the AAAS representative argued, then admissions procedures would not be altered substantially if admissions tests were waived for handicapped applicants but could be improved if nondiscriminatory tests were available.

A representative from the Deafness Research and Training Center at New York University testified about problems in assessing deaf people. Two factors that must be considered in the assessment of deaf people are degree of impairment and age of onset, both of which affect linguistic competence and general experience. Problems in the administration and interpretation of tests may or may not be obvious or severe. Recent studies have shown that deaf children tend to distribute themselves normally on performance on intelligence tests and that the predictive value of the scores is the same as for hearing children.

In response to a question, the spokesperson reported that the Deafness Research and Training Center's experience with work samples has been promising. Researchers videotaped and signed instructions for certain work sample instruments and administered them to deaf examinees. Preliminary data suggest the work samples are good predictors of performance on the job.

The representative summarized research results showing that deaf secondary school students go to college about one-fifth as often as hearing students. He also cited a study at a college for the deaf that showed that, of the instruments examined, the best predictor of college grades for deaf students was a particular verbal test. He believes, based on research and experience, that employment discrimination against handicapped people lies in the job description rather than in the tests.

**LIST OF INVITEES TO OPEN MEETING OF PANEL ON TESTING OF HANDICAPPED PEOPLE
NATIONAL ACADEMY OF SCIENCES**

**MARCH 14-15, 1980**

NOTE: The organizations marked with an asterisk (*) either testified at the hearings or submitted documents.

*Alexander Graham Bell Association for the Deaf
*American Association for the Advancement of Science
*American Association of Collegiate Registrars and Admissions Officers
American Association of University Affiliated Programs for the Developmentally Disabled
American Association of Workers for the Blind
American Association on Mental Deficiency
American Automobile Association
American Coalition of Citizens with Disabilities, Inc.
American College Personnel Association
*American College Testing Program
American Council of the Blind
American Dental Association
  Division of Educational Measurement
American Educational Research Association
AFL-CIO
  Industrial Union Department
*American Foundation for the Blind
American Medical Association, Education and Research Foundation
American Personnel and Guidance Association
American Printing House for the Blind
American Professional Society of the Deaf
American Psychological Association
  Board on Social and Ethical Responsibility Division on Evaluation and Measurement
*  Division of Industrial and Organizational Psychology
  Division of Rehabilitation Psychology
*  Task Force on Psychology and the Handicapped
American Rehabilitation Committee
American School Counselors Association
Arthritis Foundation
Association for Children with Learning Disabilities
Association for Education of Visually Handicapped
Association for Students with Handicaps

Association of American Law Schools
Association of American Medical Colleges
Blinded Veterans Association
*Bureau of Education for the Handicapped, U.S. Department of Health, Education, and Welfare
California Association for the Handicapped
CTB/McGraw-Hill
Center for Independent Living, Berkely, CA
*Center for Unique Learners
Children's Defense Fund
Citicorp
*The College Board
Council for Exceptional Children
Council of State Administrators of Vocational Rehabilitation
Deaf Community Analysts
Department of Rehabilitation, Sacramento, CA
Disability Rights Center
Disabled in Action
Disabled American Veterans
Educational Rehabilitation Services, Wayne State University
*Educational Testing Service
Fight for Sight
Foundation for the Handicapped
*Gallaudet College
Goodwill Industries of America
*Human Resources Center and Abilities, Inc.
Institute on Attitudinal, Legal and Leisure Barriers
International Center for the Disabled
Jewish Braille Institute
Joseph P. Kennedy, Jr. Foundation
Lions Eye Bank and Research Foundation
Mainstream, Inc.
Manufacturer's Hanover Trust
Mental Health Association, National Headquarters
Muscular Dystrophy Association, Inc.
National Association for Visually Handicapped
National Association for Retarded Citizens
*National Association of the Deaf
National Association of the Deaf-Blind of America
National Association of the Physically Handicapped
National Braille Association
National Center for Deaf-Blind Youths and Adults
National Center for Law and the Deaf

National Center for Law and the Handicapped
National Council on Measurement in Education
National Easter Seal Society for Crippled Children and Adults
*National Education Association
*National Federation of the Blind
National Foundation—March of Dimes
National Industries for the Blind
*National Institute of Handicapped Research
National Institute of Neurological and Communicative Disorders and Stroke
National Multiple Sclerosis Society
National Paraplegia Foundation
National Rehabilitation Association
National Society for Medical Research
National Society for the Prevention of Blindness
*New York State Office of Vocational Rehabilitation
*New York University Deafness Research and Training Center
Office of Handicapped Individuals, Office of Assistant Secretary for Human Development, U.S. Department of Health, Education, and Welfare
*Office of Personnel Management
The Orton Society, Inc.
People-to-People Health Foundation
Perkins School for the Blind
President's Committee on Employment of the Handicapped
President's Committee on Mental Retardation
*The Psychological Corporation
Public Interest Law Center of Philadelphia
Rehabilitation Commission, Boston, MA
Rehabilitation Services Administration, U.S. Department of Health, Education, and Welfare
Research to Prevent Blindness, Inc.
Harold Russell Associates
Science Research Associates
Spina Bifida Association of America
*Uniformed Services University of the Health Sciences
*United Cerebral Palsy Association
*Veterans Administration
Stout Vocational Rehabilitation Institute, Menomonie, WI
Texas Institute of Rehabilitation
Vocational Rehabilitation Services, Lansing, MI
West Virginia Research and Training Center
Xavier Society for the Blind

APPENDIX **C**

# Biographical Sketches of Panel Members and Staff

NANCY M. ROBINSON is Associate Professor of Psychiatry and Behavioral Sciences and Adjunct Associate Professor of Psychology and Pediatrics; Head, Psychology/Education, Clinical Training Unit, Child Development and Mental Retardation Center; and Director, Child Development Research Group, University of Washington, Seattle. Her work has focused primarily on mentally retarded and gifted children, with particular attention to educational interventions, clinical treatment, and cross-cultural perspectives. She is a fellow of the American Psychological Association and edits the *American Journal of Mental Deficiency*. She received her BA, MA, and PhD in psychology from Stanford University.

MARGARET E. BACKMAN is currently a psychologist in private practice in New York City. Previously she was the Director of Program Development Services at The College Board, and prior to that, Director of Vocational and Social Science Research at the ICD Rehabilitation and Research Center. Her work has focused on research and test development in education and rehabilitation, specifically vocational evaluation of handicapped people. She received her PhD in psychology from Columbia University, where she specialized in measurement and evaluation, and has pursued postdoctoral studies in clinical psychology at New York University. Her MA from Teachers College, Columbia University, and her AB from Barnard College are both in psychology.

EMERSON FOULKE is Professor of Psychology, Associate in Education, and Director of the Perceptual Alternatives Laboratory at the University of Louisville, Kentucky. His work includes research on the development and evaluation of methods of presenting information in aural and haptic form to blind people, the development of methods to aid blind people in scanning aural recordings, the improvement of methods for constructing tangible displays, research on the perceptual and cognitive processes on which the mobility of blind persons depends, plus other research on sensory and perceptual processes. He received his BA from the University of Arkansas and his PhD from Washington University, St. Louis, Missouri, both in psychology.

JOSEPH S. HIMES is Excellence Fund Professor Emeritus of Sociology at the University of North Carolina at Greensboro. He is founder and first president of the North Carolina Sociological Association, former president of the Southern Sociological Association, and member of the American and of the International Sociological Associations. His research has focused on racial and ethnic relations, political sociology, and the family. He received his AB and AM from Oberlin College and PhD from Ohio State University, all in sociology and economics.

IRA J. HIRSH is Professor of Psychology at Washington University, and Director of Research at the Central Institute for the Deaf, St. Louis, Missouri. His research has focused on psychoacoustics, perception of complex auditory patterns, including speech, music, and other time-varying signals, and applications to audiology and to the education of the deaf. He is a member of the National Academy of Sciences, a fellow and former president of the Acoustical Society of America. He received his AB from the New York State College for Teachers (Albany), his AM in speech pathology from Northwestern University, and his MA and PhD in experimental psychology from Harvard University.

WILLIAM G. JOHNSON is Professor of Economics, The Maxwell School, Syracuse University and Senior Research Associate of the Health Studies Program, The Maxwell School and the Upstate Medical Center (S.U.N.Y.). He is also Professor of Administrative Medicine, Upstate Medical Center. His research has centered on the relationship between health and productive activities, analysis of public programs and policies relating to health and welfare, and the economics of occupational health and safety. He received his BS from the University of Pennsylvania, his MA from Temple University, and his PhD from Rutgers University, all in economics.

NADINE M. LAMBERT is Professor of Education at the University of California, Berkeley. Her work has centered on school mental health, educational measurement, special education, nonintellectual attributes associated with learning, adaptive behavior in public school children, and hyperactivity in children. She is a fellow of the American Psychological Association and the American Orthopsychiatric Association. She received her PhD in psychology from the University of Southern California, her MA in education from Los Angeles State College, and her AB in psychology from the University of California at Los Angeles.

JACK C. MERWIN is Professor of Educational Psychology in the College of Education, University of Minnesota. He has worked principally in educational and psychological measurement and evaluation. He is a fellow of the American Psychological Association and a former president of the National Council on Measurement in Education. He received his EdD and MS in educational psychology and his BS in mathematics education from the University of Illinois.

STEPHEN J. POLLAK is a partner in the firm of Shea and Gardner, Attorneys at Law, Washington, D.C. He served as Assistant Attorney General in charge of the Civil Rights Division of the U.S. Department of Justice under President Johnson. He has been president of the District of Columbia Bar and co-chairman of the Lawyers' Committee for Civil Rights Under Law. He has participated as counsel in major lawsuits dealing with the use of standardized tests in selection of people for employment and educational placement. He received his LLB from Yale Law School and his BA from Dartmouth College.

NORMAN S. ROSENBERG is an attorney and Director of the Mental Health Law Project, a Washington, D.C.-based public interest law firm that specializes in advocacy on behalf of mentally ill and developmentally disabled people and those so labeled. He has worked principally in developmental disability law, the provision of educational services to handicapped children, and mental health administration and the law. He received his JD from the State University of New York at Buffalo, School of Law, and his BA from Hofstra University.

I. RICHARD SAVAGE is Professor of Statistics at Yale University. He has done research in mathematical statistics, nonparametric techniques, and control theory. He is a fellow of the American Statistical Association and the Institute of Mathematical Statistics. He received his BS from the University of Chicago, his MS from the University of Michigan, and his PhD in statistics from Columbia University.

WILLIAM A. SPENCER is President of The Institute for Rehabilitation and Research, and Chairman and Professor of the Baylor College of Medicine. His work has focused on poliomyelitis, infantile paralysis, physiology, and rehabilitation medicine. He is a member of the Institute of Medicine, a fellow of the American Academy of Pediatrics. He served as Acting Director of the National Institute of Handicapped Research. He received his BS from Georgetown University and his MD from Johns Hopkins University.

HERBERT A. ZARETSKY is Chief of Psychological Services and Assistant Director of the Department of Rehabilitation Medicine at the New York University Medical Center, Goldwater Memorial Hospital, and Clinical Assistant Professor at New York University School of Medicine and the New York University College of Dentistry. He is also Adjunct Professor of Psychology at Hunter College of the City University of New York. His research interests include psychological aspects of disability, pain, chronic illness, and aging. He is a fellow of the American Psychological Association and the New York Academy of Sciences. He received his BS from Brooklyn College, his MA from the University of Pennsylvania, and his PhD from Adelphi University.

SUSAN W. SHERMAN is study director of the Panel on Testing of Handicapped People and also senior research associate with the Committee on Ability Testing. Previously she served as staff officer with the Committee on Community Reactions to the Concorde and the Committee on Vocational Education Research and Development, both in the Assembly of Behavioral and Social Sciences. Her principal professional interests include educational and psychological measurement and policy issues in the social sciences. She received her PhD and MA in quantitative psychology from the University of North Carolina at Chapel Hill and her AB in psychology from Queens College, Charlotte, North Carolina.

ALEXANDRA K. WIGDOR is study director of the Committee on Ability

Testing and also senior research associate with the Panel on Testing of Handicapped People. Previously she served as historian with the National Study Commission on Records and Documents of Federal Officials. Her particular interests include the legal dimensions of testing and the development of government equal employment opportunity policy. She received an MA in history from the University of Missouri and pursued advanced studies at the University of Maryland, the Free University of Berlin, and the Folger Shakespeare Library.

NANCY E. ADELMAN served as research associate to the panel for six months. She had been a teacher and principal in public schools, worked with handicapped students, and taught in college. She received an AB from Pembroke College, and an MA in curriculum and teaching from Teachers College, Columbia University, where she also did advanced graduate work.

RITA L. ATKINSON served as research associate to the panel for nine months early in the project. She is the co-author of the fourth through eighth editions of *Introduction to Psychology*. She received her MA and PhD in clinical psychology from Indiana University and her AB from Randolph-Macon Woman's College.